Integrative Approaches To

Family
Art
Therapy

SECOND EDITION

Integrative Approaches To

Family
Art
Therapy

SECOND EDITION

SHIRLEY RILEY, MA, ATR-HLM, MFT

observations by
Cathy A. Malchiodi, ATR-HLM, LPCC.

Published by
Magnolia Street Publishers
1250 West Victoria Street
Chicago, Illinois 60660

ISBN: 1-890374-03-2
Library of Congress Catalog Card Number: RC489.A7R556 2004
616.89'1656--dc22   .2004050482

Editorial Assistance: Mimi Sandeen, WF
Cover Design: Sarah Reinken

Printed in the United States of America
  4 5 6 7 8 9 10

This Book is Dedicated
to my Family.
My husband, our sons,
their wives and children.

Publishers Note:

SADLY, SHIRLEY RILEY PASSED AWAY JUST AS SHE COMPLETED THIS NEW EDITION, BUT BEFORE SHE WAS ABLE TO SEE AND HOLD IT IN HER HANDS. WE WILL MISS YOU SHIRLEY AND HOPE YOU APPROVE.

CONTENTS

REEVALUATING FAMILY THERAPY

It is a tribute to the lasting importance of family therapy that this volume continues to have value for practitioners. I, for one, have never lost faith or interest in the central importance of the family and how it has influenced all the clients I have seen in my practice. Traumatic events often occur in the earliest years of our lives, and these years are most often spent in the family environment. It is those early years, and the ongoing influence beyond those years, that most persons in therapy are attempting to understand. It is in pursuit of this understanding that I have found a continuing satisfaction in the use of art in the therapeutic conversation as it makes achieving the client's goals more possible. And now, with the advent of a focus on the importance of attachment between child and caretaker, along with the ability, through the neurosciences, to examine the neurological patterns that are created through relationships, I have developed a newly expanded devotion to family therapy, as well as the role of art in that therapy.

I hope that all therapists feel the excitement of sharing this recent material with the people they see in treatment. My belief is that imagery in the therapeutic conversation makes more sense than it ever did, and I also believe that further exploration of the marriage of image and narrative will be a boon to therapists in many fields. Ten years ago, when this book was first published, I had a beginning notion about the brain-mind-body interaction and the importance of art as a conduit to information best conveyed through the use of imagery as we now understand it. Some of my awareness is inferred in the writing: Chapter Two illustrates the power of nonverbal, non-interpreted solutions to a serious problem where the realignment of neuronal pathways probably helped with the solution. Chapter Three suggests the fusion of left and right brain (cognitive and emotional) functioning as an essential in the practice of art therapy, as well as exploring the use of nonverbal knowing brought forth through cognitive interpretation and language. Later on, Couples Therapy again utilizes the knowledge of the power of patterned responses and the need to introduce new pathways in the emotional mind before acceptance in the cognitive mind. Chapter Four, a family with a history of schizophrenia, shows clearly how we learn what is "normal" in our family of origin, and how that "normalcy" is passed down though the generational belief system. Chapter Ten addresses the same issue by exploring domestic violence. Throughout, the clinical literature can be enhanced if, as the art therapist reads the case material and the treatments in the chapters, he/she brings with them some fundamental background knowledge of psychoneurology and interweaves speculations of how the mind-body has had a formative impact on clients.

As the author of this "revisited" text, I hope the reader will also take into consideration some of the new material, presented in the two chapters added to Section Three, that I now find essential to my understanding of treating families and clients today. There will be more advances in science that will bring psychology and neurology even closer together. I firmly believe clients and therapists will all benefit by this association. It is of great satisfaction to me that my choice of thinking about, and working with, families continues to fascinate me. It is a gift to do daily what is called work when it seems more like pleasure. I seem to have a hard time with retiring, having failed to do so several times. It is irresistible not to continue to be involved in the field of family art therapy when new information continues to arise.

Along with the involvement in my work, I have made many friends and enjoyed many rewards and awards. I am grateful that the thoughts I have written have been useful to readers and I am delighted when someone refers to some notion I have had about treatment. I thank all my friends, Cathy Malchiodi, in particular, who keeps me in touch with reality, my caring and lovely family who show me daily that family is the core of my universe, and my supportive and stimulating work companion, Noah. I am fortunate to have had the kindness of the art therapy community over these last ten years. My best wishes for all readers in finding the family that makes them happy.

INTRODUCTION
Shirley Riley

Putting this book together provided me with a rare opportunity to re-experience my own evolution as a family therapist. As I reviewed, rewrote and added to the group of articles published over the last decade, I found myself in the reflexive position of observing myself. I began thinking about my thinking.

In my present reality, through a post-modern lens, I identify myself as a social constructionist or narrative theorist, but, strangely, it is a stance I find most familiar. I just never knew until recently to call myself by that name. However, the broad and flexible designation of social constructionist does not complete the picture for me unless I include my identity as a clinical art therapist.

My identification as a clinical art therapist has grown since this book was first published; some rather amazing concepts of neuropsychology have broadened the understanding of why visual language enhances psychotherapy and in turn this information has influenced my practice. For art therapists this recent validation (through neuroscience) of the worth of adding art expression to verbal discourse is, to my way of thinking, a way to make additional sense of all the theories and techniques that are explored in this text. How the brain processes information, the value of nonverbal right brain intelligence, and the larger concept of how the body-mind appreciates states of stress and makes those reactions known, gives the therapist new tools and new confidence to use these tools.

To explore these more contemporary modes of addressing art therapy treatment based on neuropsychology I have added a chapter that demonstrates how an experienced therapist may synthesize systems, post-modern and neuroscience knowledge into a flexible approach that is most successful for the client's treatment. Obviously art therapists, such as myself, are just laymen (laywomen) and cannot pose as neurologists, but a beginning course in neuroscience offers enough information to value how our minds (brains) develop interactionally and thus validates the process of psychotherapy.

Some years ago, I read Lynn Hoffman's article in which she included "lenses" as part of the title ("Constructing Realities: An Art of Lenses", Family Process, 29: 1, 1990). Her view of constructing realities seemed to fit with an art therapist's vision. The difference is that lenses we wear to consultation are bifocal! We *see* our theories and the application of treatment through the externalized art products of our clients. We *listen* to language and the stories our clients tell. Through this duality of knowing we co-create alternative meanings to these tales. We rely on the silent information provided through the visual illustrations of the narrative which inform our contributions and observations. This combination results in the formation of alternative views of the client's tale.

What has become apparent to me is that the narrative of my engagement with therapy is demonstrated by the succession of the articles contained in this text. These theoretical stories (theories) structured my clinical life and colored my vision. In conversation with my clients the meanings we attributed to their experiences were influenced by the story I was currently living. When I adopted the view of considering myself a co-author of the therapeutic plan, rather than the inventor of the goal, a shift in my engagement in the process came about.

I did not discard the learning of the past, but I released the idea that theories are a form of "truth". I entered into the therapeutic relationship with the notion that my perceptions of reality were no more real than my clients'. The method of working together would entail an open exploration of possibilities, with the client's preference of first importance. This practice of the co-construction of new alternatives gave the clients a sense of actively assuming a capacity to shape their own lives. As the therapist, the use of curiosity, supportive questioning and opportunities to externalize through art expression were the skills I brought to the relationship.

Rather than giving up the abilities I had struggled to improve over the years, I found that all the talent I could bring to the therapy was easily shared and became more available to the client(s) through this form of therapeutic practice.

In a recent article, Lynn Hoffman confesses to being a "closet" empathetic human being in therapeutic relationships, blurring the traditional role of therapist. I identify with that confession. I often failed to keep the proper neutrality when I was strategic, nor did I hold fast to the clear delivery of the paradox when I chose that intervention. My heresy went even further: I knew a softer, more feminist approach, which entered through the art therapy imagery and was the more effective treatment. However, it was a struggle to question the "masters" whose theories I read so avidly.

As you, the reader, will observe, the stages of my own evolution were somewhat parallel to the growth of family therapy as a defined specialty. I lagged behind a few years, since I learned through books and conferences, but, with each new development in the field, I relied on my clients' responses to their art and exploration of their stories to help me validate my choice of theory and practice. I was fortunate to have many families stay with me through their conflicts and resolutions and provide me with a multitude of world views. They taught me their methods of dissolving their problems.

Each family is a unique experience and calls forth a singular approach during our therapeutic time together, one that cannot be duplicated or generalized. This uniqueness rests, to a large degree, on the power of art expressions that the majority of the time lead the way to change. No artist makes a mark identical to another artist. As artists of their own personal dialogue, externalized into visual expression, the individuality of each family member is commanding, as suggested. It is impossible to grow tired of the wonder of meeting new persons and the delight of seeing and hearing their stories.

My observation is that a therapist's style, to a degree, is an extension of their own life experience and personality. For some unknown reason I have always enjoyed seeing all around a situation— the corners, the hidden aspects, the surprises that make sense of what appears to be nonsense. In addition, I have been impressed with how often each of us has had to deal with "impossible" or paradoxical situations in our own lives. I think that is why students and professionals have such a fascination with paradoxical interventions. They are drawn to the tension and excitement of thinking through a paradox, just as they have been caught in the same tension in their own lives. I think that is true for me. I believe paradox is common to us all.

As a therapist matures, experiences, education and study inform their own lives. Comfort evolves with the knowledge that you have knowledge. I believe that all the drawings that have passed before my eyes have enriched my visual/silent knowing; I believe that all the stories that I have heard have immensely expanded my knowing of the world; I believe that sharing the private visual/verbal metaphors of my clients has changed me. I think falling in love with many theories and getting high on a successful session is a fantastic way of life. I hope I have the talent to convey my enthusiasm for the process of clinical art therapy integrated with the theories of family practice. Perhaps the case examples in the chapters that follow will in some way give the reader an entree into my delight in searching for a therapeutic path with my co-constructors, the families. We worked together toward alternative ways of handling whatever situation they presented as a difficulty.

Returning to the reality of the book, I would like to linger a moment to acknowledge my co-author Cathy Malchiodi. She did what I have not been able to do until now— make the task of creating this book possible. Working with her on this book has been a pleasure. There is in my colleague a very pragmatic but creative drive that speaks to me in a way that imbued me with the courage to move forward.

I am grateful for her prodding, delighted with her humor, amazed at her organization, and eternally thankful for the stimulating exchange of ideas that this project has offered us. Her contributions are invaluable.

I wish to thank Lori Jayne Gloyd, who, without complaint, retyped the many versions of my articles as I struggled to make them clearer. She was essential to much of the original work herein.

I have been fortunate to work with colleagues who are intellectually challenging: Helen Landgarten, Noah Hass-Cohen and Richard Carr— all friends whose opinions I respect.

Perhaps the greatest credit should go to the families in therapy who gave their trust to me during difficult times. They presented a challenge and worked hard to show me what they needed.

Lastly, I wish to acknowledge the students whom I have taught and supervised. Their acceptance (and occasional rejection) of my lectures and supervision helped me clarify my thoughts and my theories.

My goal has always been to be aesthetically pragmatic. That means, to me, an artistic, creative approach to helping families solve hard problems in their immediate world. I have worked most of the time in a clinic where social systems, financial restraints, political pressures, cultural tensions, and rising crime were the environmental surroundings. I also acknowledge that living in Los Angeles is a factor in my stylistic preferences. I consider it a privilege to live in a city where the polyglot of ethnicities push the therapist to deal with "today", since the future is a mix that has yet to be formed. The therapeutic principles of the past must be transformed; by pressing on we release old methodologies and move into the postmodern mode of thinking and conducting therapy.

Section One: Theoretical Applications

The first chapter reflects my social constructionist thoughts about how the illustrations of the families' stories may construct the core of therapy. Following is an exploration of the method a family chose to control their solution to dis-solving an abusive situation. Thirdly, there is an examination of the importance language plays in art therapy, challenging the notion that words used in art therapy are not essential. The next chapter presents a family in chaos, bearing the label of schizophrenic. The chaos called for structure and a structural approach to therapy is demonstrated in this case study. We then have a look at the way paradoxical, or as I prefer, positively connoting behaviors, can be explored and integrated into the art therapy. Seeing an individual in a family context and using strategies and rituals in treatment is the focus of chapter six. Chapter seven turns the lens of treatment on couple work, and the exploration of family of origin within a systemic treatment plan.

Section Two: Specific Issues

Treatment of handicapped members in a family and the advantages of multifamily group therapy are described as a treatment approach. Secondly, the challenge of treating adolescents and their families is confronted; in this case, difficulties are heightened when the parent has not moved beyond adolescent development him/herself. Next, we examine if art therapy is useful as a treatment choice with families who have experienced domestic violence. Lastly, the various practical and clinical reasons that make art therapy a successful modality to include in outpatient clinic services are presented.

Section Three: Postmodern Issues

The postmodern world is dominated by social issues that have disrupted our way of life and impinged on our families. The first chapter in this section reflects on the resurgence of the role of grandparents as primary caretakers in today's world. Second, a glimpse of the Los Angeles riots of 1992 is presented through art therapy expressions as responses to crisis. The third chapter in this section is the most contemporary addition to the text; it addresses the direction in which art therapy is going at the beginning of the 21st century. Neuroscience, psychology, attachment theory, inter-relational developmental theory, brain scans, trauma resolution, and controlled observations, greatly broaden the foundations on which to build, and justify, the use of art therapy. These concepts point the way to understanding how nonverbal expressive statements augment and enrich the therapeutic relationship and the outcome of treatment. This approach is fresh and has not been widely taught, but I am convinced it is basic to our growth as a profession. Lastly, a call for change (personal and professional) in our world views and a plea for awareness of the deconstruction of old ways of knowing are offered. The necessity for building new views of art therapy for the future is discussed.

The experience of redefining the material presented in this text has resulted in two reactions with which I will close. The immediate response was one of pleasure. I recognized again how many aspects of treatment benefit from the integration of art therapy and family therapy theory. This recognition was immediately modified by the flash of memory of countless other clinical opportunities I have witnessed and neglected to record, examples which might have offered a more succinct message to the reader. The second reaction came about as I experienced the realization (again) of my own limitations. My hope is that talented art therapists and therapists from other disciplines will find some of this information useful and continue to explore the integration of visual ways of knowing with verbal descriptions of knowing. There is a lot of looking, seeing, speaking, and hearing left to be done.

Shirley Riley, MA, A.T.R., MFCC
April 14, 1994 - November 1, 2004

SECTION ONE: FAMILY ART THERAPY—INTEGRATING THEORY WITH PRACTICE
Cathy A. Malchiodi

Throughout this first section of the book Shirley Riley presents the theoretical foundations of her integrative approaches to family art therapy. The term "eclectic" might have been substituted for the word "integrative", given the rich variety of approaches that Riley has investigated and successfully applied to clinical work with families. However, the term "integrative" more accurately describes her philosophy for two distinct reasons: 1) The clinician who works with families should have an understanding of the variety of theoretical viewpoints in family therapy theories and be willing to use these theories in combination to meet the unique needs of the client and 2) the clinician has the opportunity to integrate the art process and resultant product in therapy, enhancing interventions and clarifying the parameters of the family system.

It is important to note that there have been many important contributions to the development of the field of family art therapy over the last thirty years that have been precursors to the material presented in this book. Some of these contributions include: family art evaluation and art-based assessment of families and systems (Bing, 1970; Kwiatkowska, 1967a, 1978; Kwiatkowska & Wynne, 1971; Landgarten, 1987; Rubin, 1978; Rubin & Magnussen, 1974; Levick & Herring, 1973; Zierer, Sternberg, Finn, & Farmer, 1975a, 1975b); family art therapy (Kwiatkowska, 1962a, 1967b, 1975, 1978; Kwiatkowska, Day, & Wynne, 1962; Landgarten, 1987; Mueller, 1968; Sobol, 1982); child/parent dyads (Lachman-Chapin, Stuntz, & Jones, 1975; Landgarten, 1975; Rubin, 1978; Malchiodi, 1990); couples art therapy (Wadeson, 1973, 1976,1980). Many of these authors have focused on the use of the art process for communication and insight with families;

others have drawn upon the major theories of family therapy in general, utilizing these theories to enhance the use of art expression to effect change, assist insight, identify system dynamics, and understand the communication patterns of families and groups.

In contrast to the majority of writings on family art therapy, Riley offers a unique set of experiences in her contribution to the field. Her history as a therapist is rich in direct work with a variety of populations who come from diverse socioeconomic and cultural backgrounds. As a clinician, supervisor and educator, Riley has written numerous papers about her observations as a family art therapist, describing the use of art therapy with a variety of clinical populations and from a variety of perspectives. Her major strengths are the application of art therapy to family work and her ability to integrate and synthesize family therapy theories in work with clients. In this postmodern era of single parenthood, blended families, and reinvented family roles, as well as economic distress and societal violence, Riley's approaches to clinical intervention with families are in the forefront of the necessary evolution of the practice of family art therapy.

The Role of Theory in the Practice of Family Art Therapy

The integration of theory, whether it be a family therapy theory or other conceptual frameworks, is of chief concern to the beginning student or practitioner when approaching work with families. Over the last several decades there have been many theories proposed addressing the treatment of and intervention with families. It is often difficult for a beginning student or practitioner to find a level of comfort in integrating theory into practice; adding the concepts of art therapy into practice with families poses an additional concern.

Families themselves present another challenge, given the varying dynamics, ages and developmental levels of family members, and the unique world views each member brings. This complexity is cogently described by Goldenberg and Goldenberg (1991) in their definition of a family:

> A family is a natural social system, with properties all its own, one that has evolved a set of rules, is replete with assigned and ascribed roles for its members, has an organized power structure, has developed intricate and overt forms of communication, and has elaborated ways of negotiating and problem-solving that permit various tasks to be performed effectively. (p. 3)

With these multifaceted aspects in mind, it can become both anxiety producing and frustrating for a novice therapist, as well as a seasoned clinician, to conceive of ways to intervene successfully within a family system. The situation becomes even more complex when a multitude of theoretical frameworks are available as possible ways to intervene with and treat troubled families.

In the first section, Riley presents a philosophy that is interwoven throughout this book: that first one must understand and utilize a solid theoretical foundation in work with families, and second, that a practical application of theory is enhanced by introducing the art process into the session. To fully illustrate this premise, chapters demonstrating the use of art therapy as integrated with some of the most important theories in family therapy are presented.

The social constructivist view is predominant in Riley's therapeutic vocabulary (and is more fully described in Chapter One "Illustrating the Family Story"). Of constructivism, Neimeyer (1993) said "... is a view of human beings as active agents who, individually and collectively, co-constitute the meaning of their experiential world". (p. 222) A relatively new development in the field of family therapy, social constructivism argues that objective descriptions of the family by the therapist are illusory; reality itself is a social construction and therefore, there is no reality that exists independent of human perception and invention (Watzlawick, 1984). The parties in communication with each other (in this case, the family art therapist and the clients) "co-construct" reality. An important premise of constructionism is that the relationship between the client(s) and the therapist can serve as catalyst in helping to recreate the clients' world views.

To further illustrate the concept of constructionism, Anderson (1990) gives the following definition:

> Constructivist therapy is not so much a technique as a philosophical context within which therapy is done, and more a product of the *zietgeist* than the brainchild of a single theorist.... These approaches work with a part of the human psyche that is surprisingly neglected in many schools of therapy— the form-giving, meaning-making part, the narrator who at every waking moment of our lives spins out its account of who we are and what we are doing and why we are doing it. (p. 137)

Riley has chosen to emphasize the use of constructionism because of inherent connections between this way of working and the use of art expression in therapy. The act of art making itself includes not only constructing an image, but can include deconstruction and eventual reconstruction of the elements contained within an image. This varied process is a powerful metaphor for both expressing and reframing reality for the family working through issues of crisis and/or interpersonal problems.

Other major theories are emphasized throughout the text, particularly in this first section. In the field of family therapy, Minuchin is well-known for his seminal work in the area of structural family therapy (1974,1984; Minuchin & Fishman, 1981). He believes that therapists can identify the underlying pattern of subsystems, functions of family members, hierarchies, and boundaries. In Chapter Four, Riley presents an interesting case of a family whose history of schizophrenia and serious mental disorders were initially not recognized by the family as intrinsic to their discomfort and dysfunction. A structural approach was applied in conjunction with art interventions, capitalizing on transactional patterns and encouraging a hierarchical organization within the family to stabilize it. Like Minuchin, Riley's application of a structural approach to family art therapy was directed to the family's current structure, with particular focus on their current crises which included a seriously ill parent, a schizophrenic daughter, and a suicidal incident. Structured art interventions were used to challenge their rigid patterns, allowing them to reorganize their interactions into a healthier, more productive mode, and to cope with the serious problems that threatened the family system.

In Chapter Six, a systemic approach is presented with an emphasis on the concept of "paradox". Among family therapists, Selvini-Palazzoli and other members of the Milan Group (Selvini-Palazzoli, Boscolo, Cecchin, & Praza, 1978) are best known for this approach to treatment. Systemic therapy is characterized by clarifying the connections between family members and perceptions of each family member concerning a particular event or situation. Other theorists in the area of systemic therapy include Hoffman (1981), Papp (1983), and Kerr (1981).

Interviewing techniques such as hypothesizing, circular questioning, and positive connotation come to mind when thinking of this approach. These techniques also emphasize a visual component of family dynamics, a component uniquely suited to the use of art-based interventions in treatment. Riley presents several examples of how art therapy can be utilized to help both the therapist and the family "see" systems of communication and behavior; additionally, she emphasizes the concept of the systemic paradox (see Haley, 1973; Papp, 1983, for a more detailed definition of paradoxical interventions). Riley notes that "the art therapist has the advantage of observing in the art product more covert interactions than the clients have been willing to discuss". Because of this therapeutic advantage, the art therapist can more effectively design a suitable paradoxical intervention to address the problems of the family.

In Chapters Six and Seven, strategic family therapy is examined. Strategic family therapy originated from the work of the Mental Research Institute (MRI) group (Bateson, Jackson, Haley, Weakland, Satir, Watzlawick, to name a few of many names associated with this group) in the '50s and '60s, and was based in general systems theory, cybernetics, and information theory. A major premise of strategic therapy is that all communication within the family takes place on two levels— the first or surface level, and a second level called *metacommunication.* Directives are important in the strategic approach and Riley gives several examples, demonstrating the integration of strategic approaches with the art process and resultant product.

Finally, an exploration of a little discussed topic in the field of art therapy: the importance of language in process of art therapy (Chapter Three). Language is an important aspect in the social constructionist view, since the use of language can affect the direction of therapy and can either be a tool for communication or miscommunication of the family's story. The combination of language with the nonverbal aspects of art therapy strengthens the therapeutic discourse according to Riley, because both the visual and verbal aspects provide different lenses through which to view the family. When both are used effectively, there is a greater possibility that additional themes, communications and realities will be discovered and amplified.

A Note for Students, Instructors and Supervisors

It is the authors' intention that this book be of practical use in learning and understanding family art therapy. However, much of what is considered in this book is presented with an understanding that the reader is familiar with the basic foundations of family therapy in general. To assist readers who may not have had such training, readings are suggested at the end of most chapters that represent the major theories of family therapy. There are several good texts available on the basic principles of family therapy; two of these texts are *Family Therapy: An Overview* (Goldenberg & Goldenberg, 1991) and *Family Therapy* (Nichols, 1984).

Instructors of art therapy or family therapy coursework and supervisors working with interns who see families in their practice will also find this text useful. The material included in this text—philosophy, methodology, cases and commentaries— is presented with the intent of stimulating discussion about the theory and practice of family art therapy from a variety of viewpoints. Instructors and supervisors are encouraged to engage with students in critically considering the material presented in each chapter and the major theories of family therapy. Case material may also be hypothetically considered from other theoretical perspectives, in addition to the ones being described. Lastly, teachers are encouraged to design experientials for the classroom, thereby allowing students to experience firsthand the methodology and theories discussed.

It is also important to continue to stay contemporary in the field of family therapy in order to understand how art therapy can be best integrated in clinical work. Collecting journal articles and starting a journal club in the area of family art therapy and family therapy in general is one way for instructors and their students and supervisors and supervisees to share current knowledge and increase understanding in changes in therapeutic thinking and treatment. *Family Process* and *Family Therapy Networker* (both of which are referenced throughout the text) are two journals to consider; the former discusses the clinical application and research in the field and the latter focuses on more contemporary issues. Occasionally, journals in the field of art therapy have articles on family art therapy (see *Art Therapy: Journal of the American Art Therapy Association, American*

Journal of Art Therapy, and *The Arts in Psychotherapy).*

Concluding Thoughts

In a recent book on the importance of ritual in families, Imber-Black and Roberts (1992) make an observation that might also describe the application of art therapy to family work:

> All human systems must deal with relating, including questions of who is in and who is out, who belongs, who decides who belongs, who is close to whom, and who is distant. Rituals can help us to see aspects of our relationships and enable us to rework relationship patterns, rules, roles, and opportunities.... The relating aspect of rituals occurs daily during meals when seating arrangements, allowable topics, and allowable emotions metaphorically define and redefine family relationships. Who gets invited, who chooses to actually attend, and who is left out of any ritual is, of course, an implicit comment on relationships. Where a given ritual is held... may tell you a lot about who holds power or influence in family networks. (p. 28)

The integration of the art-making into family therapy yields much the same result: a clearer understanding of family dynamics, roles and rules, ways to reinvent communication and behavior patterns, and the expression of individual and family metaphors in a more complete way than through words alone. In contrast to past methods of family treatment based in psychoanalysis and behaviorism, family therapists today are more and more interested in helping families to tell their stories than in merely identifying their underlying psychological structures. Art expression is obviously one viable way to help families communicate the uniqueness of their story, both as individuals within a system and as members of a group.

It is also important to note that there is a history for the utilization of nonverbal, action-oriented interventions in the field of family therapy. The family sculpture (Duhl, Kantor, & Duhl, 1973; Satir, 1982) and family choreography (Papp, 1976) were early applications of nonverbal techniques that employed visual methods to help both clinicians and their clients understand interactional patterns and facilitate change. Today, many family therapists continue to employ these types of interventions. There is an increasing emphasis on understanding personal and cultural meanings, as well as restructuring and clarifying the roles and communication patterns of each family member; therapists are looking for ways to honor families' unique viewpoints while also providing them an appropriate format for communicating their problems, crises, etc. The infusion of the art process into therapy is clearly one viable way to address the multilevel needs of both the therapist and client.

Over the last decade, increasing attention from the creative arts therapies, including art therapy, has been directed toward families (Johnson, 1991;

Landgarten, 1991). Johnson (1991) notes that the arts therapies "should be able to help the family to play: bring greater intimacy to a disengaged family, more freedom and spontaneity to the rigid or enmeshed family" (p. 187). He also notes that "arts therapies have not had a significant impact on the practice of family therapy", possibly due to the inherent resistance of families to arts media and the lack of access to families in general. Although this observation may bear some truth, I feel that it is our lack of clinical literature about the application of art therapy to family work that has held back our impact and perhaps even our access to clientele. Shirley Riley has certainly taken a large step forward in addressing this lack of practical information with this book, demonstrating that a wide range of families and the problems they bring to the therapeutic session can be successfully engaged through family art therapy and helped in their transformation.

References

Anderson, W. T. (1990). *Reality isn't what it used to be*. New York: Harper & Row.

Bing, E. (1970). The conjoint family drawing. *Family Process, 9*, 173-194.

Duhl, F., Kantor, D., & Duhl, B. (1973). Learning, space, and action in family therapy: A primer of sculpture. In D. A. Bloch (Ed.), *Techniques of family psychotherapy: A primer*. New York: Grune & Stratton.

Goldenberg, I., & Goldenberg, H. (1991). *Family therapy: An overview*. Belmont, CA: Wadsworth.

Haley, J. (1973). *Uncommon therapy*. New York: Norton.

Hoffman, L (1981). *Foundations of family therapy*. New York: Basic Books.

Imber-Black, E., & Roberts, J. (1992). *Rituals for our times: Celebrating, healing, and changing our lives and our relationships*. New York: Harper.

Johnson, D. R. (1991). Introduction to the special issue on the creative arts therapies and the family. *The Arts in Psychotherapy, 18* (3), 187-190.

Kerr, M. E. (1981). Family systems theory and therapy. In A. S. Gurman & D.P. Kniskern (Eds.), *Handbook of family therapy*. New York: Brunner/ Mazel.

Kwiatkowska, H. Y., Day, J., & Wyneem L. (1962). *The schizophrenic patient, his parents and siblings: Observations through family art therapy*. U.S. Department of Health, Education & Welfare, Public Health Service. Washington, DC.

Kwiatkowska, H. Y., & Mosher, L. (1971). Family art evaluation: Use in families with schizophrenic twins. *Journal of Nervous and Mental Disease, 153* (3).

Kwiatkowska, H. Y. (1962). Family art therapy: Experiments with a new technique. *Bulletin of Art Therapy, 1* (3), 3-15.

Kwiatkowska, H. Y. (1967a). The use of families' art productions for psychiatric evaluation. *Bulletin of Art Therapy, 6*, 52-69.

Kwiatkowska, H. Y. (1967b). Family art therapy. *Family Process, 6* (1), 37-55.

Kwiatkowska, H. Y. (1975). Family art therapy: Experiments with a new technique, In E. Ulman (Ed.), *Art Therapy in Theory and Practice*. New York: Schocken.

Kwiatkowska, H. Y. (1978). *Family therapy and evaluation through art*. Springfield, IL: Charles C Thomas.

Lachman-Chapin, M., Stuntz, E., & Jones, N. (1975). Art therapy in the psychotherapy of a mother and her son. *American Journal of Art Therapy, 14* (4), 105-116.

Landgarten, H. (1975). Group art therapy for mothers and daughters. *American Journal of Art Therapy, 14* (2).

Landgarten, H. (1987). *Family art psychotherapy: A clinical guide and casebook.* New York: Brunner/Mazel.

Landgarten, H. (1991). Perspective: Family creative arts therapies: Past and present. *The Arts in Psychotherapy, 18* (3), 191-194.

Levick, M., & Herring, J. (1973). Family dynamics— as seen through art therapy. *Art Psychotherapy, 1* (1), 45-54.

Malchiodi, C. A. (1990). *Breaking the silence: Art therapy with children from violent homes.* New York: Brunner/Mazel.

Minuchin, S. (1974). *Families and family therapy.* Cambridge, MA: Harvard University.

Minuchin, S. (1984). *Family kaleidoscope.* Cambridge, MA: Harvard University.

Minuchin, S., & Fishman, H. C. (1981). *Family therapy techniques.* Cambridge, MA: Harvard University.

Mueller, E. (1968). Family group art therapy: Treatment of choice for a specific case. In I. Jakab (Ed.), *Psychiatry and art: Proceedings of the IV International Colloquium of Psychopathology of Expression* (pp. 132-143.) Basel: Karger.

Neimeyer, R. (1993). An appraisal of constructivist psychotherapies. *Journal of Consulting and Clinical Psychology,* 61 (2), 221-234.

Papp, P. (1976). Family choreography. In P. Guerin, Jr. (Ed.), *Family therapy: Theory and practice.* New York: Gardner.

Papp, P. (1983). *The process of change.* New York: Guilford.

Rubin, J., & Magnussen, M. (1974). A family art evaluation. *Family Process,* 13 (2), 185-220.

Rubin, J. (1978). *Child art therapy.* New York: Van Nostrand Reinhold.

Satir, V. (1982). The therapist and family therapy: Process model. In A. Horne & M. Olsen (Eds.), *Family counseling and therapy.* Itasca, IL: Peacock.

Selvini-Palazzoli, M., Boscolo, L., Cecchin, G., & Prata, G. (1978). *Paradox and counterparadox.* New York: Aronson.

Sobol, B. (1982). Art therapy and strategic family therapy. *American Journal of Art Therapy,* 21 (2), 43-52.

Wadeson, H. (1973). Art techniques used in conjoint marital therapy. *American Journal of Art Therapy, 12*(3), 147-164.

Wadeson, H. (1976). The fluid family in multi-family art therapy. *American Journal of Art Therapy, 13* (4), 115-118.

Wadeson, H. (1980). *Art psychotherapy.* New York: Wiley.

Watzlawick, P. (1984). *The invented reality.* New York: Norton.

Zierer, E., Sternberg, D., Finn, R., & Farmer, M. (1975a). Family creative analysis: Its role in treatment. Part 1. *Bulletin of Art Therapy, 5* (2), 47-63.

Zierer, E., Sternberg, D., Finn, R., & Farmer, M. (1975b). Family creative analysis: Its role in treatment. Part 2. *Bulletin of Art Therapy, 5* (3), 87-104.

Suggested Readings on Family Art Therapy

Kwiatkowska, H. Y. (1978). *Family therapy and evaluation through art.* Springfield, IL: Charles C Thomas.

Landgarten, H. (1987). *Family art psychotherapy: A clinical guide and casebook.* New York: Brunner/Mazel.

Rubin, J. (1978). *Child art therapy.* New York: Van Nostrand Reinhold. (chapters on family work)

Wadeson, H. (1980). *Art psychotherapy.* New York: Wiley. (chapter on couples work)

Suggested Readings on Family Therapy in General

Becvar, D. & Becvar, R. (1993) *Family Therapy: A Systemic integration,* Boston, MA: Allyn & Bacon.

Goldenberg, I., & Goldenberg, H. (1991). *Family therapy: An overview.* Belmont, CA: Wadsworth.

Nichols, M. *(1984). Family therapy: Concepts and methods.* New York: Gardner's Press.

ILLUSTRATING THE FAMILY STORY: ART THERAPY, A LENS FOR VIEWING THE FAMILY'S REALITY

This chapter explores current trends in theoretical thinking in the practice of family therapy: social constructionism, structure determinism, and the aesthetics of therapy. The compatibility of these theories with family art therapy treatment will be questioned.

Art therapy products created by a family in treatment have proved valuable as assessment tools, fresh modes of communication, and levers for change. However, therapists most often use these products to move toward goals that fit within a particular family treatment theory. For example, structural family art therapists look for hierarchical imbalances, strategic family art therapists seek out repetitive patterns of problem solving, and family of origin devotees scan the art for examples of continuing ties to the family of birth. The capacity for the images to support all these (and more) approaches has been seen as a strength and a delight for art therapists involved in family work.

However, in the past few years, the family field has been shifting toward another convincing attitude for family treatment. The constructionist framework appears to this author as a natural synthesis with art therapy expressions. The artwork has always led sensitive therapists to an awareness of the message embedded in the product. When the emphasis is on the family telling their story and how they have invented their reality, the clinician is able to find a window to this world through the visual illustration. The art therapists can move with the art first and choose the proper theoretical

This chapter originally appeared in *The Arts in Psychotherapy, 20*, 253-264 (1993), and is reprinted with their permission.

approach second. The family and each member in the family can be known more intimately when therapists accept a social constructionist approach toward learning and understanding their unique world as presented in therapy.

The search for a lens in family therapy encourages the therapist to inquire how the family has constructed their knowledge of social phenomena, developed their language, created an attitude toward gender-sensitive issues and have taught each other what to believe in. Art products are the avenue to the meta-messages, an entree into second-ordered views and the invented reality of the family.

Art therapy has been recognized, since its formalized inception in the 1950's, to have the ability to be receptive and reflective of a broad spectrum of theoretical approaches (Landgarten, 1987; Rubin, 1987; Wadeson, 1980). However, in this chapter I intend to limit my focus on clinical art therapy as it is integrated with family theory and treatment. I also intend to challenge the notion that the art is solely a tool that conveys the goals set by the therapist. Rather, given the proper receptivity, the visual expressions of the family can be the prime indicator for the choice of theory best suited to treatment.

I also wish to propose that it would be useful to adopt a method of thinking that introduces creativity into treatment and allows the art, the families' illustrations, to take a dominant role in the therapeutic process. The theory to which I refer is social constructionism and the created reality (Berger & Luckman, 1966; Watzlawick, 1984).

Below is a brief description of constructionism presented by Duncan, Parks and Rush (1990):

> The constructivist position holds that individuals do not discover "reality", rather, they *invent it* (Watzlawick, 1984). Experience orders and organizes the environment; it does not directly reflect it.
>
> Reality is evident only through the *constructed meanings* which shape and organize experience; simply put, meaning is reality.... The construction of reality/meaning by individuals is a highly creative process which is limited somewhat by prevailing sociocultural limits and expectations. The creation of meaning frames and organizes perception and experience into rule-governed patterns through which individuals may predict, describe, and direct their lives.... The constructivist paradigm bears implications for a flexible, eclectic strategic practice. Therapists, like clients, are engaged in the struggle to create a predictable structured reality. Models of psychotherapy and individual/family development serve to assist clinicians in the struggle to order their own perceptions and experience regarding the client's presenting problem. In addition, theory functions to structure the assumptions and goals of the interactive process which is designated "psychotherapy" (Beutler, 1983). Paradoxically, the structure which the therapist selects also limits the search for solutions. From a constructivist vantage point, theoretical language and content conceptualizations may be viewed

as metaphorical presentations which explain and organize the therapist's reality. (p. 166)

As I assume the role of an interpreter of social constructionism in this chapter, I am aware that the theory becomes a vision filtered through my lens: the personal and social experience of my person. My view reflected my interest in examining the relationship of the philosophy of constructionism to art therapy theory. As Watzlawick (1984) has written:

> Each of us have invented the world in which we live. We do this by the way we use words (language) and how we interpret the events of our lives, both in the present and in the past, and how we connect these events sequentially. (p. 113)

In this world of invented realities, the motivation to change reality comes when a world view, an understanding, a conclusion, a truth, the perception of how events are sequenced has proven false or unsatisfactory. To regain equilibrium these events must be viewed in a different way. When we accept that events themselves and their sequence does not change, the *view* of the situation may change, and the difficulty may be resolved.

In the manner as described above, families build up a world of "truths", Over the generations, they describe to each other how to interpret an event, how to understand it "correctly". They reference back to historical and time-honored stories and the sequence of events that have become significant.

"Reality is not discovered through objective means but is agreed upon continually through social interaction, through conversation. Things 'are' what we agree to call them" (Real, 1990). Families operate within a matrix of agreed-upon realities. However, problems arise as each member experiences additional events outside the family and hears society's conflicting descriptions of truths. She or he then incorporates an expanded notion of reality that differs to some degree from the family's beliefs. Even the meaning of language changes (so well demonstrated by the ever-shifting adolescent vocabulary). Words have a life and meaning of their own and impact the reality of the individual within the family system. This complexity and enrichment embedded in the meaning of language, which leads to variations of the explanation of "truth", is often an overlooked and unacknowledged component of family difficulties. As a result of this enriched experience, many world truths exist secretly and in conflict within the boundaries of the generic world view, substantiated by the common complaint of families that they have "poor communication".

Taking the viewpoint of a social constructionist, I believe, provides the family art therapist with an encompassing overview of relationships and behaviors. It allows for a broad variation of individual beliefs within the large picture, while maintaining the view of the family as a system (Efran, Lukens & Lukens, 1990).

The constructionist approach relieves the therapist of the responsibility of "having the answer", knowing the "proper" treatment for the family. However, it is essential that the therapist put aside the invented realities of her own world and keep her bias from being intrusive in the therapy. The best entree into the family's world is to invite the members to relate their story in their own language. As they tell their tale, they will instruct the therapist about their dissatisfactions with certain behaviors and outcomes of sequences. The family story will shape the therapist's approach to treatment, one that will "fit". Only after the therapist grasps a glimpse of their world view and becomes sensitive to the meaning of their words and symbols will she or he be in a position to suggest alternative variations on the family script. This understanding does not come about by examining content of the first level communication, but by being receptive to messages that are contained in the second-order view. According to Hoffman (1990):

> Second-order view merely means taking a position that is a step removed from the operation itself so that you can perceive the operation reflexively. These views are really views about views. They often make you more aware of how your own relationship to the operation influences it, or allows you to see that a particular interpretation is one of only many possible versions. (p. 4)

Given the freedom to not have the answer, the therapist becomes the student of the family. Learning from them opens opportunities to offer unique interpretations of events, to reframe the meaning of a sequence of behaviors, speak the language they understand and appreciate their reality. Quoting Anderson and Gooloshian (1988):

> The role of the therapist is that of master conversational artist— an architect of dialogue whose expertise is in creating a space and facilitating a dialogical conversation. The therapist is a participant-observer and participant-manager of the therapeutic conversation. Just as systems are fluid, so are our ideas about them. Our theories, as well as our practice of therapy are meant as temporary lenses rather than representations that conform to a social reality. (p. 372)

As the therapist studies the world within the family, she or he must be acutely aware of the biased personal lens through which all therapists and the family look at reality. The lens is a composite of social constructions in life, in family, in color, in gender and in myths and beliefs that are held from childhood. With this awareness alive in the therapeutic relationship, there is little chance that the therapist will take an omnipotent stance and direct the families to fit a mold she or he has pre-selected.

For example, one family may desire structure and clarity of their hierarchical positions, the next may be greatly distressed by trying to keep old family traditions alive in a world in which they no longer fit. Each will direct the therapist to the theory— not because of theory but because of need.

When the family begins telling their stories, imagining a new ending, finding new truths, they are becoming creative. Being aware of these variants should improve the chances for a good outcome to therapy. The block to success is that of language. It takes many years for newlyweds, for example, to understand what their spouse really means. How can therapists, newly wed to the client family, learn the "foreign" language and exotic legends of their clients rapidly enough to be effective?

It is helpful to think about family legend in this manner. Byng-Hall (1988) wrote:

> Family legends have a particular place in family mythology. They are those colored and often colorful stories that are told time and time again—in contrast to other information about the family's past, which fades away. Although they are ostensibly told because they are interesting, the way in which they are told frequently indicates how the family *should* behave—a form of moral tale....
>
> What neither narrator or audience are usually aware of, however, is that legends are continually being re-edited by altering the metacommunications or reshaping the content in order to build up a story that fits present family attitudes. The past is usually seen as creating the present, not the present molding the past. (p. 169)

To amplify our understanding of the legend, to create visible illustrations of the story, we choose clinical art therapy. Pictures need few words and speak an international language. Art therapy is a bridge between the invented reality of the family and the ability of the art therapist to appreciate that reality. Not only the therapist, but other family members as well will "get the picture". Through art therapy, the family is provided the opportunity to illustrate the family story and, aided by these illustrations, to discover a new, alternative ending to that legend. The introduction of the image, followed by discussing the meanings of the art product, encourages creativity and gives breadth, depth and excitement to the process of therapy.

When the therapist takes a social constructionist view of reality, the therapeutic art tasks are presented and utilized in a manner that is integrated with the family's concept of reality (Hoffman, 1990). No longer is there a need for a specific "school" of art therapy, but a therapy more directly connected to the expressive, creative thrust of each family member. The variations that become available through the concrete expression are countless, and the images, laden with symbols, metaphors and messages, give clarity and a new visual truth to the unique tales of each person. The art task is given the same respect as that given to an illustrator of a piece of fiction who attempts to bring his or her creative and artistic vision to a literary piece. I often think of the power the illustrations by John Tenniel had for me as a child reading the original *Alice in Wonderland*. Alice became real to me when I entered her world via the drawings. The descriptive words illuminated by the illustrations invited me into a strange world. Now, in a similar manner, the clients' stories and artwork provide me with a fresh lens to "see" their world and their troubles.

Case I

A 50-year-old African-American woman (Priscilla) came to the clinic with her 11-year-old foster son (Joseph). The court had recently ordered conjoint therapy after the boy had been removed from the home of his natural father, who had been charged with being physically abusive. The father's fifth wife had punished Joseph by forcing him to kneel on dried beans for several hours at a time, sometimes more than once a day. It was a painful punishment and made him lame. In due time, he ran away to the home of his now foster mother, Priscilla, who was his father's third wife. His natural mother, Sarah, had not married his father and had never taken full responsibility for her son's care; at her request, Priscilla had raised him during a large part of his youth. It was a natural transition for him to live with Priscilla permanently. The court assigned her as legal guardian and he was content with the decision.

Initial problems presented in therapy were his uncooperative behavior at school, his nightmares and his constant fear that his father would kidnap him and return him to the bean torture. Priscilla wisely realized that his acting out at school was a manifestation of his anger, anxiety and tensions around the question of the permanence of his placement and the trauma of his father's cruelty. While in therapy, the negative behavior at school de-escalated rather quickly, but fears and anxiety continued to distress the boy daily. He had a hard time going to and from school because he was convinced that his dad would force him into the car and abduct him. It all revolved around the "beans". Fear equalled beans. Therefore, it seemed pressing for me to do something with the beans.

However, before we could move in this direction, I found myself confused about the various relationships in the extended family. To solve this problem "for me", Priscilla and Joseph did a family map (Figure 1).

They told me that Joseph's natural mother, Sarah, was the father's acknowledged mistress during the time that Priscilla was the wife. She shared the boy with her from infancy. The relationships with all the past wives and multiple mistresses were actively acknowledged and were part of the social world of the family. There were half-brothers and relatives from past associations who also were active in Joseph's life. Drugs and illegal transactions were the normal business of the father; however, Priscilla had never joined in these activities. Joseph's father's present wife was from Asia. He had married her through a contract to provide her with United States citizenship. As one might imagine, the courts were hard pressed to know which of the many members of this tribe should be responsible for Joseph, but miraculously found the right person in Priscilla. As I listened to their explanation of their spontaneously created genogram, I was able to resolve my confusion.

The free form of the genogram and use of color to indicate emotional attachment added greatly to their personal statement and gave "life" to the many persons involved. I could better enter into their world view when I saw the complicated relationships and cultural implications, and they were delighted to draw this description of their interwoven family system. They were fully aware of how unusually enmeshed they were, and how much it puzzled outsiders. It was not a family, it was a clan! Priscilla was fond of saying that she was the only one not intimidated by this powerful man, who, she said, acted like a "godfather".

The next step was to address and transform the beans. Joseph decorated the outside of a shoe box with collage pictures (Figure 2) representing aspects of himself. The box had a mailbox slot cut into it. After he was finished, we moved to the next task. His face turned grey when he saw me cutting large beans out of brown construction paper. With his foster mother's help, he handled the beans. They both wondered how Joseph would utilize the beans. What could be done with them? He reluctantly decided to use them as the place on which he could write "things he wanted to forget". He then put them in the box (inside himself). At each session he proceeded in this manner, first recalling the misery at his father's home and writing short sentences, such as "I'll never go back there again". In time he moved to phrases that indicated he felt secure in Priscilla's home. Much later in treatment, I brought him green paper beans and told him that the hurtful brown beans were nearly used up. He could now start on the beans that would grow into his future. Joseph followed the suggestion and wrote messages about growing up, playing football and being permanently at home with his "Mum", Priscilla. During one brief time of his regression at school

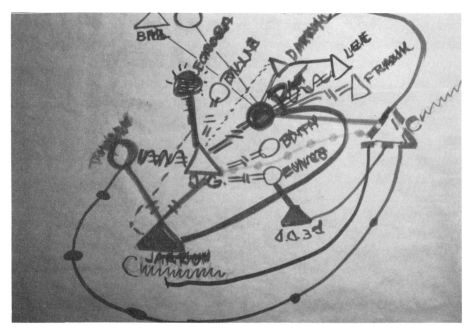

Figure 1: Multi-colored, free form "family map"

Figure 2: "Bean therapy"

I gave him some dried kidney beans to carry in his pocket. When he felt the real beans, he would be reminded that *he* was in charge of the beans (his conduct), not his father.

My perception of this task was that it would be helpful to take a sad, painful story, embrace the key metaphor (beans, with all the trauma inferred) and transform them into a vehicle for therapy. Joseph would be able to find a new ending to his frightening story, contain his fears in the box, be in command of his future by actually putting his hands and his words on the abuse and thus, give himself a sense of power. He transformed his tragedy through an art task, which he learned to enjoy and even request in his sessions. It became a healing ritual.

As a therapist, I also experienced his pleasure. It is not often that a way can be found to alleviate the effects of abuse for an 11-year-old who has few emotional resources and has lived in a family system where the word "constancy" was not included in the vocabulary. As he learned to view his world in a new way, I was privileged to share in his construction of a more acceptable reality.

Needless to say, there were many other issues addressed in the course of this treatment, but it was my first "bean" case, and it demonstrated how redefining an event and introducing new interpretations for a toxic sequence can enhance the course of therapy. How could that issue have been addressed within the reality of Joseph's life experience without the art task? Varela (1989) states: "First, therapists do not simply provide a commentary on meanings that are shared by everyone.... Second, they do not seek some 'intrinsic' or fundamental meaning for the actors or the family" (p. 22). The art gave the young client the freedom to deal directly with the abuse and provided a means to gain control. He invented the way to direct his fears, deal with his trauma and to find creativity in the process as well.

Discussion

Treating children who have been abused is always a delicate and difficult challenge. In spite of the abuse, a child (such as Joseph) is torn by a divided allegiance to his father and to his foster mother. As he worked with the symbolic representation of his abuse he reevaluated the messages of his primary socialization (Berger & Luckman, 1966). He questioned his early belief, "love your father under all circumstances", through the opportunity to objectify his abusive experience. He was able to make the move of transferring his loyalty from his father to his foster mother by understanding that there is more than one interpretation of an event or a relationship. When the art task provided him with the circumstance to take a reflective stance, he was able to personally create alternative realities. Discovering cohesion in his story of abuse was therapeutically possible through listening, encouraging and collaborating with the boy as he searched for an understanding of the events congruent with his world view.

Case II

In a second case, the major concerns were ethnic and social issues. A couple, desperate to repair their failing marriage, asked for help at an outpatient crisis center. The husband was distant and noncommunicative according to the wife. From his viewpoint, she was unreasonable and over-demanding. The complaints had not varied over their entire seven-year marriage. Each charged the other with an inability to change or to attempt to communicate clearly. This was their third attempt to resolve their distress through therapy.

Both Hideo and Anna presented themselves as intelligent, educated and not overly defensive persons. However, although they seemed able to hear the therapist, they appeared to be deaf to one another. The husband's quiet manner of speaking was in great contrast to his wife's more passionate rapid delivery. Each asked the therapist to find a way to make their partner change and to be more like themselves. He was to warm up and she was to cool down. Neither member of this dyad seemed the least interested in investing energy to resolve this challenge, although they both said they were hoping to improve and maintain their marriage. The husband was of Asian/African-American parents. His mother was Japanese and had been the dominant influence in his youth. The wife's family was Costa Rican and her father was her leading parental figure. Both families of origin were intact in spite of turbulent marriages.

From the outset of therapy the contrasting cultural backgrounds were obviously a major dissonant factor influencing their world views. However, discussion pointed in that direction led to vociferous denial from both. They insisted that this issue had no relevance to their concerns. As the present therapy was their first encounter with an expressive modality, it was an opportunity to see if a more concrete look at their families' realities made any difference. They were asked to "draw how it was (in their youth) when one opened the door and entered into their family home". What colors were around? What music was being played? What noise level was heard? How many people were present? Were they talking or being still?

Anna's drawing opened the door on a room full of people all talking excitedly at the same time music was blaring; reds and oranges vibrated to the high intensity of the close contact between many persons (Figure 3).

Figure 3: "Anna's family"

Figure 4: "Hideo's family"

Hideo's door opened upon a blue-green room, serene and calm, one child reading by his mother's side and music softly playing in the background (Figure 4). The couple was amazed at these illustrations of their families and the contrasting colors and forms. It may seem curious that these drawings made such a tremendous impact upon Hideo and Anna, because one almost might have predicted from their previous verbal descriptions that this art task would lead to these products. But these two apparently had never really *seen* their differences. Through art therapy they illustrated their social reality and they saw through each other's lens the contrasting manner in which each partner viewed the world.

Their expressive product eliminated the pejorative aspect of right/ wrong in the relationship; only differences remained. Apparently all the past words about this difficult ethnic issue had not made a sufficiently powerful impression (one that was defined and believable enough) to impel them toward understanding how their past lives in (and influences) the present. The lenses they wore were color-coded early in their lives and continued to tint how they saw their relationship.

After this, the therapist asked Hideo and Anna to speak to each other about their feelings for one another. They said they wished to express continued care for their partner. The therapist asked Hideo to verbalize his sentiments in Japanese and Anna to respond to him in Spanish. They complied with feeling and tenderness. The contrasting sounds of the languages, the music of the communication, added another dimension to the impact of the drawings. The language reinforced the visual component of the experience. They closed the session by acknowledging that they had never considered how differently they had experienced the world and each other.

In a later session, after this fresh information was absorbed and integrated, the task moved to finding an "international language" of their own, a search for a vocabulary that would bring these two very diverse backgrounds into the same arena for negotiation. We moved into second level meanings. This communication task was introduced by an art directive that pointed out how their beloved little daughter was a blend of the father's cool Asian traits and her mother's fiery Central American personality. If she could handle it, why not they? In the next session they talked about communicating during the week in a more comprehensible way. They were no longer "deaf". This brief crisis treatment came to an end with each having a more hopeful attitude and commitment to continue in longer-term couples' therapy.

My hope is that this example points out how language alone is insufficient to convey the color and texture of many situations. Drawings such as those described above bring the client back to his/her origins and are loaded with multiple messages much greater than the mere art product appears to convey. The illustration provides the other partner with an opportunity to briefly (and safely) dip into the environment of his or her spouse. This type of encounter opens doors to change and allows each client to don the lens through which the spouse sees the world. In this example, a lack in comprehending ethnic values and the cultural nuances buried in their partner's language of origin had made both "deaf" to one another. The message was not conveyed. It was important to find a way for them to really hear the words in their basic purity to complete the picture and complement the pictorial form. It was interesting to note that he was expecting his Latino wife to be like his Japanese mother, and she wanted her Asian husband to perform like her Hispanic father! No wonder they needed to find a translator! They continue in treatment and find talking through their art their preferred mode of therapy.

Discussion

"Social constructionist therapists come to the therapeutic relationship without preconceived notions of pathology or dysfunctional structures. They have no set idea what should or should not change" (Hoffman, 1990, p. 10). Therefore, the art psychotherapist enjoys the freedom to offer creative tasks to the clients and then builds on this experience collaboratively. With a couple such as described above, the function of communication had broken down and there was no longer useful dialogue between them. In service of providing an opportunity to expand the process of speaking the "unsaid" (Anderson & Goolishian, 1990), the alternative mode of conversation through the drawings opened the narrative and moved the therapeutic dialogue forward. The addition of the "music" of the language of origin of each partner was a creative leap suggested by the therapist as she became more aware of their conflicting views of the world and relationships. Therapist and clients participated in an experience that offered a possibility of co-creating a conversational context that allowed for some mutual collaboration.

Case III

This final example was chosen because of the complexity of the circumstances, social and racial, that added great difficulties to the therapists' attempts to achieve the goals set by the clients. The family was treated by my colleague, Jane Walter, who was the family art therapist. I was the supervisor. As always, we have severely modified the circumstances of this case to conform to standards of confidentiality.

Marcy, a 14-year-old girl, had recently returned home to live with her mother, Nancy, after a year at a residential center. The mother had lost her own mother just prior to the time Marcy was placed in residence. Upon the death of her mother, Nancy had given up drugs and alcohol. She had been abusing both substances since her marriage failed 10 years ago. Marcy was 4 years old when her stepfather moved away; he never made contact again. Marcy did not know he was not her real father until he left. Nancy was unsure which of three men had fathered her daughter, as they were all casual affairs entered into before her marriage. All the potential fathers were black men; Nancy was white and Marcy appeared black.

Nancy raised Marcy in the same home with her mother until the girl was placed in the therapeutic environment, about a year before current treatment began. Both mother and daughter presented the same complaint: "the fighting in the family was unbearable". Marcy fought for extravagant material possessions that her mother could not afford. She argued that she could not go swimming at the local beach unless she had a complete wetsuit and fins. The girl knew that there was barely sufficient money to meet basic expenses and that luxuries were out of the question. However, Nancy was unable to state the financial facts clearly and set proper limits because she felt guilty about the drug environment in which she had raised her daughter. She avoided confrontations by going to work mid-morning through evening, school several times a week, Alcoholics Anonymous (AA) every evening and gym after the AA meeting. The two rarely saw one another, and when they did the intensity of their contact bordered on the dangerous.

The issues that emerged from the start of treatment were: (a) Marcy demanding "goods" to compensate for what she perceived as mother's withholding of responsible, loving parenting during her childhood; (b) Marcy's rage at being rejected and sent away from home by Children's Services; (c) her resentment that her mother had changed from the drugged, alcoholic mother of her youth to this AA woman she hardly knew; and (d) her loss of power in the relationship. From a mother's perspective, her daughter was a child who demanded contact and expensive objects, who interfered with her recovery, and who constantly (by her very presence) reminded Nancy of all her years "lost" in the haze of drugs. Finally, from the therapists' viewpoint, we felt that Nancy had not yet developmentally achieved adulthood and would be overly stressed by attempting to assume parental responsibility of a teenaged child. She still struggled with her own individuation (Riley, 1991). Conversely, Marcy, who for so many years had run the house and taken care of her drugged mother, was determined not to give up her dominant adult role.

From Marcy's fourth year until her twelfth, the mother/daughter dyad had lived in a time capsule. Drugs and drug people were their lives; their language and world view were specific to this group. Moreover, the ethnic question of color was avoided. Marcy grew up in a reality constructed in a manner that was unique. Being removed into the "real" world of residential treatment was traumatic. For the first time she was identified as a black girl. She had a color label placed on her. In addition, the way people spoke, the words they used often did not have the same meaning to which she was accustomed. She was an outsider.

Nancy experienced a parallel culture shock as a recovering substance abuser. She was now supposed to be able to operate as a parent and a responsible member of society. She had not functioned in society for a decade, and therefore was gravely ill-prepared to take on the duties imposed on her. She experienced anger and frustration at her own lack of competence and she wished that her daughter would demonstrate that she was proud of her mother's recovery instead of being angry at her efforts. The role of the mother was an unrewarding experience. Finally, the major obstacle to treatment was the absolute determination of both to avoid dealing with the "black daughter, white mother" issue. Marcy demonstrated in her art work that this was a very significant part of her anger, but she would not verbalize her feelings. The mother's art also expressed her avoidant attitude toward the issue of color.

In the third session, Marcy explained the meaning behind her choice of collage pictures (Figure 5). In the upper left is a picture of a black man in obvious distress half buried in the dirt. He is surrounded by white men in military fatigues. Marcy said, "This is me. Like the black man, I'm trapped in the pit, oppressed". The knives, pictured below, translated into, "Mother stabbed me in the back by her recovery". The bird's beak and the claws represented "her nit-picking, she no longer masks her feelings, and below, she claws at me". "The fire and explosion pictures are my feelings, but I'm not angry." In the upper corner the clown represents "the image of a mother who has no respect for her daughter", and the image of a man behind the safety glasses holding the red-hot metal is "mother looking shielded and dangerous, never showing her anger". The two pictures, one of a black man stabbing a recumbent black man, and the other of the Christ on the Cross, give the message "being black is like being stabbed and on the cross." She continued by declaring she was *not* angry because she was a girl of color. She aggressively refused to discuss it. The therapist wisely accepted her protests and took in her images without interpretation. The collage was a revelation but also a warning not to trespass too soon.

Figure 6 shows Nancy's rendition of her "wall of drugs in brown and

Figure 5: "Marcy's collage"

Figure 6: Nancy's wall of drugs and recovery cycle

black that protected my scattered feelings for so long." The undulating blue line demonstrates her mood swings and self-doubts after recovery with the barbs along the way that "set me off and interfere with abstinence."

The mother showed her single-minded focus in her art expressions, a determination to continue to make recovery the primary concern of her life while parenthood took a distant second place. In spite of these conflicting issues both Nancy and Marcy said that, except for fighting, they were "fine".

When these determined stances became very clear to the therapist and myself, we had to ask the question, who most wants to initiate change? We decided we wanted change more than the family did. We assessed that, given the present situation in this relationship, their refusal to make a major move was correct. The difficulties were insurmountable to them at this time. They needed the passion of the fighting to keep the emotional warmth high enough to preserve the relationship. We were outside their reality. We had to listen and see that it was necessary to remain in the present reality before making a move. We took some small comfort in the fact that the fighting had become limited to verbal expression and that there were short periods of time when mother and daughter found some pleasure together.

It was very difficult to come to this conclusion. However, reviewing their artwork we saw that they were aware of the major issues; they understood each other; they were just not ready to chance any more change.

Discussion

To clarify where we felt we had moved away from the social constructionist position and had become less effective in the therapy, I quote Real (1990):

> A second order cybernetic, or constructionist, therapy asks the therapist to view himself or herself not as standing apart from and acting *upon* a system but, rather, as positioned in potentially useful ways *within* the system. Thus, the therapist is asked to forego the mantle of 'expertise' in the favor of the role of participant-observer. (p. 259)

When this concept was brought back into the therapeutic relationship we were open to greater appreciation of their dilemma and allowed the therapeutic dialogue to resume. Although social circumstances would still pressure this family, their ability to restructure their relationship was within the realm of possibility when we relinquished our leadership and moved in a co-constructionist stance.

This is a case that dramatically underscores how hard it may be at times to accept the family's reality. Coming from our perspective we wanted them to want what we wanted for them. Only when we reevaluated the clear nonverbal messages they had shared with each other through their art were we willing to concede that they had a right not to change. Paradoxically, at this moment of conceding our "defeat", Nancy began to be more assertive in her parenting style and Marcy, struggling to maintain control, decided to come to therapy "only when she wanted to!" Previously, she had "never" wanted to attend.

We appreciated the extent of their trauma. Until a year and a half ago, they had been safe and closely united in the drug world, but then the grandmother died. Her death changed their world. They no longer were protected. Nancy was forced into a mother position because she could no longer be a daughter. Marcy found her sober mother greatly changed, a woman she hardly knew. They had previously been in a "sisterly" relationship; now the "real" mother (grandmother) was dead and her "sister" was now her mother! Immediately following this major loss of the grandmother, the "system" intervened.

Marcy was removed by the Department of Children's Services and Nancy went sober. When Marcy entered the residential facility she completely lost her identity. She was cut off from any culture, any reality she had ever known. She had no ethnic foundations in the African-American culture, but she was treated as an African-American. Neither did she have the usual white cultural base. Her life had been rooted in the drug-dealing world as her grandmother, her mother and she had run a crackhouse, living outside the law and society. In addition, after a year of living apart, Marcy returned home speaking "residential-talk" and found Nancy "AA-talking". They had lost their common language. They were enraged when thrust into a society that did not see them as mother and daughter because of their contrasting skin color. Their family ties were hidden from the casual observer. They turned in pain to one another in a struggle to correct the collapse of their world. Thus, a frozen continent had to be heated with emotion. We modified our goals and plan to sustain them through the "ice-age" and continue to hear their story. We hope to find a new ending after they speak the same tongue and re-invent a world in which they both can fit.

As I speculate on their future, it saddens me to project how the impositions of society will continue to make reuniting a remote possibility. The prejudices and privilege of color will force them into experiencing the world in very different ways. Marcy will be faced with discrimination and loss of privileges because she is seen as a black woman. Her partial whiteness is covered by her color and very few situations will provide the opportunity for her to explain her background. She has already felt the pressure in residential placement, discrimination that her mother will never feel. Nancy may try to step into her daughter's shoes, but she will always be protected by the privileges of her white skin (Hurtado, 1981). As the world impacts on them in very different ways, the challenge to their understanding of one another will be at constant risk. The mediation of therapy as a bridge between their world views will become an increasingly important need.

This mother/daughter family example demonstrates how helpful a social constructionist viewpoint is to the therapist. Listening through their language, seeing through their art, and sensitized by their perception of reality allowed us to fit our goals to their needs. Difficult as it was to "fail", it was only in failure that we began to move slowly toward success.

Summary

In conclusion, I wish to suggest that as therapists and as individuals we all struggle with the difficulty that lies in the recursive position of a human being. We are unable to observe our observations because one cannot stand outside of one's world. Therefore, observations are self-referred. With the use of art therapy this dilemma can be improved, to some extent, by utilizing the images produced in treatment. Like all art, after completion by the maker, the symbolic expressions assume a life of their own. They are another "observer". In this manner the art representations provide an opportunity to look at a situation "once removed". The art task offers families a lens to observe themselves as though they were outside their system. Discussing the illustrations stimulates the language and the conversation in the family. There is a better chance to find new themes, new histories, create an alternate view of their problem, to invent a new reality. Fresh explanations that remove a negative label on the problem—to view the situation in a fresh light—leads to the process of change. Referring to a talk given by Bateson in 1980, Allman (1982) quoted a syllogism in Bateson's talk: "Grass dies. Men die. Men are grass". He discussed linear logic and poetic logic. Allman wrote,

> The pragmatic view of mind seeks to define singular contexts governed by linear chains of causation, whereas an aesthetic view searches for nonlinear, metaphorical connections. In the metaphor 'The eyes are the windows of the soul,' we can see how we must disconnect from traditional subject classifications to see eyes as windows and souls as having windows. Metaphors are made of patterns of images, which in turn structure the tapestry of our minds. (p. 47)

Looking at the self-created art therapy images encourages the use of metaphors, which lead to seeing aspects of situations that are more fluid, nonlinear and open to dialogue. This in turn leads to evolving a more poetic meaning to the situation at hand.

As professionals caught in the paradox of living in our created realities, we offer a therapeutic solution by bringing in a third reality, that of art therapy. This gives the power to an observer (the art) who through metaphor and image moves into the second-ordered world of the family. The windows of therapy are opened and let in the light needed to create change.

Throughout this chapter and in the case examples, the goal has been to demonstrate that it is beneficial to the therapist, the family and the course of treatment for the art therapist to look at life through the lens of a social constructionist. Each case presented needed a philosophy that allowed the clients to model their own treatment, illustrate their own invented truth and find, with the support of the art therapist, a more acceptable reality to embrace their lives.

References

Allman, L. R. (1982). The aesthetic preference: Overcoming the pragmatic error. *Family Process*, 21, 43-56.

Anderson, H., & Goolishian, H. (1988). Human systems as linguistic systems: Preliminary and evolving ideas about the implications for clinical theory. *Family Process*, 27, 371-394.

Anderson, H., & Goolishian, H. (1990). Beyond cybernetics: Comments on Atkinson and Heath's 'Further thoughts on second-order family therapy'. *Family Process*, 29, 157-163.

Berger, P., & Luckman, T. (1966). *The social construction of reality*. New York: Anchor Books.

Byng-Hall, J. (1988). Scripts and legends in families and family therapy. *Family Process*, 27, 167-180.

Duncan, B., Parks, B., & Rush, G. (1990). Eclectic strategic practice: A process constructive perspective. *Journal of Marital and Family Therapy*, 16, 165-179.

Efran, J., Lukens, M., & Lukens, R. (1990). *Language, structure, and change*. New York: Norton.

Hoffman, L. (1990). Constructing realities: An art of lenses. *Family Process*, 29, 1-12.

Hurtado, A. (1981). Relating to privilege: Seduction and rejection in the subordination of white women and women of color. *Journal of Women in Culture*, 14 (11), 834-846.

Landgarten, H. (1987). *Family art psychotherapy*. New York: Brunner/Mazel.

Real, T. (1990). The therapeutic use of self in constructionist systemic therapy. *Family Process*, 29, 255-272.

Riley, S. (1991). Couples therapy/art therapy: Strategic interventions and family of origin work. *Art Therapy: Journal of the American Art Therapy Association*, 8 (2), 4-9.

Rubin, J. (1987). *Approaches to art therapy*. New York: Brunner/ Mazel.

Varela, F. J. (1989). Reflections on the circulation of concepts between a biology of cognition and systemic family therapy. *Family Process*, 28, 15-24.

Wadeson, H. (1980). *Art psychotherapy*. New York: Wiley.

Watzlawick, P. (1984). *The invented reality*. New York: Norton.

REACHING THE CLIENT THROUGH HIS/HER OWN CHOICE OF SYMPTOM DIS-SOLUTION

This chapter describes a situation where the problem presented by the client at the beginning of therapy seemed to mask the "serious" issues that the therapist felt needed to be addressed. The challenge of maintaining a neutral and non-intrusive stance toward the client and accepting her preferred method of symptom dis-solution is the focus of this narrative.

The term "dis-solving a problem" is derived from Anderson and Goolishian's article (1988) wherein they examine language and problem-organizing systems:

> ...systems do not make problems; languaging about problems makes systems. We think of such defined systems as a problem-organizing, problem dis-solving system... the process of therapy is elaborating on, and remaining in conversation until the problem disappears... Therapeutic conversation is not the process of finding solutions. No solution is found; the problem dis-solves...the changing language and meaning of problem definition yield a dis-solving of the problem-organizing system. (p. 383)

The above quote emphasizes therapeutic conversation; however, there are many clients who are ill at ease with dialogue, and others who refuse to converse at all, actively avoiding confrontation of problems. In such situations, art expressions can become a meaningful avenue for communication of information and therapeutic conversation. Imagery gives the client mastery over his/her fear of verbal disclosure and provides an opportunity for dissolution of the problem-organizing system.

51

Overview

When a client calls the clinic asking for treatment, the way s/he presents the problem is the introduction to the problem-organizing system. The first responsibility of the therapist is to take the client's view seriously (Riley, 1993). However, in matters of suspected but unacknowledged violence, it is particularly difficult not to rush in and re-interpret the presenting problem. Unless the client is ready to let you in and open the door to this painful situation, the therapist will surely lose the client and the family. More importantly, the therapist will lose the chance to find an avenue to protect this client from the abusive behavior which is secretly suffered and pridefully protected from outside scrutiny.

Case Example

A young woman in her early twenties requested treatment in an outpatient clinic for her son, John, age seven, who engaged in unacceptable behaviors at the school (although he was compliant at day care), which coincided with the time she started to work a forty hour week job which often increased to fifty hours with overtime, and moved in with a boyfriend. She asked for a therapist who could teach her parenting skills and had the ability to modify her son's school behaviors.

This young mother was very clear and passionate about her love for her son, and easily recalled their pleasures together and the close relationship they maintained. The little boy was polite, appeared happy and comfortable with his mother, and agreed that he was "bad" at school, but that he "couldn't stop it". His behavior consisted of driving the teacher crazy by wandering around the room, not paying attention to directions, and leaving his school work unfinished. In contrast, he easily finished his homework if his mother was home with him. When she was working late, he consistently forgot to complete his assignments.

On the surface, this appeared to be a usual case of inconsistent parenting, a child's call for attention, and his wish to have his mother home a greater amount of time. However, from the start of therapy, the manner in which the mother avoided questions which explored the living conditions in the home, and her relationship with her own parents, made me somewhat concerned about the story that was *not* being told. It was a puzzle why the son seemed particularly anxious when he had to stay with his sitter away from home on the weekends when Lisa worked, and why he demanded to sleep in her bed every evening.

In the session I found it difficult to stay with her request to be only taught parenting skills, particularly when she looked distraught, was unable to focus, and seemed acutely depressed. She firmly refused to respond to even the slightest reference to these distressing symptoms. If I had pressed her for more information, or interpreted her appearance, there was no question that she would have terminated treatment.

Therefore, in spite of my concerns, we talked about parent/child love and child-rearing; we explored how naughty behaviors were not the same as a naughty boy; we talked about respect, closeness, and distance, and of freedom versus running away. In short, the loving relationship between mother and son was illuminated and the background was left in the dark. The therapeutic relationship grew firm and the stacks of problem-solving collage tasks grew higher (collage was the only media with which they were willing to work). Each collage was introduced in a similar manner: "together create a solution to the problem you discussed in the session today". The art images silently became the path to reducing the reserve and shame about the background of the symptoms. Gradually, images of an angry man emerged and violent social scenes were picked by the family from the collage box. The mother and son were not ready to acknowledge these images verbally, but their message began to visually enter the foreground through the art product, providing me with a way to speculate and enlarge the field of therapeutic conversation.

A serious issue emerged at this time: should Lisa be confronted about the art expressions which indicated that there was violence in the home? I weighed this situation carefully, coming to the conclusion that I would continue to be attentive, but remain silent about the matter a little longer. Lisa was not yet ready to talk about any issue other than her relationship with her son. If the boy had shown or disclosed any signs of abuse, I would have reported the case immediately. However, since he was improving in school and seemed comfortable at home, I decided to wait. In a case like this one, I prefer to keep the family in treatment, rather than lose them and any hopes of monitoring the situation.

The Role of Art Therapy

Let me briefly interrupt the narrative of this case to focus on the mother's firm decision to use collage and her determined rejection of any other form of art expression. Initially, she had been offered a wide range of media, but her choice was clear. How could that choice be understood within the context of the treatment? First, my natural inclination is to go along with any media chosen by the client if it is comfortable for the client; there is no reason to enter into a power struggle on this level. My conviction is that power struggles lead only to therapeutic failure. Second, upon reflection I respected how wise her choice was in this case. The collage images allowed the greatest amount of peripheral information to "accidently" slip into the art task, since magazine photos are often very complicated in their content and visual attributes. In addition, Lisa felt that her own hand was not responsible for creating these revealing images, which would have not been the case had she made drawings, for example. In this way, she could use denial for protection, making the excuse that a photo was the "only one I can find in the box" or that "I hadn't noticed" a specific detail in the image, one that she was not yet ready to verbalize. Also, the collage gave equal weight to the imagery produced by her son—thus John's interpretation of events or attempts to problem-solve were described in a visual manner. The respect we both gave his products reflected his importance in her life. Unquestionably, this choice of collage was the most effective and efficient vehicle to reach her goals and the one most syntonic with the process she needed to change her world view.

Dis-Solution

> ...In the therapeutic conversation, newness is continually evolving toward "dissolving" the problem and cultivating a new sense of agency and freedom for the client. Problems are, therefore, not solved but dissolved. Dis-solution of the problem may be born of the client's newly acquired sense of agency and self-capability. This sense can evolve from an altered understanding of the problem, which is then no longer viewed or experienced as a problem and may actually be dissolved through actions. Change, whether in the cognitive or behavioral domain, is a natural consequence of dialogue. (Anderson & Goolishian, 1991 p. 325)

As we continued to explore "what constitutes a loving relationship", permission to have a variety of views and descriptions of events was introduced within the framework of parenting skills. This revised understanding of giving and taking nurturance stimulated a parallel understanding of how adult relationships could be negotiated with respect and care on both sides. Lisa slowly and carefully experimented with a new set of lenses. Second-level modification of reality was occurring simultaneously with first level conceptualization of alternate ways of knowing.

As Lisa practiced loving her son and, at the same time, developed the ability to not love some of his behaviors, she also generated a meaning for herself that was new to her world view. This led her to redefine her own position in her primary relationship with her parents. As Lisa grew up, she had not been seen as an unique individual. She was taught, and in time she accepted, the notion that she was created to serve and respond to the variety of needs that her mother demanded of her. Her role in the family was negatively defined so consistently that she discarded as untrue any conflicting positive information that filtered in from the outside world. It followed that in therapy, or as Anderson and Goolishian (1988) define it, "the conversation organized around the problem" (p. 322) of her son's behavior, she was not yet ready to accept a direct confrontation concerning her relationships or her gender-defined roles, past or present. A changed world view remained outside her reality.

Gradually, as we redefined and co-created a new meaning to the difficulties she experienced with her boy, fresh meanings infiltrated her larger view. They became acceptable because they were generated through the only channel that was available to her at the time (the problem of his school behavior). She slowly began to make the connection that her adult position was similar to that of a child who was not getting the kind of nurturing or respect that she had learned was effective and rewarding. She began to apply this new knowledge to herself and to her son.

Lisa's active involvement in the co-creation of ways to express security and love to her son was the only useful path to dissolving the boy's problem and to concurrently examine her own problem of self-worth. The construction of a loving relationship was generalized to the full context of her entire life rather than only between herself and her child. When this became real to her, she then timidly introduced a description of the relationship with a male that she was enduring at home. She slowly moved away from this abusive adult relationship as she re-examined the destructive role to which she had been delegated in her own childhood. In the course of therapy, her ability to love and be loved was confirmed and her ability to redefine her position was supported. She developed a new understanding that to care for another did not include neglecting her own desire for autonomy. Exercising independence did not equate with suffering rejection and abuse from her male companion. As Lisa developed the strength to ask for a complementary adult relationship, her partner reacted in a progressively more controlling and abusive manner. Finally, her positive growth and his inability to join her in this change resulted in the termination of the relationship.

Problem Dissolved

Therapy was not completed until Lisa allowed herself to mourn the loss of love she felt for this man and deal with the guilt she felt because her son witnessed so many scenes of verbal, emotional, and, later, physical abuse. When the boy felt that his mother was strong enough to be her own person, he could give up being protective and strong for her. He lost interest in those school behaviors that were needed to distract his mother from her depression.

The final task in therapy was a careful review of primary belief systems that Lisa had learned as a child. Understanding her parents as products of their own abusive childhoods and creating a new adult relationship with them, freed her to retain her new-found self respect and parenting skills.

Throughout this entire process the art products produced in every session never varied from collages reflecting mother/son conflict and eventual resolution. Lisa observed that the art contained the power to "open her eyes" to repetitive patterns of painful behaviors and brought past and present together in a nonthreatening manner.

In this case, the focus on achieving positive parenting skills gave the mother an understanding of a loving relationship. A person who has not experienced love and respect translates this lack into a perception that s/he is unlovable. As Lisa learned to honor and express her love for her son and to accept his love, she ceased to feel unlovable. Once this transition was made, she no longer had a reason to tolerate an abusive partner and remain in a second-class position with her companion; she had become worthwhile.

Through learning parenting skills, Lisa effectively parented not only her son, but also herself. She had discovered a perfect vehicle to introduce change in herself as well as her relationships with others.

Summary

This case demonstrates that women who deny that they are being abused must be "believed" until they see the situation differently. Going slowly and following the path the client leads is sometimes a difficult course to maintain, but is, in the long run, the more effective choice where the violence is agressively denied. Untimely confrontations are disrespectful of the client's right to reveal painful events at her own pace. Each client will define her situation in an individual manner, and a redefinition will also emerge in an equally unique way. Dis-solution of the problem-organizing system occurs through both verbal dialogue and the silent language of art expression. This process does not preclude the legal reporting responsibilities of the therapist in cases of abuse, but it does provide the framework for treatment.

Trust the art product to do its magic for foretelling the next productive step in informing the therapist and the client on how to creatively bring new meanings to view in an acceptable and effective manner. It is tempting to immediately share the perceived meanings that surface in the art work. Revelations by the therapist may be motivated by a decision to bring new material into the session; it also may be an irresistible desire to share his/her own view of the client's art expressions. In both cases, the move may be premature and can stand in the way of the client making his/her own discoveries. An important therapeutic issue is rarely lost and the persistence of the imagery in the art products can validate the therapist's perception of the situation.

Therapists can use other techniques to illuminate the material rather than hastily interpreting the art. Co-constructing alternate views of the imagery assists the client in creating alternate meanings with the therapist. The dissolution of the problem comes about through observations and descriptions of both the verbal and nonverbal presentation of the narrative in a joint effort between client and therapist. Comparing narrative to illustration gives flexibility to the process and can result in the reinvention of a new ending to a dysfunctional tale.

References

Anderson, H., & Goolishian, H. (1988). Human systems as linguistic systems: Preliminary and evolving ideas about the implications for clinical theory. *Family Process, 27* (4), 371-393.

Riley, S. (1993). Illustrating the family story: Art therapy, a lens for viewing the family's reality. *The Arts in Psychotherapy, 20,* 253-264.

Suggested Readings

Anderson, H. & Goolishian, H. (1985). Systems consultation to agencies dealing with domestic violence. In L. Wynne, S. McDaniel & T. White (Eds.), *The family therapist as consultant.* New York: Guilford Press.

Finkelhor, D. (1983). *The dark side of families.* Beverley Hills, CA: Sage.

Goldner, V. (1985). Feminism and family therapy. *Family Process, 24,* 31-47.

Goldner, V., Penn, P., Sheinberg, M., & Walker, G. (1990). Love and violence: Gender paradoxes in volatile attachments. *Family Process, 29,* 343-363.

Hare-Mustin, R. (1987). The problem of gender in family therapy. *Family Process, 26,* 15-27.

Malchiodi, C. (1990). B*reaking the silence: Art therapy with children from violent homes.* New York: Brunner/Mazel.

Naitove, C. (1982). Art therapy with sexually abused children. In S. Sgroi (Ed.) *Handbook of Clinical Intervention in Child Sexual Abuse.* Lexington, MA: Lexington Books.

Pynoos, R., & Eth, S. (1986). Special intervention programs for child witnesses to violence. In M. Lystad (Ed.), *Violence in the Home.* New York: Brunner/Mazel.

LANGUAGING: EXAMINING THE VERBAL COMPONENT OF ART THERAPY TREATMENT

I am concerned that the public and health professionals suffer from a general misconception about the field of art therapy. Often brochures, literature and presentations give the impression that art therapy is solely a nonverbal modality. In my opinion, the majority of art therapy expressions are explored verbally with the client as an integral part of the therapy session. Progress toward change is manifest in the dialogue between the therapist and client in reference to the expressive product.

This leads to the inquiry: does the discourse exploring the art expression demonstrate that there can be an awareness of both first and second level meaning simultaneously in therapy? One must still grapple with the paradox that although descriptive language is created by the client/family, they are bound by their linguistic structures in the verbal expression of these views. The art therapy product may be thought to lie between these two levels of reality. It is created primarily to reflect the clients' personal views, but is forced to accommodate language when attempts are made to reveal or interpret its meaning.

This dialogue, exploring the art, and the aesthetics of the verbal components of the art therapy process have seldom been examined in our field (Andrus, 1990). The neglect is particularly noticeable in light of the serious attention given to languaging in the literature of allied professions (Allman, 1982; Goolishian & Anderson, 1992; Efran, Lukens, & Lukens, 1990; Epston & White, 1991; Sluzki, 1992). My own focus on the verbal

This chapter originally appeared in *Art Therapy: Journal of the American Art Therapy Association,* 11 (3), (1994) in a slightly different form and is reprinted with permission.

component of art therapy is not meant to diminish the central importance of the art product. The aesthetics of languaging only add to the visual product and the effectiveness of the psychotherapeutic process.

Hearing client's language does not negate the process of looking at the art product. It is a synthesis of two creative means of communication. The union of the client's oral story and the illustrations of their story gives a depth and dimension which introduces new contructs into the client's recursive, symptom-bound tale (Riley, 1993).

It should not be a threat to art therapists to accept the holistic aspects of art therapy: the visual product, the verbal exploration of the art expression, and the experiential components of the process. Each of these aspects contributes to and supports the other. We are people who primarily appreciate our ability to think symbolically and create visual metaphors with our clients. We also give thought to our images and those thoughts are translated into an internal verbal dialogue. Those words rising from the image are then expressed in some manner with the client, sometimes verbally and other times through art expression. I wish to focus our attention on this junction between the visual product and the verbal enhancement of this expression.

Reflections on Languaging

Let us start with a concept of the knowing process. We have, I believe, two ways of understanding our world. We have a knowing process that is purely symbolic, impressionistic, with no words attached. We also have cognitive knowing that attempts to explain and describe these silent images and emotive qualities. Tinnin (1990, p. 9) states that "when one's nonverbal memories conflict with what one consciously remembers and that conflict is troubling, it may be necessary to bypass the obligatory censorship and rescue the nonverbal message in its wordless form 'in art'". Later, he continues, "the therapist must be careful when converting a message from pictures into words to avoid unintentional distortion by the therapist's own verbal censorship". His article addresses both the split and the synthesis of symbolic and cognitive knowing.

Generally two kinds of art expressions are presented in the art therapy session. One type of work is closer to nonverbal knowing of our own inner symbolic world, a more aesthetic art work, and the other a more pragmatic expression which may be closer to the cognitive and language-bound understanding of the narrative we live. How the art product is perceived and utilized by the client is important. A symbolic image usually does not reveal all its meaning until the client has had time to contemplate it. A pragmatic expression is often more directly focused on a problem or the situation surrounding the problem. In this case, the art maker is conscious of the meaning of the image, although unexpected meaning may also emerge. If therapists are aware of the verbal techniques more appropriate to each style, I believe that we will be more useful to our clients.

Gergen (1991) states: "We must break away from the time-honored practice of explaining cognition primarily as something that individuals do in their heads. Instead, our attention must shift to the communal organization in which symbols arise and without language could not have come into being". This author goes on to say that the lens of knowing that language provides becomes so familiar to us that we become blind to other truths of perception. It appears to me that treating "blindness" is one function of art therapy.

I again emphasize the sensitivity that the therapist must maintain to find a path which leads from the client's art product to the meaning of the work. The client's lenses are surely not our own. Therefore, the significance s/he attaches to the illustration is information we must learn from them.

The importance of the symbol in family work is stated by Connell, Milten and Whitaker (1993):

> Symbol formation is an ongoing process of the mind. In a healthy family, a free-flowing interaction exists between the world of experience and the world of symbols...current experiences constantly reshape the symbolic....Conversely in a dysfunctional family there is a split between the world of experience and the world of symbol. Thus symbols become fixed and rigid, inhibiting growth. (p. 246)

At the point that the symbolic art expressions of the family demonstrate these dysfunctional patterns, the therapist looks for ways to co-create more successful patterning in the family relationships. To see the patterns through externalization of the symbols makes this split clearly visible to client and therapist.

One of the distinctions to which we must attend is described by Goolishian and Anderson (1992):

> We believe description and explanation are distinct activities, a difference pointed to exactly by Wittgnestein. 'Our mistake is to look for explanation, when we ought to look at what happens' (1968, p. 654). Mistaking descriptions for causal explanation is a result of being imposed upon or even duped by language to the point of our forgetting how our notions developed from figures of speech and the interactional process of therapist and client taking turns talking together. (p. 456)

It follows that sensitivity to language is a prerequisite to the process of art therapy.

The quotes and notions I have presented here are a basis for considering some techniques that I believe would blend well with an individual or family art therapy practice. The goal is to eliminate the split between the visual and verbal communication within the therapeutic process.

Circular Questioning: An Example of the Integration of Art Therapy with Verbal Technique

Imagine a situation where a family gathers in the art therapy room and in response to the therapist, "How did things go this week?", they produce four different versions of the conflicts in the home. The mother, relieved that her mother has moved out, draws a sun smiling down on her home. The daughter of eight draws rain and drooping flowers with a grey environment; she misses her grandmother. The husband draws himself flattened on the chaise watching TV (dead tired from the conflict in the home). The older son draws himself in an empty, desolate field playing baseball all alone; the boy feels that no one is on his "team". The family's conflicting opinions of what happened of importance during the week is quite a common occurrence in a family art therapy session. However, what evolves next may be "uncommon". It is at this moment of exploring the meaning of the art, the introduction of the verbal component, that a multitude of opportunities are available, depending on the therapist's style and belief system.

I feel that at this juncture, the family's world view, expressed in both art and language, creates a challenge to a therapist's sensitivity, creativity and aesthetic awareness, thus presenting an opportunity to provide a significant window for growth. Let us consider some options regarding the above family example. Do we simply ask the family to discuss the content of their pictures? Do we limit the family to their stories of the art piece? Do we ask each member to take another family member's drawing and find meaning in it? If we choose the latter approach, the family's perceptions and misperceptions are conveyed to each other, the magical thinking is unveiled, and the communication system is made visible through the family's interaction with each other's art products. The art process then leads to a form of circular questioning (Penn, 1982).

Thomm (1985) describes circular questioning in this manner:

> "Circular questions tend to characterize about the possible connectedness of events that include the problem, rather than a precise need to know the problem... These questions are reflexive in that they are formulated to trigger family members to reflect upon the implications of their current perceptions and action and to consider options."

Circular questioning is often referred to as "family gossip"(Palazzoli, Cecchin, Prata, & Boscolo, 1978), where one family member tells about another. The therapist is able to include others in the gossip by asking questions that unsettle the rigid belief system of the clients.

I use the technique of circular questioning in conjunction with art expressions made in a family therapy session to show how images are often the most important knowing that we experience. For example, one way to do this is to give each person a chance to speculate on the other members' art expressions. This punctuates how projections and personal convictions often have little to do with the message the creator intended to convey. In a family session, as each person looks at and discusses the other members' art work, they can recognize discrepancies between the message they imagined the art conveyed and the message that the art maker really had in mind. By using the technique of circular questioning to help the family investigate how misinterpretation might affect a third party, the entire family can be included in the dialogue. The opportunity to open up countless alternative explanations becomes viable, and the original "truth" becomes only one option.

I have lingered on this technique of circular questioning, not only because it is useful for a family to engage in creative thinking, but also because it demonstrates how visual expression can be enriched by verbal knowing. It also adds to the process of clarifying the intended meaning in nonverbal communication. Additionally, the metacommunications can be observed through the family's unique comments on how meaning is assigned to both words and actions. In other words, the ways of communicating and symbolizing in the family become less mysterious.

In spite of the power of the art to enlarge the family's understanding, they still will not "hear" the therapist unless s/he speaks in a language that stylistically reflects this particular family group. Therefore, attentive listening for the metaphor, or even better, to extract the visual metaphors from the drawings, gives the therapist a dictionary that mirrors their unique way of perceiving the world and understanding events. Also, the therapist should be sensitive to any cultural or societal messages in the art expressions specific to the family's way of knowing their world.

In using circular questioning based on art expression, the image both stimulates and reflects each family member's perception of an event. The individual creator of the images has the opportunity to correct the perceptions of others with his/her own narratives. In this manner, the therapist learns how each family member views the world and begins the process of co-creating a synthesis of these views. The desired outcome is to find a new vision for the family. The language the therapist uses in the discussion reflects the family's mode of communication. The description of the art work and explanation of the meaning allows more possibilities for communication and resolution of problems within the family and their social context.

Fish (1993), observes the therapeutic process in this manner: "Families and individuals do construct their lives, including their own stories; these stories both make possible and constrain their existence. But, as Leipnitz (1988, p. 146) has observed, they have not made these stories 'just to please'. Nor may we assist them to construct new stories, 'just as we please'. There are circumstances which are, inevitably, directly encountered, and these are the result of past individual, group, and institutional processes"(p. 230). So even as we attend to our client's narratives, we also acknowledge the impact of society and the larger system. Aesthetic and pragmatic problem-solving skills are brought into the dialogue; realities of the social system's impact are not ignored. The narrative of the clients is modified through alterations in the story which lead to a change in how the problem is perceived. Both aesthetic and pragmatic knowing informs the dialogue; image and language form the constructive process.

Enhancing Transformations Through Art Therapy

Continuing along the line of reasoning that attempts to blend the art, words and therapeutic techniques, I would like to turn to Sluzki's article (1992) on the subject of transformations. This essay suggests, in regard to therapeutic conversation, "... an encounter can be defined as therapeutic when a transformation has taken place in the family's set of dominant stories to include new experiences, meaning, and (inter) actions. This has the effect of loosening the thematic grip of the stories of symptomatic problematic behaviors" (p. 217). He proceeds to consider some transformative micro-practices which act as a force to provide variables in the dimensions of the client's tale.

I am interested in Sluzki's theory for two reasons. First, it in essence describes the process of change; second, I believe, each of these techniques is enhanced when associated with art therapy. I will attempt to interpret some of his ideas as they relate to art therapy as I practice it.

Briefly, Sluzki looks at the following:

1) *transformation in time*; shifts between descriptions that do not present temporal fluctuations and one that does. A search for exceptions to "an event unmovable in time" can be well addressed through the art, by having the client find illustrations of a time when the symptom did *not* impact the family, or create pictorially how it would be in the future if the symptom disappeared. This directive has the client find fluctuations in time of their own making.

2) *the use of nouns/verbs*; shifts between the definitions of events and descriptions of actions; i.e., when dealing with a situation that the client describes as possessing immutable attributes, the art therapist first asks the client to draw the situation. S/he then asks, "When is it more or less intense? How do you react when this situation occurs?" The execution of the drawing is an action in itself that implies an action is possible in the problematic circumstance; to imagine more or less intensity denies permanence.

3) *Ahistoric/historic*; shifts between a story devoid of historical roots and context vs. one with a scenario; this intervention is particularly well-suited to an art therapy task that asks the client to illustrate a past event and subsequently invites them to draw, cut, and paste changes directly on the original product. This intervention brings the past rigid patterns into the here and now of the session and symbolically changes history by changing the art work.

Sluzki continues to describe his micro-practices in transforming causality, symptoms/conflicts, roles/rules, and values of the story. These fundamental moves are concepts of interest for most therapists; however, when we have more to work with than words alone, when the client can "transform" an art object, the process becomes more personal, more believable and more securely anchored in their belief system.

Additional Observations

A radio discussion about an adolescent training program used a homily that struck me as pertinent to our profession. The quote was, "Tell me what to do and I'll forget; show me what to do and I'll remember; let me do it and I will learn". This is our way of doing therapy. We utilize all the capabilities of the person: doing, showing, telling. The silent knowing through the symbol speaks non-verbally to the hand that transforms it into seeing. "Seeing" is then translated by the cognitive mind. When the cognitive mind has access to this material it informs the person and the therapist through words. Based on this information the therapist proceeds to redefine the meaning of the patterns with client/ family by utilizing new ways of co-constructing alternative realities. First-level explanations are changed by second-level descriptions (Golann, 1988).

A final example of how aesthetics has become a concern in the field of family therapy is from Cecchin (1978) in an article about therapeutic curiosity.

"Another idea central to developing a stance of curiosity is the concept of aesthetics. In describing artists he was teaching at the California School of Fine

Arts, Bateson recognized that they were 'responsive to the pattern which connects' (1972, p. 8). An orientation toward pattern, as opposed to an orientation toward discrete entities, is more suggestive of the realm of art... To adopt an aesthetic orientation, interaction not only shifts our focus toward pattern, but also emphasizes the multiplicity of possible patterns... Through the myriad of stories, we begin to see descriptions, and subsequent explanation, in more neutral ways".
(p. 406)

This quotation emphasizes a therapeutic orientation that, in my mind, implies that the family's descriptions and stories can be refocused through art expressions. Patterns of behaviors and the notions of a created reality have been a core concept from the beginnings of family therapy. The term aesthetics has also been used regularly (Allman, 1982). In the field of art therapy, the term often has a much closer relationship to the "production of beauty" rather than the creation of successful clinical sessions.

The component of curiosity which Cecchin notes refers to the therapist's ability to puzzle with the client on how patterns were created and if they are the kind of recurring behaviors that have benefited the family in the past, and now in the present. These patterns, when expressed through art, can be visual statements that are often creative and beautiful in their own way.

I have chosen a constructionist's theoretical lens to illustrate a holistic approach to treatment; this may not be the theoretical choice others would make. However, I believe that most would agree that the following premise is true. Therapists work in ways that fit their understanding of therapy and that perspective will be a part of their clients' experience. Therefore, it seems to me that we should embrace a description of art therapy that includes languaging as an integral part of the entire therapeutic process. The services we provide will be more effective if we include, rather than exclude, a broad range of theories that may be utilized in our practice of art psychotherapy.

Case Examples

I would like to share a few examples that demonstrate two types of art expression that I have observed. A full clinical description of these cases is too lengthy for this chapter

The first example (see Figures 1-6) is client work completed at home and then later processed in the session; this is work that took time and contemplation to produce. An aesthetic knowing was the dominant process. The client (Margaret) had a great deal of trouble understanding the message and the potential in her drawings. Gradually, the power of the image emerged into her conceptual knowing and became the vehicle for change.

Margaret, self-referred to my private practice, had sought art therapy

Figure 1: "I watch - they fly"

Figure 2: "Black hearts in a coffin. How can I get away?"

Figure 3: "You can't eat me—turn my heart to excrement"

Figure 4: "so hard to break away. The phoenix rises out of the
graves of my parents"

Figure 5: "The phoenix breaks out of the black egg"

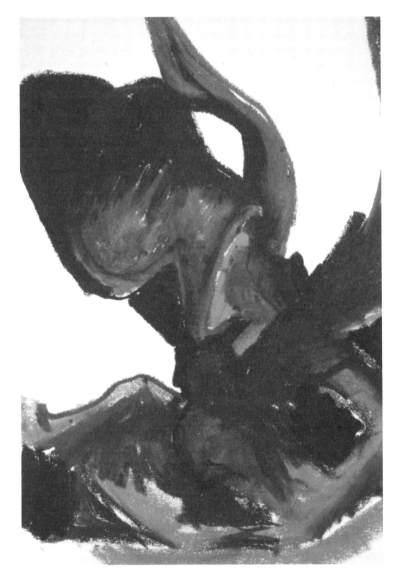

Figure 6: "The bottle of tears opens, sadness pours out,
takes form—flys away"

after she had read about it in a bookstore she owned. She had a strong interest in the arts, having created ceramic vessels as an ongoing artistic outlet. Middle-aged and married for a second time, she was discontent, depressed and had to cope with a medical problem which was not life-threatening, but uncomfortable. She had several periods of depression where she chose hospitalization to protect herself from suicidal impulses. Margaret was very intelligent, well-educated and held an advanced degree in literature. She had previous therapy in which she came to terms with her abusive childhood.

She was convinced that art therapy would be of benefit because she said "when I talk my thoughts go all fuzzy and I can't seem to focus on the ideas that I start out with". I also was aware that following her conversation was difficult. She often changed the direction of her thoughts or began to make tangential references to the subject being discussed. For Margaret, it was essential to have a firm image that remained tangible and concrete.

The six illustrations have been selected to demonstrate a "Phoenix Rising" theme that continued over an eight-month period of therapy and seemed to be her vehicle for change. Many drawings were done in an art therapy personal journal; the second theme was the "emergent woman" which appeared concurrently with this theme of the "Phoenix rising". (This second theme is not illustrated in this paper.)

I have quoted lines from the free associations she made after finishing the drawings. She recorded her thoughts on the page opposite from the image in her journal. She was making the first step toward turning the wordless image into awareness through language. The drawings are black lines with blues and greens intermingled; the lines flowing upward with the phoenix form were always in vermilion and cadmium orange. The contrast was visually dramatic.

The art revealed to her that there was a woman fighting to emerge from the ashes of her destructive past. The metaphor of the "Phoenix Rising" gave words to the image and power to the vision. The dynamic drawings gave her an idea of her own potential that had been repressed and neglected during her youth and marriages. She was energized out of a depressive state and stimulated to take the chance to change. She concluded that her life-style could become congruent with her more passionate interior life. She continues to work in this manner in art therapy sessions.

The second case is an example of a family of three: mother, age 30, son, age 9, and daughter, age 7, who were dealing with divorce and feelings of rejection. This was a pragmatic problem that required creative solutions in order to reframe a situation that appeared out of the family's capacity to accept.

The type of art product and the use of the expressions were in keeping with the immediate problem-solving needs of the family. Clinic environment also affected how art therapy was presented, e.g., once a week, for one hour sessions. The art therapy was also modified by the developmental levels of the family. An adult woman, a pre-adolescent boy, and a latency age girl have different ways of expressing themselves, both verbally and graphically. Also, the children had a different awareness of the problem than did their mother. They benefited from sharing these contrasting views and finding new meanings through drawing which accommodated their various levels of development and understanding.

Specifically, the mother was unable to emotionally release her ex-husband in spite of the divorce. He remained her main focus of concern and, because of this stance, she kept the children in a scenario where they were delegated to act out her emotions. They substituted for the affection she felt was owed her; they acted out the fear she taught them and conveyed this fearful message to their father. He reciprocated by moving directly across the street with his partner who eventually became his new wife. The client lived behind closed blinds and came in with the same closed attitude toward change.

The case evolved from the position of blaming all the troubles on the ex-husband, to a realization that the hierarchy in the home was the most disturbed feature of the therapy. Living in the home were four generations of the mother's family: great-grandmother, grandmother, the client and her children. The roles were clear: the great-grandmother acted like "mother,' the grandmother took the position of daughter, my client assumed the responsibility for all of them in the capacity of the great-grandmother role. The children were aware of this confusion and the only male—the son—was pressured to disengage from the only male role model in his life, his divorced father.

The boy acted out this pressure by developing asthmatic attacks that came on every morning as he was about to leave for school. After a medical examination that showed no physical reason for these attacks, it seemed possible that he wheezed when he became anxious about leaving his mother. He seemed to think that his father would force entry into the home and frighten his mother, part of a script that he had been taught.

He gave up this solution when the therapist insisted that his mother walk him to school and sit next to him in his classroom all day, so that he could see that she was safe. His embarrassment at having his mom at school was stronger than his fear-induced asthma. He was encouraged to take this new control over his life into his visitations with his father.

Through a series of drawings, these enmeshed and confused relationships were examined and the children's voices were heard through the art products. Figure 7 is an example of a group drawing in which the family (after several sessions) was able to acknowledge that the divorce was indeed a final act. They titled the drawing "The Old House is Gone", which they explained was the home they lived in when their father was part of the family.

Figures 8, 9 and 10 were drawn in another session. In Figure 8, the son drew a happy outing with his father (this was very risky for him to do since he was not supposed to have pleasure with his dad). In Figure 9, the mother drew a casket with roses on the lid. She just "happened" to remember the death of a friend. Lastly, in Figure 10, the daughter drew a "I love you" drawing to diffuse and repair the intense emotion that was evoked from the boy's drawing of a "good fishing day". These drawings allowed the images to communicate in a way that usual conversation in this family prohibited.

Figure 11 is a family drawing directed toward the question "what needs fixing?". Daughter drew great-grandmother in bed, demanding service, with the ghosts of the past around her bed; on the opposite side of the paper the son also drew the grandmother and great-grandmother having supper as he waited on them; in the center of the paper the mother is confused with words "What shall I do?" and "Pick up (the pieces) of everyone's life". This more straightforward confrontation of the generational stress in the family gave the family and therapist an opportunity to speculate on readjusting the hierarchy and freeing the children from adult responsibilities. Clearly, these drawings were not on an aesthetic level of communication, but they described the family system and its troubles. They informed the family and illustrated their symptom-bound story.

The therapy progressed from this base of information. The outcome was a partial success, although the power of the generational female role assignments was impossible to break. However, there was some bending of the rules and the children did benefit. In particular, the ex-husband/father was divested of his "evil" character and the boy and girl could enjoy their visits with him. Also, the shades of the front room were raised about fifty percent.

The therapeutic plan in this case was much more action-oriented than the previous vignette. The shift in emphasis came more through environmental change than emergent awareness in the art work alone. These children and their mother used the art tasks to externalize their problems. Once viewed from a distance through art expression, they could begin to follow suit and

Figure 7: son "The old house is gone"

Figure 8: mother "Happy day with father"

Figure 9: mother "Death of a friend"

Figure 10: daughter "I love you mother"

Figure 11: "What needs fixing?"

disengage from their destructive pattern. They learned to accept reality and still have appropriate feelings of loss.

Summary

In the cases presented, the art therapy products differ greatly; however, each was appropriate for the given situation. Basically, the therapeutic approaches were similar, with the therapist introducing speculations of change by creating transformations in the stories told by the clients, transformations informed by the art expressions and spoken about in the sessions.

In the first case, the primary agent of change was the nonverbal, impressionistic, emotive imagery that informed the direction of the therapy. Through the exploration of the symbolic expression, the language of cognitive knowing released the silent meaning. The merging of the two, nonverbal and verbal, capacities of the client gave the woman the motivation to enter into the process of change. She identified with the "Phoenix Rising" as her own flight into a more desirable reality. Her art was powerful but until she was able to give words to the images, she was unable to cognitively access the potential in her new scenario.

In the second case, the art expressions served as a form of communication, closer to words than symbols. This family benefited from the encouragement given in the art therapy sessions to find more creative ways to solve their problems and to transform the immutable obstacles into difficulties they could manage. Words had not been sufficient to break through the rigid patterns of behavior. The therapist provided opportunities for transformations in the family's perceptions of their problems.

We can make the observation that recognizing at least two systems of knowing must come into play to assure a greater possibility of success in art therapy treatment. By holding fast to the belief that creative solutions come about in a holistic manner syntonic with the individual's way of perceiving and experiencing their world, the interaction of language and art expression throughout treatment resulted in individualized therapy that was judged by the client as satisfactory.

Art therapists who are interested in working within a social constructionist framework in their practice of art therapy are advised to carefully consider the dialogue between therapist and client(s). A basic concept of the social constructionist view is that the therapeutic session is time spent in conversation, co-constructing a new outcome to a problematic situation presented by the client(s). Therefore, unless the concept of "languaging", the dialogue that arises from exploration of the art product, is attended to and understood, the desired outcome of therapy may be at risk.

The author regards the art product as an illumination of the world view of the client(s). The art product is a visual guideline which informs the therapist in which direction to proceed and encourage new possibilities for resolution of the dilemma under discussion. Therefore, how that art product is discussed is the core of successful therapy.

References

Allman, L. (1982). The aesthetic reference: Overcoming the pragmatic error. *Family Process*, 21, 43-56.

Andrus, L. (1990). Art therapy education: A tool for developing verbal skills. *Art Therapy: Journal of the American Art Therapy Association, 7*,

Bateson, G. (1979). *Mind and nature*. New York: E. P. Dutton.

Cecchin, G. (1966). Hypothesizing, circularity, and neutrality revisited: An invitation to curiosity. *Family Process*, 26, 405-413.

Connell, G., Milten, G., & Whitaker, C. (1993). Reshaping family symbols: A symbolic-experiential perspective. *Journal of Marital and Family Therapy*, 19 (3), 245-254.

Efran, J. Lukens, M., & Lukens, R. (1990). *Language structure and change*. New York: Norton.

Epston, D., & White, M. (1991). *Experience contradiction, narrative and imagination*. Australia: Delwich Center Publications.

Fish, V. (1993). Poststructuralism in family therapy: Interrogating the narrative/ conversational mode. *Journal of Marital and Family Therapy*, 19 (3), 223-234.

Gergen, K. (1991). *The saturated self.* New York: Harper Collins.

Golann, S. (1988). On second-order family therapy. *Family Process*, 27, 51-57.

Goolishian, H., & Anderson, H. (1992). Strategy and intervention versus non-intervention: A matter of theory. *Journal of Marital and Family Therapy*, 18 (1), 11.

Palazzoli, M. S., Cecchin, G., Prata, G., & Boscolo, H. (1978). *Paradox and counterparadox.* New York: Jason Aronson.

Penn, P. (1982). Circular questioning. *Family Process,* 21, 267-280.

Riley, S. (1993). Illustrating the family story: Art therapy, ideas for viewing the family's reality. *The Arts in Psychotherapy*, 20, 253-264.

Sluzki, C. (1992). Transformations: A blueprint for narrative changes in therapy. *Family Process*, 31, 217-230.

Thomm, K. (1985). Circular interviewing: A multifaceted clinical tool. In D. Campbell & R. Droper (Eds.), *Application of Systemic Therapy: The Milan Approach.* London: Grune & Stratton.

Tinnin, L. (1990). Biological processes in nonverbal communication and their role in the making and interpretations of art. *American Journal of Art Therapy,* 29, 9-13.

SCHIZOPHRENIA AS A SOLUTION TO FAMILY DISORDERS: USING A STRUCTURAL APPROACH TO TREATMENT

The following clinical case example explores how the therapist responded to a family's crisis and felt directed to choose a structural family therapy approach to treatment. This case will also punctuate the dilemma felt by the therapist when the family failed to be aroused by symptoms of serious illness. This casual attitude resulted in one instance in a tragedy, and in the other instance, therapeutic intervention was needed to provide protection for a second family member.

When a family seeks treatment their perceptions of danger, family interactions, and issues of importance are not necessarily matched by the clinician's view of their situation. Finding a balance between searching for their world view and a plan of actions that would not neglect a client at risk is the main topic of the following discussion.

In the framework of treatment from the first phone call, followed by the early assessment sessions with a family, the therapist searches for the theoretical approach that best fits the family's way of perceiving (or misperceiving) their difficulties. As their story unfolds, the family reveals patterns that recreate situations as though they were authoring a clinical theory. When their needs direct us to a plan of action, the clinician can begin to think along therapeutic terms and clarify goals on the family's behalf.

The family discussed in this chapter demonstrated a need for structure, clarity, and a realignment of the family hierarchy. A serious disorder in one of the children labeled schizophrenic seemed to be viewed benignly by the entire family; this was out of the norm and a puzzle. In contrast, the chaos in the family was apparent. The schizophrenic oldest daughter (16 years) directed the interactions in the family and interceded between her parents. The next child, a boy of 14 years, was by choice almost entirely nonverbal; he modeled after his father's behavior. The third child, a girl of 10 years, was "perfect" and advised her mother on finding the correct solutions to the family's problems. The father appeared deeply concerned about his family, at least in the sessions, but the family reported that he was very distant and spent his time in the garage workshop. He had recently had a serious melanoma removed and was receiving chemotherapy, but no other family member regarded this as a serious illness. The mother disregarded her husband and found her family identity with her daughters.

The only thing that seemed to be clear to the therapist was that the family system was very skewed. The teenage girl was the leader and the center of the family's actions; the father and son had formed a subsystem which removed them from daily activities. The mother had joined with the girls in another subsystem wherein the youngest daughter was parenting her parents. These confused boundaries and enmeshed interactions led the therapist to believe that a structural approach to treatment would be the best choice.

Salvador Minuchin outlined structural family therapy treatment techniques in 1974 in *Families and Family Therapy*. He observed that functional families work best when: 1) clear boundaries are set between the nuclear family and their families of origin; 2) there are closed boundaries around the marital subsystem to insure privacy; 3) boundaries clarify the parental dyad, but are accessible to children in matters of parenting; 4) limitations also exist around the children subsystem, designating privileges and tasks according to the age of the siblings. Crossover alliances, triangulations, enmeshments, and diffused boundaries result in a dysfunctional family system.

In addition, the structural approach requires an active stance by the therapist. S/he looks for self-reinforcing sequences and behaviors in the family that are attempts to eliminate the symptom and at the same time sustain it. As the problem is being attacked, it is simultaneously being supported covertly by conflictual behaviors. A criticism of this approach says that to recognize and successfully intervene in these difficult situations takes a skilled and charismatic personality. Also, a great deal of training is necessary before a therapist can recognize these invisible patterns in the family system (Hoffman, 1981).

The addition of art products created by family members in therapy greatly enhances the possibility that the therapist will see these invisible dynamics. The family most probably will not be aware that they expose the first and second levels of their transactions in their artwork. In their innocence, they inadvertently give the therapist through their art expressions access to knowledge that will ultimately lead to change in the dysfunctional patterns of interactions.

Hopefully, the art therapist who undertakes this type of approach will be well trained and experienced in working with families. However, the addition of clinical art therapy to the overall treatment plan makes the family patterns so much more visible that s/he can proceed with added confidence.

Case Example

The case described below demonstrates an enmeshed family pattern where behaviors labeled as "schizophrenic" served a function in the family system. This observation does not intend to contradict the biological explanation for this psychic disorder, but to demonstrate that as these symptoms emerged, the family appeared to have directed the behaviors to serve a purpose in their relationships. The family's diffused thought patterns and tangential thinking needed structure and limit setting. Thus a structural approach to art therapy was utilized in this case.

History

The outpatient clinic received an emergency call from the local psychiatric teaching hospital. The intake person was advised to anticipate a call from the family of a 16-year-old girl with the diagnosis of acute schizophrenia. They cautioned that the girl was still at risk and that the family had been asked to leave the hospital treatment due to their lack of cooperation. The adolescent treatment team had recommended continuing care, after discharge, in a closed residential setting, but the family had refused the suggestion. Under these circumstances, the hospital released the girl to the family's care and made it clear that this decision ran counter to the plan they felt was therapeutically correct for her. They, in fact, felt very concerned and recommended immediate treatment.

The family's call for help was taken on the clinic's crisis line, and because of the serious nature of the problem, was referred directly to the Family and Child division. The family consisted of father and mother, each in their late '40s, in a second marriage of 18 years; daughter, 16 years, son, 14 years, and youngest daughter, 10 years. The father had a daughter 32-years-old by his first wife, and the mother had two thirty-something daughters (both married) and a son 25-years-old by her first husband. The son was a patient in a psychiatric hospital; these older children had been out of the home for some time.

The precipitating event that brought on the schizophrenic break occurred about six months before this therapist met the family. The father decided to take his son and older daughter to Australia to spend some time with their grandmother. The trip was arranged so that there would be small island visits on the way. At the third island visit the father "forgot" to see that his daughter was on the plane and they left without her. By the time they arranged a return flight, the girl had become disoriented, fearful and was actively hallucinating. They flew back home and entered her into the hospital immediately where she was treated on the adolescent unit for three months.

During the hospital stay, the family consistently subverted the family therapy hour. These sessions were led by a very experienced, well-known and respected family therapist. Because of their noncompliance, the treatment plan was not implemented and goals were not achieved. The family's behavior incurred the anger of the staff and they expelled the patient with written instructions, but gave up on following through with future treatment plans.

When the family was assigned to this therapist, the information I had received seemed formidable, but most disturbing was the issue of noncompliance and the "at-risk" condition of the 16-year-old girl. To provide the kind of protection this child needed it was necessary to enlist the parents' cooperation and a positive, primary joining with them was of the greatest importance. My plan was to immediately set up a "suicide watch" until medication stabilized her and a routine was created for her daily activities. A member of the family would be by her side constantly. The four to six-hour watch periods would rotate from father to mother and/or another responsible adult, including both day and night hours.

The first goal in the treatment of this family was to fulfill the obligation of insuring the primary client's safety. Ethical responsibility was of the greatest importance in this case. A strategy needed to be created that would be acceptable to the family and effectively protect the child. My hypothesis was that establishing an executive parental position was the most effective first step in achieving a positive change in this system. Clarifying the boundaries between parents and children was the structural change that would best serve the family's needs at this time.

Minuchin (1974) expressed the goals that I had in mind for this family:

> This is the foundation of family therapy. The therapist joins the family with the goal of changing family organization in such a way that the family members' experiences change. By facilitating the use of alternative modalities of transaction among family members, the therapist makes use of the family matrix in the process of healing. The changed family offers its members new circumstances and new perspectives of themselves vis-a-vis their circumstances.

84

The changed organization makes possible a continuous reinforcement of the changed experience, which provides a validation of the changed sense of self. (p. 14)

Treatment

The family required new skills to organize themselves and provide a cessation from the chaos of their daily patterns. I also needed a structured approach to give me freedom to set goals with the family and focus their attention on achieving them.

At the first session, the family was strangely lacking in the ability to explain why they were at the clinic. Although the daughter looked distraught, they directed their complaints to the distant position of the father in the family and the general lack of communication between members. The girl's problems were mentioned very casually.

The lack of ability to stay with the presenting problem (the 16 year-old's hallucinations and suicidal ideation) was demonstrated both by tangential discourse and unrelated subject matter in the art expressions. The one exception was the youngest girl who asked for help in the art product. In Figure 1, the father depicted everyone facing away in his collage; Figure 2

Figure 1: "Father's first collage of isolation"

Figure 2: Mother's collage "Denial of problem"

Figure 3: Son's nonverbal surfing drawing

Figure 4: Schizophrenic 16-year-old daughter's drawing

Figure 5: Ten-year-old daughter's prescription for happiness

shows that the mother was focused on "making friends with animals", another tangential theme; in Figure 3 the son started a surfer series which had little significance at this time; in Figure 4 the oldest daughter created a drawing/collage which depicted her inner visions; in Figure 5 the youngest daughter asked for help, showing a crippled family, how "lightning struck" if they tried to talk.

After the first three weeks of medication the daughter's crisis was controlled and the immediate threats to herself were diminished. By the third session, the art work revealed how much the mother was involved with her daughter; indeed, she seemed to be one of the "girls". The mother drew as a "pupil" of her youngest daughter and copied her imagery, presenting art work that was filled with happy representations which avoided the crisis of the daughter's condition and the confusion in the family. Her son, modeling after his dad, aligned with his father in a silent partnership of withdrawal. He began to draw the same image at every session. It was a picture of a surfer riding a large wave into what appeared to be destruction on a large rock. At this time, I was unaware that this drawing repeated over and over would inform me of the family's progress. The surfer moved from danger to eventual success and victory over the waves.

The parental and sibling boundaries were askew. The main focus of treatment was directed toward realigning the system into more functional hierarchy. We spent several weeks encouraging the mother to disengage from the children and bringing the father "in from the garage". Having an executive team (the parents) that worked well together was, in this case, a necessity. The schizophrenic 16-year-old needed to be kept safe through rules and consistent parenting that would counteract her inner voices who were suggesting self-destructive actions. As she was attended to, the other two children could better proceed with their lives.

One of the first interventions in the art therapy session was to ask the parents to sit together on one side of the art therapy table and the three children on the other. The therapist was positioned at one end of the table. The configuration silently divided the parental executives from the children, with the therapist in neutral space between the two groups. Thus, boundaries were put into place rather than discussed. "Cognitive constructions per se are rarely powerful enough to spark family change... a therapeutic message must be recognized by family members, meaning that it needs to be received in such a way that it encourages them to experience things in a new way" (Minuchin & Fishman, 1981, p. 117).

As the sessions continued, the parents drew issues that concerned them, the children each drew events from their world. Separation of adult and child worlds was emphasized and demonstrated by the contrasting content of the art products. The verbal sharing was also structured: father and mother would first lead the dialogue in referring to their art expressions, and then they would be encouraged to interface with the children in a leadership role. The teenage girl often responded with rage and blaming. She recalled her many grievances against one parent or the other, but, having been removed from her preferred seat between her parents, she found it disconcerting to face them both. The mother and father also learned a great deal more about the abuse that she had suffered at the hands of her cousin. Up until now, the girl had told pieces of her story to each parent separately, using situations that kept each off balance with partial truths. Also, because of her additional disclosure of her abuse, her brother and sister were more fully informed of her victimization and sympathetically made excuses for her aberrant behavior, finding ways of rationalizing the schizophrenia.

I wish to remind the reader that the 16-year-old was seeing the clinic psychiatrist weekly for evaluation and medication; given the circumstances, psychotherapy was not enough. Encouraging regular consultation with the physician was a comfort for the patient as well as an ethical responsibility for the art therapist.

To further the emphasis on clear boundaries, we began to focus on the daily functions of the family members. Much of the art work done in the sessions had to do with household tasks. The drawings about doing dishes and taking out the trash are not diagnostic in themselves. However, issues of who delegated responsibilities and who followed through on consequences was like teaching a foreign language to this family.

A second key theme emerged: not surprisingly, the parents were having marital/sexual difficulties. Mother insisted on joining the children during the dishwashing after dinner time to avoid joining her husband in the living room. When she finished, he went upstairs to the bed as she was ready to watch TV. They had perfected a dance of avoidance.

A drawing that dramatized this split came about in this manner. The parents were asked to "take a vacation together" on a large sheet of paper (Figure 6). He drew a boat, she an island. The husband then drew a black line down the middle of the page. The wife, enraged, said, "That's what you always do! Keep us apart!" The husband was shocked into observing his own behavior. He protested that he did not want this division and he wished he could change the black line. There it remained, as everyone looked miserable and the wife wept. In a while, allowing the situation to reach its full impact, I just touched the white oil pastel on the table. The dad took the hint and quickly marked white over the black line, verbalizing how he would

Figure 6: Two conjoint drawings, top/mother and father, below/three children

Figure 7: Daughter's "bodiless horse" doodle

like to have this symbolic gesture translate into reality. I cannot imagine how this conflict could have been illuminated with such clarity by words alone. A long-standing pattern has to be *seen* in a new light to fully catch the attention of both members of the dance.

The wife quickly followed her husband's move by populating her island with a loving couple, arms around each other; her spouse put a couple on his boat. Then he drew a heavy anchor! Without going into an interpretation that there was a possibility of the anchor keeping him in the same place, we focused again on the removal of the black line and how that could be translated into real world actions.

In contrast, when the children drew their "vacation" picture, there were signs of greater chaos than before (Figure 6). The teen-aged girl drew a bodiless horse, and the siblings copied her, creating even more disorganization. Their positions and relationships in the family were changing and discomfort was experienced by all. As the parents drew closer, the children felt the move and responded with anxiety.

The patterns revealed in the art expressions also provided the opportunity to interrupt the behaviors they had established. The drawing offered the spouses a chance to make a change that symbolized a shift in their reciprocal avoidance pattern. Simultaneously, they could comment on the anxiety and lack of organization in the children's art work and see how change is always threatening, even when it offers a more harmonious way of living together. This key drawing was the topic of discussion in the family for several weeks, putting the parents in the managerial position and freeing the children to attend to age-appropriate developmental tasks.

Shortly after this move forward, it appeared that the family system returned to its former state of disarray. I was very puzzled why the apparent progress had turned to regression. At this point, let me digress in order to discuss the symbol of the horse head drawn by the girl. This drawing (Figure 7) was her constant "doodle", particularly when there was stress in the session. Other free drawings indicated her internal conflict and, although they were not fully explored, they provided extremely important information to the therapist. Since her medication and enforced therapeutic school attendance, as well as some parental guidance, had gone into effect, the girl's behavior had begun to settle down. Her rages were more tempered and her stories were more believable. My guess is that without the art to give a picture of her inner psychotic world, we might have assumed that she had stabilized. The drawings made it obvious that she needed continuing care; this was particularly important to a family who was so casual about severe mental illness. For example, when the "horse without a body" was later drawn as a

Figure 8: Letter to stepsister from oldest girl

Figure 9: Parent's conjoint mourning drawing

complete animal, I felt that she had made a significant move toward integration. This more complete image was a positive sign and helped with the ongoing assessment of her condition.

Returning to the progress of the family, the sudden signs of disorganization mentioned above, as well as the frantic production of the "bodiless horse" drawing by the oldest daughter, were not explained until the youngest girl let it slip that their stepsister, the father's daughter from his first marriage, had moved in. She was sleeping with the teenage girl and was "sick." As the story unfolded, it was reported that the stepsister was rapidly decompensating and, according to their description, was showing flamboyant signs of severe mental illness. Again, the almost cavalier attitude toward these behaviors was very hard for me to comprehend. By cajoling and then confronting I was able to insist that they introduce this woman into the day treatment program at our clinic, where she was later diagnosed a paranoid schizophrenic.

It was shortly after this incident, when we were dealing with rules to keep the teenage girl from sharing a room with the stepsister, that a profound statement was made by the mother. She turned to me and remarked, "Why is it, Shirley, that whenever we have a problem in our family we go schizophrenic?" She then proceeded to tell a story of all the incidents that applied to this scenario. She had three major breaks and hospitalizations after the birth of three of her children. The last break was after the teenage daughter's birth when she remained in the hospital four months after the baby was born. The other two incidents were with her first family. The adult son of this marriage was hospitalized as schizophrenic. Her mother had the same history. Father's first wife had been diagnosed a functional schizoid personality and now his daughter was in a full blown episode. This tale was told in such a matter of fact manner you might have thought that she was telling about traits of left-handedness in the family tree.

No wonder I had been feeling that there was something "off" about the treatment. It became clear that the symptoms of schizophrenia had been an organizing factor in the family. That is not to say that the family members created this behavior, but once it was named, they then fit it into their plans in a way that would have greatly disrupted many other families. The symptomology was all too familiar to this family to be a threat.

Another factor to consider was how late in the therapy the revelation of these very dramatic facts occurred. Some might label this as resistance or defensive behavior; perhaps that may be the case. I believe that although we were five months into therapy, the story was never told because, to these people, it was not an unusual fact or really worth bringing to therapy.

Sadly, the indifference to the condition of the stepsister had very serious consequences. After she refused treatment in our day care program and checked out without permission, she became homeless. Since she was an adult we could not hold her against her will. The father searched for her everywhere and the mother grieved with guilty feelings because she had never liked his daughter.

One terrible morning the mother found this young woman hanged from the tree in their backyard; she had committed suicide. The family immediately came into the clinic and we had a crisis session. To alleviate and ventilate a little stress, each person wrote on a large piece of paper all the words and messages they wished that they had said to the departed half-sister (Figure 8). Each member read their good-bye message out loud. As they heard how each one felt s/he had failed to prevent this tragedy, they were able to give and receive support, sharing their mutual fears.. We continued to focus on this loss for many weeks. The image of the backyard tree was drawn over and over; it became the symbol for all the regrets and mourning (Figure 9).

Out of this tragedy a new system was born. The moves that the mother and father made to be a unit solidified. The mother was very comforting to the father in his grief and he acknowledged her support. The children were relieved of the guilt that they had caused the death and the teenage girl's illness was seen in a different light. They no longer accused her of acting weird just to gain attention and gave her real attention in an appropriate way. She was relieved of her fear that she was fated to go the way of her stepsister and had intensified individual therapy in addition to the family sessions. On some level she seemed to understand that she had a serious problem and that she needed to take some responsibility for her treatment. She no longer railed at her parents for being the sole cause of her psychosis.

Termination

The end of treatment came with a second period of case management. This included: making plans for the girl's future and the other two children; finding a social support system for the parents; and continuing the girl in individual therapy.

When a family has realigned their system, experienced their strengths and modified the truths by which they live, they no longer need therapy. Termination is supported by the therapist as s/he reviews and punctuates their new world view and their ability to take on new challenges. The outsider (the therapist) that has visited the family now is politely invited to leave. With fond regards, but nevertheless leave!

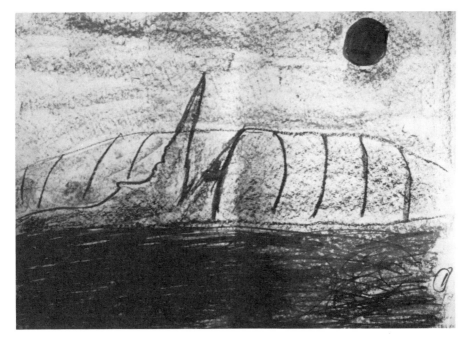

Figure 10: Surfing, 2 months

Figure 11: Surfing, 5 months

Conclusion

This case demonstrates how it was first necessary to clarify the parental and child subsystems to provide not only function, but also safety for a child at risk. The triangulation of the girl within the marriage and the difficulties with boundaries where the mother joined with the children and the father and son stood outside the system were issues that took some time to face. The unexpected (and concealed) addition of a secret family member to the family disorganized the emerging functional structure. When the stepdaughter's role was revealed as one of fusion with her father, enemy of the wife and identifier with the girl, the work of therapy began again. Her death threw everyone into shock, and in that time of flux the more organized family structure was reinforced and appeared to remain fairly solid up until the time of termination.

The art tasks were vital to building the family's coping skills. They externalized their grief and shared their feelings through their drawings. They gave ritual and form to a departed member of the family. They actively dealt with their guilt through many art products together with writing. A drawing said a more complete good-bye to their relative than words alone.

Structural family therapy was the treatment that they required. The family indicated this choice by their behaviors, their needs, and their disorganized response to a life-threatening illness. They required a clear, structured approach to therapy which would give them new tools to realign their dysfunctional family system. With the emphasis on the need for a parental team and boundaries set around the child subsystem, the psychotic girl no longer ruled the family. She could be helped rather than burdened with reaching out for structure in a family where none was provided. The family did not come together sufficiently to prevent a sad loss to the family, but they did restructure sufficiently to provide a positive environment for their daughter at risk.

I believe that the therapeutic dilemma demonstrated during the course of this family's treatment addressed two considerations that appeared illogical at first. Why was schizophrenic behavior viewed with such complacency by the family, and, secondly, why did they seem so unsure of how to set their goals?

The therapist was puzzled when the family came to treatment with an obvious crisis, but appeared to choose to focus on less important concerns first. In a case like this, the clinician must trust his/her own reactions to the clients and use these reactions as a basis for exploring the family system. For example, if the therapist is confused, perhaps the way the family functions is

Figure 12: Surfing, 7 months

Figure 13: Surfing, 9 months

Figure 14: Termination, 11 months

confusing. If the therapist needs some structure in order to protect the teenage girl, then perhaps the family needs some structure also. Using oneself as a barometer is a form of empathy and can be a very important clue to the family's world view.

The strength of structural family therapy (Minuchin, 1974, 1984; Minuchin & Fishman, 1981; Minuchin, Rosman & Baker, 1978; Minuchin, Montalvo, Guerney, Rosman & Schumer, 1967) has reemerged in clinical practice today. This theory was originally based on Minuchin's work with families in the inner city. However, the approach he developed is applicable to families in contemporary society where violence and poverty undermine the family structure and greater clarity in relationships is needed. Minuchin and his co-authors describe specific techniques that can be utilized by both the advanced and novice practitioner. These techniques include joining, planning, reframing, working with boundaries, unbalancing, and searching for strengths in the family system. With the addition of a sensitivity to women's issues, which the original texts on this subject neglected, the principles have withstood the test of time and are still valid for a large majority of families in treatment.

In the case described in this chapter, the therapist also needed to convince herself that it was therapeutic to ask the family to engage in structured art tasks. Coming to a session with a preconceived task is generally antithetical to my personal style of working with a family. I favor open-ended questioning that leads to concretizing the issue the family brings to the session that day. However, this particular family with their dysfunctional relationships and alliances seemed to demand a more defined form of art therapy intervention. Asking them to address conflicts or relationships in visual form was necessary to clarify the confusion.

The issue of schizophrenia was illuminated by art tasks that revealed a family history where "crazy" behavior went unnoticed and neglected; no one was visibly in charge to regulate actions or propose solutions. The father was accustomed to his first wife's schizoid tendencies, and subsequently did not react to his daughter's identical pattern of behavior. In the second marriage his wife had postpartum depressions and his oldest daughter acted similarly to his daughter in the first marriage. The second wife's mother was institutionalized for schizophrenia, and her son from her first marriage was in and out of mental facilities. Her ability to discriminate that the oldest daughter of the current marriage was behaving in bizarre ways was clouded by all these past experiences.

The art expressions of the 16-year-old girl, which were radically different from the drawings of the other members of the family, helped them to recognize the pathology in their family system. The drawings of the 14-year-old son also gave the therapist a running assessment of the changes taking place in the family (Figures 10-14). By observing the position of the surfer, first falling off his board and then gradually becoming more secure, and how the surfer was initially headed for the rocks and gradually took a safer course, the therapist was able to deduce the progress the entire family was making in treatment. His drawings were a barometer of the changes taking place in himself as well as in his parents and siblings.

Finding the rationale to pursue a course of action with a family is a serious and difficult task. When a family is a puzzle to the therapist, it takes some time to find a way into their world. When the family is at immediate risk, then the therapist must trust his/her reactions to the family; this may very well be the best guide to knowing what they need. In this particular case, reducing confusion, attending to the endangered client, and providing structure and rules by which the family could function were the guiding principles for treatment. It would be unethical to choose a form of treatment that delayed action and did not protect a family member from harm. Providing safety by structuring the treatment was syntonic with the specific needs for case management in this family: intervention for the daughter at risk of suicide and confrontation of the family to urge the stepdaughter into day treatment.

Using art therapy in a parallel and structured manner enforced new patterns that offered a more positive, functional outcome and achieved the treatment goals.

References

Hoffman, L. (1981). *Foundations of family therapy.* New York: Basic Books.

Minuchin, S. (1974). *Families and family therapy.* Cambridge, MA: Harvard University Press.

Minuchin, S. (1984). *Family kaleidoscope.* Cambridge, MA: Harvard University Press.

Minuchin, S., & Fishman, H. (1981). *Family therapy techniques.* Cambridge, MA: Harvard University Press.

Minuchin, S., Montalvo, B., Guerney, B., Rosman, B., & Schumer, F. (1967). *Families of the slums: An exploration of their structure and treatment.* New York: Basic Books.

Minuchin, S., Rosman, B., & Baker, L. (1978). *Psychosomatic families: Anorexia nervosa in context.* Cambridge, MA: Harvard University Press.

DRAW ME A PARADOX?
. . . FAMILY ART PSYCHOTHERAPY UTILIZING A SYSTEMIC APPROACH TO CHANGE

This chapter supports the notion that family art therapy can be successfully integrated into the systemic approach to family therapy. Moreover, the use of creativity—basic to both theories—produces a positive interaction resulting in a process that enhances family art therapy.

In a paper delivered as a keynote address at the Family Therapy Network Symposium held in Washington, D.C., March 1983, Peggy Papp of the Ackerman Family Institute, New York, discussed "The Links Between Clinical and Artistic Creativity". Papp stated:

> The major goal of therapy, as of art, is to change a basic perception so that one 'sees differently.' Through the introduction of the novel or unexpected, a frame of reference is broken and the structure of reality is arranged.

This remark seems to address the family art therapist and leads one to question why family art psychotherapy plays a minor role in the growing field of family therapy.

Other family therapists have referred to the need for the therapist to bring a creative and innovative view to the work of psychotherapy, and this could be one of the family art therapist's contributions. Stanton (1984) offers a theory of systemic change which includes this hypothesis:

> The extent to which change is total will depend upon the similarity between the intervention and the actual interactive process addressed by the intervention.

This chapter originally appeared in *Art Therapy: Journal of the American Art Therapy Association*, 2 (3), 116-123, 1985, and is reprinted with their permission.

The more elements or dimensions—visual, auditory, kinesthetic—attending or composing the intervention, the more effective that intervention will be in bringing about change. (p. 159)

The interactive process mentioned by Stanton can effectively incorporate these elements by the use of a variety of visual and kinesthetic art media that are natural tools of the art therapist. This hypothesis reinforces the importance of the use of concrete imagery which has been an integral part of art psychotherapy from its beginnings.

With this thought in mind, I have taken some of the key theoretical principles of systemic family therapy and have attempted to demonstrate how these techniques have been utilized by this art therapist. These principles are: 1) viewing the family as a system; 2) using positive connotation; 3) prescribing the symptom; 4) utilizing metaphors; 5) understanding family ritual; 6) using paradoxical interventions; 7) understanding a therapeutic double bind; 8) maintaining homeostatic properties; and 9) terminating treatment. By examining these principles and demonstrating how art therapy may be incorporated may help to clarify how the "addition of art" is effective in enhancing therapeutic interventions. We can also gauge whether art therapy was an aid to the family in achieving relief from symptoms they considered undesirable.

The Family as a System

The most basic concept of a systemic approach to change is based on seeing the family as operating within a system. The family as a system has often been defined as two or more people in a relationship interacting with each other in a recursive manner over a period of time, despite changes in the environment. Within a systems approach, causality is seen as a process of *circular causality*, and it is judged unproductive to see one member's behavior as separate or dissociated from the other members of the family system. The circular view of cause and effect in transactions is a radically different stance from the historically accepted linear view of events. "A causal relationship is called linear when feedback processes are not involved; in other words, when the cause and effect sequence does not lead back to the starting point" (Simon, Stierlin, & Wynne, 1985, p. 212).

Another aspect of this definition lies in the concept that the family members are usually unaware of the redundant interactional sequences that make up the bulk of their responses. It follows that family behavior can be understood when seen in the context of family rules and to observe how their rules serve to maintain the family stability or guard against its dissolution.

Here "seeing" is a key word, since we can "see" many aspects of the system in a unique manner through the art product. The therapist's task is to discover the particular form of the dysfunction and what patterns maintain what Minuchin calls "the family dance"; therefore, initial assessment should focus on the processes which appear to maintain the problem. In this assessment phase, this basic concept of causality and other aspects of family systems (not mentioned in this brief definition) present a difficult challenge for the family therapist to identify and then determine how to intervene. It follows that at the beginning of treatment an overview of the system and observation of the interactions between members are the first steps that must be considered.

One of the more common and effective techniques utilized by family art therapists when they start treatment is to have the family create a family drawing/mural. The family members accomplish this task in any way they feel comfortable. Observation of the results of this process is an immediate opportunity for the therapist to form a hypothesis about the family system and to think about interventions that will redirect the family's interactions. The task of a family drawing also enables the therapist to introduce the following concepts to the family: definition of the problem, examination of the dilemma of change, and formulation of treatment.

Let's look at some of the technical underpinnings of the family mural task:

1) The therapist has taken control early in treatment by persuading the family to use art which, for most families, is unfamiliar and sometimes even contrary to their ideas of what therapy should be. The thought of doing art as a therapy to many families seems to be a ridiculous way to solve serious problems since it includes offering pleasurable experiences such as the use of materials, color, etc. How paradoxical to expect pleasure to relieve pain! Based on their acceptance or rejection of this new experience, the therapist can begin to speculate whether the family falls into the compliant or non-compliant mode of family systems. The next move is to decide how it would be appropriate to further test their resistance to change (or new ideas) and then decide on an approach to treatment.

Interventions, interpretations, and homework are tailored to these considerations. A family that is compliant and ready for change may need only suggestions, feedback, and a new way of looking at their problems. At the other end of the continuum, a non-compliant family with a system rigidly resistant to change requires a different set of techniques.

2) In *Families and Family Therapy* (1974), Minuchin refers to the family structure as an "invisible set of rules that govern transactions... Family structure becomes visible in the behavioral transactions between family

members" (p. 52). Family art therapy provides tasks which serve to make the invisible visible and which simultaneously supplies a process to observe family behavior.

The therapist's use of the family mural can facilitate interpretation of the family system. All family members are represented through spatial, dominant and/or subdominant positions in the drawing; both verbal and nonverbal messages are sent and received, either to be rejected or acted upon. In short, so much can be observed by the therapist in the mural and in the way the family created the drawing, that s/he can proceed to use some of the following techniques if they meet treatment goals. In addition, the family is asked to discuss how they perceived the process and the product. What information did they gain from the experience? How they see their roles and reveal their motivations and messages in the art expressions are of the greatest value in forming a therapeutic alliance and setting goals.

Positive Connotation Through Art

A positive connotation of the family's motivation and behavior can be introduced in an explicit and concrete manner through art. If the therapist observes how each member has, for example, demonstrated that they "have worked with the others on the paper and have risked exposing their place in the family", or, "families who take a chance to draw together are families who demonstrate they are able to risk new experiences", the therapist may then define other behaviors in a positive manner. It is helpful to support the family's engagement in doing a mutual task that is unfamiliar to them. The messages derived from the family drawing can begin to reframe the family behavior in a manner that shifts the emphasis from a family group who is at the clinic because of an inability to solve problems, to a family which has strength to serve them in solving problems they no longer wish to have as part of their interactions.

Positive connotation of behavior or redefining behaviors is not a simple positive support of the family or an individual in the family (i.e., "you are good people"). The redefinition is based on the therapist's assessment of the family system and how each piece of behavior can be seen to be a gesture to preserve the family stability. Not all redefining is presented in the same way; certainly, with violent, illegal, or suicidal acts the therapist avoids positive connotation of the acts themselves and deals with the motivation behind the behavior. This aspect of when to avoid the use of positive connotation must be clearly defined and understood by the therapist new to this approach.

Any assumptions and interpretations made by the art therapist must be based on an honest appraisal and an empathetic feeling toward the family. In addition, it is necessary to have an attitude of respect for the family's behavior and feelings, and to do a great deal of theoretical thinking about how the family system works. This is a responsibility that supersedes any choice of approach or manner of working. However, the expressive product that results from the family's group and/or individual's efforts gives the art therapist additional avenues for appreciating underlying messages and covert alliances within the system. The therapeutic plan or tentative first hypothesis for treatment is then based on a body of information that is enriched by the material the family has provided through both verbal and nonverbal means.

Prescribing the Symptom

Prescribing the symptom is defined in this manner: "Having been defined as serving one another, both the symptom and system are prescribed. The wording of the prescription is extremely important. It should be brief, concise, and unacceptable to the family. If it is acceptable, there will be no recoil" (Papp, 1983).

Case I

A family of seven children, ranging from the age of 7 years to 19 years, and their mother, age 43, came to art therapy five months after the untimely death of their father. Before his death, the family had functioned in a normal manner; all the children were well-cared for and wanted by the parents. They had regarded themselves as a "happy family". After the father's death (which followed a stroke and five months of life support treatment), the family began to fight violently. The children demanded an outrageous and unrealistic amount of material goods as well as constant emotional support from the mother. At the first session the family promptly revealed that they had not talked with each other about the loss of their father. In addition, they couldn't understand why the mother, who had always been the disciplinarian, had become so withdrawn and lacked forcefulness as a parent. The family spent the first hour drawing a "good-bye" picture to Father and, with the therapist's support, sharing their feelings about the loss. They had been afraid to burden each other with additional sorrow and had therefore turned away from each other in their pain. The symptom of "fighting" seemed to be an outward projection of anger concerning the father's death.

After a break, they returned and did a family mural. Each worked with an individual color. They elected to draw their last fishing trip on a boat with Father. Among the multiple issues that were explored during the review of the family mural, was a major focus on the oldest son (14 years) who had drawn himself steering the boat and drawn his father up in the sky. This metaphor of "captain of the ship" was quickly recognized by the family as his attempt to take over a father role in the family. This effort to be Father had caused a major part of the verbal fighting in the sibling subsystem since not only was he very inept in this role, but additionally, he was preceded in age by three older sisters who were vying for some part of the parental position.

At the end of the session the art therapist gave the mother this *prescription* to be read at home to the family every evening. First, the family, and particularly the oldest son, were congratulated on their sensitivity to the family's needs. The boy was further supported for his willingness to sacrifice his youth to perform a role that turned him into a 47-year-old man and forced him to give up the adolescent pleasures enjoyed by most 14-year-old males. The therapist recommended that he continue to act as father, and to lead and parent the family by isolating himself from his older sisters and his friends and by studying bookkeeping and household management. Second, the sisters were to be respectful, make him his favorite foods and not be rude or sassy to such a dedicated member of the family. Third, the mother as head of the family was to monitor these actions and to point out to the family how their fighting and rudeness to one another had helped her become more perceptive and able to structure some resolution for their problems. She felt there might be ways to solutions that she had not discovered and she was open to suggestions. She had the power to modify any of the therapist's suggestions and report these changes at the next session, because as head of the household she was the final authority.

This *prescription*, or "prescribing the symptom", seemed to be necessary to push the pattern of family interaction off balance and hopefully would result in a new configuration in the system.

Paradoxical prescriptions serve as a means of isolating behaviors, requiring that behaviors occur artificially. Ritualized prescriptions must be carried out at specific and regular times. This method forced the clients to think about their situation or act it out in a prescribed fashion.

Needless to say, the recommendations made to this family failed. When this was reported at the next session, the therapist remained "puzzled", the mother took over and delegated family tasks and demanded some improved manners, the son refused to be a responsible adult figure and wanted time to be "14", and everyone reflected that no one could "father" the family the way their beloved father had when he was alive. In future sessions, they agreed to work on a new way of living together without the father.

This method had raised this family's awareness and had increased the intensity of the symptomatic behavior. The family then chose to find a "better" solution to their problems. The therapist successfully *failed* and the family was the real winner.

Utilizing Metaphors

To be able to communicate and join with a family, the therapist is best understood if s/he enters into the family's world view by utilizing metaphors particular to the family. It is here that the creative artist in the art therapist can be so successful. In the family's art products we have a greater opportunity to move into the metaphoric language by observing the product and being attentive to how the family speaks and interprets the artwork. Creatively using their metaphors strengthens the therapeutic relationship, since it is a language tailored to fit the particular family and no other. After the joining process begins to succeed, the therapist can next evaluate how the family sustains the problematic situation. Through the use of art therapy tasks which provide visual as well as verbal material s/he can begin the process of change.

Case II

A family of four came for treatment: a mother, father, daughter (15 years) and son (13 years). Their system was sustained by a constant blaming behavior that revealed the unhappiness in the family, but each expected a solution to be achieved when another member changed in some way. This was reinterpreted as "each member loving each other more than they loved themselves". Therefore, they were always being attentive to another rather than themselves. Following this reframing, the family said, "this was the first time any therapist had really understood how they felt". They agreed that the son was the person who needed to change the most and the son also supported this view. The family was judged to be highly resistant to change, but compliant to task performance. (This assessment was based on the beginning sessions.) It included a long past history of unsuccessful individual therapeutic treatment; a marriage that was endured by the couple as a formality; numerous diagnoses of the boy as learning disabled, oppositional, high I.Q. and not using his potential; the girl was "problem free" in the eyes of the parents. In addition, both the children were adopted and there were multiple unresolved feelings around this issue.

The family decided they would be willing to build their home together from construction paper, since most of the complaints were focused on activities and unfulfilled tasks performed in the home. The troubles in the home around unfinished tasks, irresponsible behaviors, and lack of cooperation made the home a suitable metaphor for art therapy. The family made every attempt to represent the home in a realistic manner. The following was observed: Father and Mother aided the construction to a minor degree while constantly correcting and criticizing each other; the daughter refrained from helping except for a mark or two in the walls; the son competently solved most of the building tasks and persisted until the home was completed. Paradoxically, the way the family recalled this process was to deny that the son had really contributed much effort, that the daughter had "meant to cooperate", and that Mother and Father alone had provided the basic structural support for the paper house. The art therapist did not modify this perception, but just puzzled about "who did what, when?". It became apparent that because of the way the process was experienced by the family they were unable to appreciate how involved and concerned the "bad" son was in building the home, how minimally cooperative the "good" girl was in the task, and how the parents failed in providing structure for completion of the task.

Understanding Family Ritual

At this juncture in art therapy with this family, the therapist was faced with a decision as to how to proceed with the treatment. Based on the conviction that the family was highly resistant to change, the therapist decided to prescribe a *family ritual*. The family ritual is a technique used to highlight a sequence of behaviors within a structured set of circumstances. The ritual itself is designed to neutralize the usual pattern of interaction. The following suggestion was made to the family at the end of the session:

They were congratulated for completing such a difficult art task and for sharing their home with the therapist by creating it during the session. It was the therapist's recommendation that every evening after dinner they place the little house on the dining table and each person point out what part they built. They were not to refer to the house or the process of creating it at any other time until they brought it back into the next art therapy session. They were, under no circumstances, to attempt to generalize the involvement of the family construction of the house to emotional and behavioral involvement of the family members and the actual functioning of the family. These instructions were written and given to the father. He was asked to read them aloud each evening before they talked about the paper construction.

The family came in the following week and made little reference to the house. However, they were concerned that "the daughter had become so uncooperative" and surprised that "the son appeared to be much more attached to the family," even though nothing had changed with the household tasks which were performed in the same manner during the week. No further mention of the "homework" (the ritual) was made except to verify that they had followed through on the directions given them.

From this session on, the boy was no longer referred to as the "problem child". The focus shifted to the daughter and, in due time, to the marital relationship. The noncritical approach aided in modifying the existing patterns of interaction and communication in this family. It succeeded in achieving the desired results by replacing an old perception of how the family members performed with a more realistic and workable view. When the family was released from the stereotypes they had assigned each other, they were able to move on from an outmoded stage of development to a new one.

Using Paradoxical Interventions

Webster's International Dictionary defines paradox as "an assertion or sentiment seemingly contradictory or opposed to common sense, but that may be true in fact...". According to Papp (1983), "designing a systemic paradox, the therapist connects the symptom with the function it serves in the system and prescribes each in relation to the other. The consequences of eliminating the symptom are enumerated and the therapist recommends that the family continue to resolve their dilemma through the symptom. The therapist must be convinced that the paradoxical messages only appear to be contradictory. It contains a double message to the family—one implies it would be good for them to change, the other implies it would not be so good—and the messages are delivered simultaneously" (p. 33).

The message in a paradoxical intervention must be delivered with conviction and sincerity and believed to be a true interpretation of the observed family transaction. Paradoxical interventions used by the art therapist are no different than if this was the treatment of choice by a therapist of another discipline. Usually, the art therapist sees in the art product more covert interactions than the clients have been willing to discuss. Since the art therapist is aware (through the messages surfacing in the art) of the second-level (covert) meanings, s/he can better tailor the paradoxical intervention to address the problem at hand. These interventions vary from the simple directive, for example, to a resistant adolescent, "Don't draw today, we want you to remain as silent as your blank page while your family talks about your problems", to a more complicated directive which involves the family doing a task in a structured way that reinforces and highlights problem-maintaining interactional patterns.

Understanding a Therapeutic Double Bind

Therapist resistance to utilizing paradoxical interventions or double bind messages is based on a fear that these techniques could be destructive, over-manipulative, and bordering on unethical practice. If the therapist understands the difference between the double bind that produces toxic behavior and the therapeutic double bind, chances are that his/her anxiety will be alleviated.

The original double bind theory by Bateson is referred to in Hoffman's book, *Foundations of Family Therapy* (1981). "The basic ingredients that create this kind of impasse are: 1) A primary negative injunction, 'Don't do that,' 2) A secondary negative injunction at another level which conflicts with the first, 'Don't listen to anything I say,' 3) An injunction forbidding comment (usually nonverbal cues reinforcing rules that no longer need to be made explicit), and another forbidding person to leave the field (often delivered by context, as when the person is a child), 4) A situation that seems to be of survival significance, so that it is vitally important for the person to discriminate correctly among the messages, and 5) After a pattern of communication containing these elements has become established, only a small reminder of the original sequence is needed to produce a reaction of rage and panic" (p. 20).

In contrast, the authors of *Pragmatics of Human Communication* (Watzlawick, Beavin, & Jackson, 1967), describe how the therapeutic double bind works. In a pathogenic double bind the patient is "damned if s/he does and damned if s/he doesn't". In a therapeutic double bind, since s/he is told not to change, s/he is in a similar trap, but with a different outcome. If one resists the injunction, s/he changes; if one doesn't change, s/he is "choosing" not to change. Since a symptom is something which by definition, one can't help, s/he is then no longer behaving symptomatically. Thus, s/he is "changed if s/he does and changed if s/he doesn't". It is a bind where a positive reward is provided upon completion rather than a negative impasse.

A mild form of therapeutic bind which we art therapists, even in our student days, were comfortable giving to clients was structured in this manner, "being able to draw your feelings is important, but difficult, so why don't you make it easier for yourself by choosing either a good feeling or a bad feeling to draw today". This is an example of *an allusion of alternatives*.

Considering, in the above example, that no one has ever seen a feeling and considering that the options for choice were constructed to gain the desired end result, it follows that when the art therapist recognizes and reinforces the value of the client performing this impossible task, s/he provides a reward that modifies this bind into a therapeutic experience. At this point perhaps one can see that the use of paradox and art therapy have been bedfellows for a long time!

Case III

An intact family of five, a mother, father, 11-year-old son, 13-year-old daughter, and 11-month-old son, requested treatment at the clinic because the teenage girl had refused to attend school for the last one and a half years. She displayed violent behavior when the parents attempted to force her to return to school (e.g., kicking a hole in the door, screaming and threatening to harm herself). The presenting problem was that they felt they needed therapeutic help to get the girl back in school.

Several observations were made in the initial assessment. The mother and father were strongly attached to one another and both perceived the other in a positive manner. This was a Latino family and the male/female roles of dominance and sub-dominance were complementary and functional at this time. The father became rather overassertive and loud when drinking beer on the weekends, but more importantly, he provided well for the family and did not distance himself. The mother was pleased with her new baby, liked her marriage, enjoyed the children (until recently), but was now ready to pick up a more active social life since the little boy was no longer an infant. The preadolescent son was perceived by the family as a "good" child. He was socially adjusted, a poor student (which was ignored), and often absent from school. He was, in fact, home about half of the school days, but this pattern was also overlooked. The toddler son seemed to be a happy, healthy baby who was thriving. The daughter described her position in the family as one of being unloved and undervalued. She resented her father's loud yelling at her mother (even though mother did not perceive it as "yelling"), she was afraid to go to school because of the noise, and she hated her younger brother and her father.

The pattern of the family was to allow the daughter to sleep late every morning. During this time, Mother went to the school and picked up her daughter's homework, which the girl accomplished during the day and thus kept her grades adequate. When school was over, the daughter's friends came by. They either swam in their pool or picked up the daughter to go out cruising. They used street drugs and alcohol and returned home very late. The daughter denied that she participated in the substance abuse in a heavy manner. This recursive behavior pattern evolved and was sustained since the mother announced her pregnancy with the last child one-and-a-half years ago.

The group drawings made by the family and art expressions made by individual family members revealed that each member, with the exception of the preadolescent son, was very anxious to make a change. However, every attempt at solving the problem only seemed to maintain the problem. The family was so locked into the system that it needed something to help family members move to a new and more satisfying set of interactional patterns.

The art work was essential in making this assessment because each member saw the dilemma and was able to illustrate the components. But even though they were able to verbally and visually lay it all out, they were stuck in their interrelational system. They projected a feeling of hopelessness. At the end of one unhappy session this paradoxical prescription was given to the family:

The daughter was acknowledged as the person who was attempting to keep the family in balance by sacrificing her normal youthful patterns of school/play. To this end, it was advised that Mother should respect her position and wait on her and bring her meals to her room, making every effort to make her life even more agreeable. The father was asked to come home early every day and check that the mother had pleased the daughter, but not talk directly to the girl. The brother was to bring his school progress record home every day and read it to his parents without Sister being present in the room. Daughter was advised that although she was giving her mother so much support, she needed to increase it and therefore no longer go out with her friends at all. She must spend more time in her room and increase her efforts to maintain the family. The more she stayed at home, the more the family would stay in this stable system. The family looked startled with this advice, but promised, in their desperation, to give it a try.

The following week the family came in very angry. Within two days of living by the new rules, the mother and father demanded that the daughter go back to school. The daughter countered by agreeing to go to school if she could go to the therapeutic school the therapist had suggested. The next day, she and her mother enrolled her in this new school. The son had "forgotten" to bring his school report home, but had attended school every day.

The family was very defiant in mood and aggressively told the therapist that "her plan was not workable and they simply had to take the decision in their own hands". The therapist then accepted her failure and congratulated them on their success.

This paradoxical prescription seemed to be successful since the family achieved its desired end of returning the girl to school and did so on the family members' own terms. The system was clarified when the connection the symptom had with the system emerged. This enabled them to modify the system and move to a new level of functioning even without "insight".

Terminating Treatment

The time when the family is ready to terminate treatment is recognized when the therapeutic process reaches a point when the patterns of interaction have changed and become more adaptive. Therapy is deemed successful when behavior and meaning are changed on both first and second levels of reality. Benjamin and Bross (1982) describe change as follows: "Evaluation of change should depend neither on the therapist's subjective judgment nor on the client's subjective report; rather it should be a matter of empirical evidence, that is, behavioral sequences and ways of attributing meaning that were observed regularly prior to intervention no longer occur following intervention" (p. 92).

If we are fortunate, and termination is a result of success, the ending is done with attention to these final goals: 1) gains are solidified by giving the family full credit for all changes; 2) success is maintained by speculating on possible future failure, which will mobilize the family to resist the prediction; and 3) follow-up sessions are offered in the future (six months) to allow for the ongoing process of change to take place and therapeutic reinforcement be available if needed.

A technique which has been a bedrock of the termination process in family art psychotherapy, namely, a review of the family's art products, can be of great use to accomplish the above goals. How better can the family members "own" their own struggles and resolution of problems than to see what they have accomplished over a period of time? If the therapist has used the strengths of the family and consistently resisted taking credit for change, and has, in fact, been "worried" at the rapid changes and has been "troubled" that the consequences might lead too quickly to problem resolution, then the therapist has helped the family to understand that they are capable of accomplishing things that they could not do previously. Often, a family will terminate rather quickly, because members feel they have been able to solve the problem better than the therapist. The "failure" of the therapist to predict the exact outcome and events which resulted in success for a family is often most clearly seen when the entire course of therapy is reviewed through the art products at the close of therapy. As family members point out the sessions where they moved from a patterned response to a new combination of more gratifying interactions in both the visual as well as verbal processes, the family and the therapist can appreciate the results achieved by the integration of systemic theory and art psychotherapy.

Conclusion

In this chapter, an attempt has been made to demonstrate how some of the basic theories of systemic therapy are compatible with theory and techniques of family art psychotherapy. Although the information offered is limited, the hope is that the family art therapist will be stimulated to pursue learning the theories of this methodology more extensively and to test if they stimulate a more creative approach and successful outcome in family work. My belief is that a positive and synergistic action takes place when family art psychotherapy is based on this epistemology. Also, the creative potential which exists within this synthesis of ideas can enhance the position of the clinical art therapist in the field of family therapy.

Reference

Bross, A. & Benjamin, M. (1982). Family therapy: a recursive model of strategic practice. In A. Bross. (ed.) *Family therapy: A recursive model of strategic practice.* Toronto: Metheun

Hoffman, L. (1981). *Foundations of family therapy: A conceptual framework for systems change.* New York: Basic Books.

Papp, P. (1983). *Getting unstuck.* Seventh Annual Family Therapy Networker Symposium. Unpublished paper.

Papp, P. (1983). *The process of change.* New York: Guilford.

Minuchin, S. (1974). *Families and family therapy.* Cambridge, MA: Harvard University Press.

Simon, F.B., Stierlin, H. & Wynne, L.C. (1985). *The Language of Family Therapy: a systemic vocabulary and source book.* New York: Family Process Press.

Stanton, M (1984). Fusion, compression, diversion, and the workings of paradox: A theory of therapeutic/systemic change. *Family Process,* 23 (2).

Watzlawick, P., Beavin, J. & Jackson, H. (1967). *Pragmatics of human communication.* New York: Ballantine.

Suggested Readings

Haley, J. (1973). *Uncommon therapy.* New York: Ballantine.

Madanes, C. (1981). *Strategic family therapy.* San Francisco: Jossey-Bass.

Weeks, G., & L'Abate, L. (1982). *Paradoxical psychotherapy.* New York: Brunner/Mazel.

A STRATEGIC FAMILY SYSTEMS APPROACH TO ART THERAPY WITH INDIVIDUALS

As a family art therapist, I believe that it is important to maintain a systemic view and, whenever possible, I meet with family groups rather than individuals. Sometimes these groups are expanded to include members of a client's family of origin or social network (Riley, 1985). It is not always feasible, however, to meet with all the members of a family or the social group, and, therefore, I developed an approach to treating individual clients from a systems perspective. In so doing I have been inspired by the theories and techniques of strategic family therapists such as Peggy Papp (1983), Jay Haley (1976), and members of the Mental Research Institute, most notably John Weakland, Paul Watzlawick, Richard Fisch, and Lynn Segal.

The Family Therapy Approach

An underlying premise of family therapy is that the family is a self-regulating organizational structure that seeks to maintain itself in a steady state despite external pressures and internal events such as births, deaths, and developmental changes. The family is greater than the sum of its parts (Bross & Benjamin, 1982). The cybernetic concept of *feedback* is often used to describe the way in which family members interact with each other. Feedback is not a cause-and-effect linear process, but a circular one, whereby one event influences a second, which simultaneously influences the first event while influencing a third and fourth event. In other words, the response to a stimulus provokes a new series of responses even as it influences the original

This chapter was originally published in the *American Journal of Art Therapy*, 28, 71-77 (1990), and is reprinted with permission.

stimulus. Feedback tends to maintain a family system in a dynamic equilibrium known as *homeostasis*, stabilizing family patterns of communication and behavior.

Causality in such a system is circular and multi-determined. An event, behavior, or symptom is not the endpoint of a particular sequence of actions and reactions, but part of a circular process in which all parts of the family system interact with and affect each other simultaneously. A particular set of results can stem from a number of different interactional sequences, but no matter where in the system an interaction begins, the same sorts of results are likely to occur. Thus, in a family where one member is scapegoated by others, the scapegoated member will be blamed for causing a family crisis regardless of who or what actually precipitated the crisis. To the systemically-oriented therapist who is helping a family or other social group solve a problem, the nature of the interactions between members is more significant and meaningful than the actual sequence of events that preceded the problem. To work with a family one does not need a complete history; one needs instead to understand the family's pattern of behavior and communication. It is the organization of the system, as manifested through these patterns–the interactional process—that determines the results of the system. For strategic family therapists, altering the sequence of interactions is the key to changing organizational patterns of behavior and communication that typically result in the symptoms from which clients seek relief.

Family Therapy and Art Therapy

I use family therapy to enhance communication among family members and to uncover, through the process as well as the content of the art task, family patterns of interaction and behavior. Landgarten (1987) has described how this is accomplished:

> The system is examined through the way in which the family functions as a unit while creating an art form together. The value of the art task is threefold: The *process* as a diagnostic, interactional, and rehearsal tool; the *contents* as a means of portraying unconscious and conscious communication; and the *product* as lasting evidence of the group's dynamics... The invading device is the art directive, which contains the appropriate media and is clinically sound. (p. 5)

For the client in individual therapy, visual expression can be an important vehicle for presenting family issues. An art work can be the means by which the client "brings the family in", and it offers an opportunity to deal with the delegation of roles within the family and issues in the client's family of origin.

The goal of treatment, as I see it, is to help clients solve the problems that led them to seek therapy, to open clients to broader perceptions of their lives, and to support a change in redundant, dysfunctional patterns of behavior. One way of accomplishing this is to alter the client's world view or frame of reference, an approach known as reframing. Art therapy offers unusual opportunities for reframing because what is presented to us in the way of client communication is an art work—by its very nature capable of being framed. Reframing in the physical sense (through cropping or repositioning) can help the client view the situation portrayed in the art work from a new perspective. Altering the physical frame is itself a powerful metaphor, one that can lead to cognitive reframing and behavioral change.

Techniques for Art Therapy from a Systems Perspective

In the cases described in this chapter, art therapy techniques were used in conjunction with a strategic family approach to individual and couples therapy. It is apparent that, due to the symbolic potential of the image as a means of communication, the combination was a fortuitous one.

Metaphors for Relationship and Change

Metaphors are analogues through which the therapist and client can communicate in a powerful, direct, but nonthreatening manner (Haley, 1963, 1973). They can be visual, verbal, or both: art expressions discussed by a client are particularly potent. Metaphors can be helpful in giving directives because when an intervention is presented in the form of a metaphor, the client may not even realize that an intervention has been made (Haley, 1976). By using the metaphor through which a client presents or describes a problem, the therapist shapes an intervention that is unique: the communication is tailored to fit the situation presented by the client and no other.

A young woman named Ann, age 26, entered art therapy with deep concerns about her 4-year-old marriage and unacknowledged anger toward her widowed mother. She and her husband Neil had recently moved out of her mother's apartment and into their own home, some 30 miles away. Ann's hobby was gardening, and she especially enjoyed spending her weekends working on the grounds of her new home.

Distance and conflict had recently appeared in Ann and Neil's relationship: she was growing anxious over his increasing demands on her time and attention. Ann's mother had also become more demanding, and Ann resented her mother's insistence that the couple visit her on the weekends, which interfered with the gardening. But Ann couldn't bear to say no to her mother.

Early in treatment, Ann began to make sketches of her lawn and garden. Her yard was an elaborately developed image she explored in drawing after drawing and became the basis for metaphorical language (Haley, 1973). Ann and the therapist used it to discuss her emotional state. Her lawn had recently become "brown and dry" and the flowers on its perimeter were "dying off". During one session, Ann told the therapist that the lawn was being taken over by crabgrass (Figure 1). At first she mused, "Wouldn't it be wonderful if one could just say 'to heck with it' and grow an untraditional weedy lawn?" She carefully considered this solution, but finally rejected it and started to plan how to eradicate the crabgrass from her yard.

The therapist expanded Ann's metaphor beyond the boundaries of

Figure 1: Dying

her drawings and designed an intervention to fit. She instructed Ann to go to the library with Neil to research the best method of eliminating the crabgrass. After they had done the reading, Ann reported that they had decided not to pull up the crabgrass after all because its roots would remain, only to grow and spread. Their choices were limited: they could till the soil and destroy the healthy grass, or apply chemicals that would kill the crabgrass, roots and all, but not the rest of the lawn. They decided to do the latter.

Their library research and yard work left Ann and Neil little time for anything else. The therapist coached Ann in explaining to her mother that she and her husband would have to limit their visits to Sunday morning breakfasts because the lawn project had to be finished before the winter rains began. In addition to helping with the research, Neil hired a man to do the heavy yard work. Ann enjoyed having her husband's support, and together she and Neil were able to curtail her mother's demands.

Neil was pleased because Ann no longer withdrew from him. In fact, she genuinely welcomed his involvement with her project. Now that Ann's mother held less sway over their daily lives, he could draw closer to his wife and express more support for her interests. Ann reciprocated by showing renewed affection.

Ann thus experienced a change in her relationships with her husband and her mother. In therapy, through the visual metaphor of a lawn full of crabgrass, she managed the difficult separation from her mother and reestablished intimacy with her husband. It would have been arduous indeed to teach her insight into her "unresolved separation from her family of origin", clarifying the problem of generational boundaries and helping her understand her "displacement of anxiety". It is doubtful that insight alone would have achieved the desired change in behavior.

In the case of Ann, an ongoing problem persisted even though she was clearly motivated to do something about it. She and Neil had moved out of her mother's home to establish an independent household. He wanted to be closer to her, so much so that she feared he would make too many demands, as her mother had done. She retreated to a solitary hobby, gardening; he complained that she wasn't paying him enough attention. The more he pursued, the more she withdrew: the cycle of behavior this couple engaged in as they struggled with their relationship only served to maintain their problems. Watzlawick, Weakland, and Fisch (1974) have noted that human problems tend to persist when people apply to them a solution that is actually "more of the same": the solution becomes the problem.

Recursive Patterns and Second-Order Change

For the clinician, symptoms and the client's previous attempts to ameliorate them are important pieces of the diagnostic puzzle. The presenting problem should not be seen as stemming from a pathological weakness within the client, but rather as recursive, patterned behavior that serves some function in maintaining the interactional sequence (Bross & Benjamin, 1982). This dynamic was clearly evident in the case of Elaine, a 42-year-old woman who was distressed because she constantly took on the responsibilities of friends and family, even though it was impossible for her to solve their problems. As a result, she felt abused and angry because the burdens "imposed" upon her were beyond her strength. She was aware that she resented the "unjust" commitment she had made, but she nonetheless continued to assist others with their unresolvable difficulties.

The therapist asked her to draw an image of how she appeared to herself as she continued to accept these unmanageable loads. Therapist and client were both surprised by what emerged: the figure of a heavy woman festooned with smaller persons clinging to her whole body (Figure 2). This figure bore no physical resemblance to Elaine, and after contemplating the figure for some time, Elaine told the therapist, with much emotion, that it represented her grandmother. This grandmother had raised her from infancy, when her mother died, until she was about 12 years old.

The grandmother's credo was "sacrifice yourself for others and never

Figure 2: Grandmother's message

say no to a request". Elaine was tearful and then angry as she remembered how her grandmother had taught her to always accommodate others. She then recalled being molested by her grandfather, a memory that had been repressed until the drawing called it forth. Suddenly, she understood why "doing for others" held such a distressing and malevolent meaning for her. As the session was concluding, Elaine decided to bury her grandmother once and for all and drew her lying in a horizontal position (Figure 2, bottom).

She declared that in so doing, she was "burying" the behavior that had kept her grandmother's beliefs alive. This intense, symbolic action was accomplished with great tension and an aura of finality.

In Elaine's revelation and decision to bury her grandmother, we see an example of what Watzlawick, Weakland, and Fisch (1974) call "second-order change", the leap to an entirely new frame or context in which to view a problem or relationship. This can be a mechanism for instigating systems change. Within a relatively stable system governed by a self-regulating feedback mechanism such as a thermostat, minor fluctuations ordinarily occur and are accommodated within the previously set limits of the system (Hoffman, 1981; Watzlawick, Weakland, & Fisch, 1974): they make slight alterations to what is going on in the system without changing the system itself. According to Hoffman (1981), second-order change "applies to any situation in which the usual range of behaviors is no longer applicable because of developments in the outer field or in the system itself", and "might be set off by any major shift in the rules governing one or more relationships in the family" (p. 197-198). Elaine's recovered incest memory dramatically altered her view of her grandmother's prescriptions and made her see self-sacrifice and accommodation in a new light. The fundamental shift in Elaine's attitude toward the family values instilled in her at an early age propelled her into a new context and range of behaviors.

Reframing

Second-order change is sometimes initiated by a change in the client's world view, which can be achieved through the tactic of *reframing* (Fisch, Weakland, & Segal, 1982; Watzlawick, Weakland, & Fisch, 1974) .

> To reframe... means to change the conceptual and/or emotional setting or viewpoint in relation to which a situation is experienced and to place it in another frame which fits the "facts" of the same concrete situation equally well or even better, and thereby changes its entire meaning. The mechanism involved here is not immediately obvious, especially if we bear in mind that there is change while the situation itself may remain quite unchanged and, indeed, even unchangeable. What turns out to be changed as a result of reframing is the meaning attributed to the situation, and therefore its consequences, but not its concrete facts.... (Watzlawick, Weakland, & Fisch, p. 95)

In *reframing* behavior, therapists frequently acknowledge that the behavior of an individual, even when it is dysfunctional, is an attempt to preserve the status quo of a system to which the individual belongs. For example, in exploring the family myths and roles that shaped their behavior, a client will sometimes recognize that he was the child "designated" by the family to engage in destructive behavior in order to save the family system. This "bad" child's actions might have distracted the parents from other issues, such as substance abuse or an unsatisfactory marriage, and forced them to join together in dealing with the child, thus strengthening their parental relationship. The child's "bad" acts can be reframed as "self-sacrifice for the good of others," which redefines the client's position in the family and may alter the client's perception of the situation. If the client still clings to a role as "the family problem," the therapist can encourage him to experiment with separation in a graphic way. After having the client make a family drawing, the therapist presents him with a pair of scissors and tells him to "cut yourself out" of the family. Once the client has made a "hole," he can speculate on how the remaining family members will relate to each other once he is out of the picture. He can also think about what he can now do as the cut-out member, liberated from the family frame. This simple metaphorical intervention can assist a client in addressing the neglected developmental task of individuation.

Giving an event or behavior a meaning that suggests value or worthiness is a form of reframing called *positive connotation* (Papp, 1983) and can drastically alter a client's perception of what he or she is doing. For example, when clients request therapy, they frequently see themselves as sick, damaged, or dysfunctional, and incapable of solving their problems. The therapist, however, usually sees the client's request as a health move, an indication that the client has forsaken the helpless stance, and can give the request a positive connotation. When the client expresses a willingness to venture into art therapy, an unfamiliar treatment modality, there is an additional opportunity to endow client action with connotations of strength, courage and determination to solve one's problems. (One caveat about positive connotation: It is not appropriate to use with clients who present issues of violence to self or others or who have a history of impulsive behavior. Therapists unfamiliar with this strategic therapy approach should not use it without adequate training and supervision, particularly in potentially life-threatening situations.)

An effective use of positive connotation occurred in the case of a 40-year-old businesswoman who aspired to be a novelist. Her second husband underused his talents and had been only partially employed during the five years of their marriage. There was affection between the couple and they did not want to divorce, but the wife had become progressively depressed as her children grew up and moved out. Her executive job seemed "cold" and "not creative enough". She complained that she "worked like a horse" because if she didn't, her family would starve, and there was never time to write.

In the second session, the therapist redefined the wife's depression as "an omen for change" and told her that unconscious desire to be creative and publish a novel was demanding that she take a sabbatical. Because this wish had been denied for so long, depression had set in. Moreover, by continuing to sacrifice her career as a writer, the wife was keeping her husband from assuming his proper role in the family. In fact, by neglecting her talents, she was giving off the misleading impression that she was too businesslike and assertive. The therapist congratulated the wife because, in spite of all these conflicting circumstances, she continued to deprive herself and carried on as the primary financial provider.

These interventions paved the way for another strategic technique: *restraining* (Madanes, 1981; Papp, 1980). After "diagnosing" depression, the therapist cautioned the wife that due to the complexities of family and work issues, any attempt at change would be premature. A rapid move to alter herself or the marital relationship could lead to unknown problems.

In the third session, the wife appeared less depressed and made a drawing of "last week's feelings and this week's feelings". Whereas "last week's feelings" were compressed and drawn mainly in black, "this week's" were expansive-looking and contained bright reds and oranges. The client was puzzled because even though her routine at home and work had not changed, her perception of it had inexplicably altered. She had decided to continue working until her husband got a job. However, she would go "on sabbatical" for a few hours every evening by withdrawing to her study to work on her novel. She was glad that the depression had given her a helpful message.

When this client recognized that, by overachieving, she dominated her husband, she decided to work at making the marriage a more equal partnership. As that change occurred, the husband surprised her by taking on part of the financial burden. The client continued to work and write, and decided to remain in art therapy so that she could explore other issues.

Restraining Through a Ritual

The paradoxical, defiance-based technique of *restraining* is often used to counter the common belief that either change must be complete and all-encompassing or else everything must stay exactly the same. After defining the symptom as benign and essential for family survival and advising a client to follow the same interactional sequence which regularly leads to the presentation of the symptom, the therapist cautions the client *not* to change. "Both the symptom and the system are prescribed. The wording of the prescription is extremely important. It should be brief, concise, and unacceptable to the family. If it is not unacceptable, there will be no recoil"

(Papp, 1983, p. 33).

Prescribing the symptom was the approach taken in the case of Steve, a 20-year-old who sought treatment for compulsive handwashing. Steve washed his hands countless times during the day and even woke several times each night with an irresistible compulsion to wash them again. When he entered therapy, Steve was still living at home with his parents and blamed his compulsion for his inability to look for work. His parents continued to let him live with them and had only recently asked that he help out with the household expenses.

The therapist hypothesized that the parents were covertly supporting the youth's handwashing compulsion because it diverted attention from their alcoholism: the symptom served both the parents' and child's need to postpone Steve's developmental task of leaving home. In art therapy, Steve drew many pictures in which he recalled ways he had previously expressed anger, such as shattering the bathroom mirror with his fist. He continued to complain about his handwashing, which by now was causing his skin to crack and bleed, but the reason for the compulsion remained a mystery.

To interrupt this sequence of compulsive behavior, the therapist designed a *ritual* (Haley, 1976). The young man was told that his handwashing was symbolic of his need to "wash his hands of his family", that is, to separate appropriately as a young adult. Therefore, the symptom could be addressed only with his family's help. The therapist told Steve that every time he experienced a compulsion to wash his hands, he should ask the family to join him. All family members were to accompany him to the bathroom and wash their hands, too. By experiencing the handwashing themselves, Steve was told, family members would be inspired to find a cure for the problem. This ritual required that Steve wake everyone in the family several times during the night.

A week later, Steve reported that his family had initially been helpful and cooperative, joining him in the bathroom throughout one full day and night. Then they grew extremely annoyed at being awakened from their sleep. In anger, the parents refused to continue to cooperate in the task and thereby made the first move to detriangulate their son. Steve slept through the next night "by accident", and other family members didn't have to get up with him. For the rest of the week, he managed to sleep all night without waking to wash his hands.

In a subsequent session, the therapist suggested that Steve trace and cut out an outline of his hands. Steve then pinned the hands on the wall of the therapy room, where he asked to leave them for a week. He was job-hunting, he explained, and constant handwashing would be inconvenient and embarrassing. He wanted the therapist to be in charge of his hands while he was looking for work.

Shortly after this intervention, Steve found a job. Within several months, his handwashing was at a near normal level, and he had moved from his parents' home into an apartment with a friend. Treatment stopped because the symptom was now resolved.

In this case, the unfinished adolescent task of separating from one's parents had to be dramatized through a ritual in order for individuation to continue. By redefining and prescribing the undesirable behavior and restraining the client from change, the therapist provoked a therapeutic recoil. As Papp (1980) notes, "By consciously enacting the cycle that produced the symptom [behavior] loses its power to produce a symptom. The secret rules of the game are made explicit and the family must take responsibility for its own actions" (p. 47). Art imagery can help make these interactional sequences visible.

Unbalancing

A paradoxical intervention was also made in the treatment of Mary, a young woman who was seen individually for short-term therapy. Mary was unhappy with her husband, who had become progressively more controlling. The couple had been married three years and enjoyed a loving relationship, but their roles were rigidly complementary with a potential for oppression. Eduardo, the husband, came from a Hispanic family in which males were supposed to be dominant. Mary had adopted the role of a submissive and protected woman.

Mary and Eduardo had one child, a toddler. The couple agreed that Mary was inadequate as a mother to this little girl, but Mary was eager to improve. The child had stimulated her desire to be competent and respected in her new role as mother. The goals of therapy were to help Mary individuate from her family of origin, in which she served the role of submissive and dutiful child; to help her to become a "mother" rather than a "daughter"; and to redistribute the power in the marriage so that it would be shared more equally.

Early in the therapy, the focus was on Mary's anger at her husband. To illustrate how he provoked her, she related an incident that had occurred when she was chopping onions. Eduardo grabbed her paring knife, insisting that she use a French chopping knife instead because it was "safe" and "the correct tool for chopping onions". This had infuriated Mary because the paring knife was one of her favorite utensils; moreover, Eduardo had intruded on her territory, her preparation of the family meal. After describing this scene,

Mary drew a picture of a stick figure who was berating her (Figure 3). She identified the scolding figure as either her husband or her mother, who "act and say the same". In discussing her husband's overprotectiveness, Mary made a connection between her current problem and the distress and resentment she felt as a child, cared for but smothered by an overinvolved mother.

To redefine the interactional sequence between husband and wife, the therapist gave the following directive:

> Each time your husband comes into the kitchen and asks you to change the way you prepare dinner, stop what you are doing and go over and give him a kiss or a hug. You may then return to preparing the meal in the same way you were doing. Do not change.

Figure 3: "You are stupid"

Mary responded with a startled and confused look but smiled as she left the room.

The therapist structured this intervention so that it would address the motives behind the husband's controlling behavior while interrupting the couple's interactional pattern. Since Eduardo was behaving in a caring and protective manner towards Mary, the kiss rewarded him for his positive intentions. But when Mary replied to Eduardo's interference with an unexpected display of sexual affection, his characteristic exercise of paternal control became unbalanced. Mary felt supported by the therapist's directive, which kept her in charge of her own method of cooking. But it also served to interrupt a redundant and toxic pattern of repetitive behavior while giving each spouse a positive reward. Seeing his startled response to her kiss diffused her anger.

The Therapeutic Double Bind

The use of a paradoxical intervention is grounded in the concept of the *double bind* (Weeks & L'Abate, 1982), first expounded by Gregory Bateson's research group as a means of understanding communication and behavior in families with a schizophrenic member (Bateson, 1972). The double bind describes a relationship in which there are two or more members, a repeated interactional sequence, a primary negative injunction enforced through punishments or other threats to survival, and a secondary injunction in conflict with the first. Another essential condition is that the subject of the double bind be prohibited from leaving the arena of the relationship. In a family where this sequence produces dysfunctional behavior, the double bind is said to be pathogenic. But sometimes, a bind can be created to work therapeutically, as when a paradox is introduced that forces the client and/or family system to make the leap to a new level of functioning. Hoffman (1981) explains the difference:

> In a pathogenic double bind the patient is "damned if he does and damned if he doesn't." In a therapeutic double bind, since he is told not to change in a context where he has come expecting to be helped to change, he is in a similar trap. If he resists the injunction, he changes; if he does not change, he is "choosing" not to change. Since a symptom is something which, by definition, one "can't help," he is then no longer behaving symptomatically. Thus he is "changed if he does and changed if he doesn't." (pp. 237-238).

Even though the subject of a therapeutic double bind receives confusing messages, he or she is in a win-win situation and is rewarded regardless of which choice is made.

In the following case, a paradoxical intervention was built around imagery that appeared in client art work. A couple entered therapy with complaints about each other's parenting, and argument about who contributed more to the household, and mutual accusations of poor communication skills. The symptoms seemed vague and out-of-focus until the couple revealed that they had physically abused the husband's son by a previous marriage during a visit six months before entering therapy. The wife had committed the actual abuse, but the husband had stood by watching and did not intervene. In therapy, the wife uncovered memories of abuse in her family of origin, and this helped her understand her own abusive behavior. But the husband continued to puzzle over why he had passively held back from protecting his son.

In an individual session, the therapist asked the husband to draw a picture of his relationship with his mother (Figure 4). He portrayed himself on his knees, bowing and protesting ineffectually as his mother loomed over him, pointing an accusing finger and saying, "You're weak, selfish, stupid, but I need you even though you wrecked my life, you bastard!" It was clear that even as an adult, he continued to believe that his mother was correct and that there was some basic flaw in his nature for which he "deserved" abuse. In early childhood, he had continually experienced devaluation and rejection and had a poor self-concept and low self-esteem, and his mother's belittling words still rang in his ears. Now, however, he could evaluate his mother's parenting abilities more realistically, and in so doing felt much anger, but also intense guilt.

In a subsequent session, the husband was asked to "draw his guilt". He explained the picture (Figure 5): "The guilt flows from my mother's pot, fills up the container, drips off the spigot. I catch the runoff and pour it back on myself". When asked what purpose this served, he replied. "If I take off the container, the volcano in my head will explode." Even after this dramatic disclosure of how he perpetuated his feelings of guilt, the husband continued to believe he had to behave in this "guilty manner" and was unwilling to attempt any change.

The therapist decided to make a strategic intervention in the form of a homework assignment. At the end of the session, she congratulated the husband for being astute enough to understand how important it was to keep the container of guilt balanced on his head. In order that he might fully experience his guilt and evaluate its role in his life, the therapist instructed him to go to family members, friends, and acquaintances individually, and ask them how he had failed them and what he could do to make reparations for his sins. The client was told to pay close attention to the heightened feelings of guilt this exercise would evoke. Reluctantly, the client agreed to perform the assigned task.

At the next session, the client brusquely informed the therapist that the homework was a "foolish plan". He had tried it several times, but trying to please everyone was "nonsense". He was now convinced that he could "give and take equally in this world" and refused to complete the assignment. The therapist apologized for mishandling the homework and wondered aloud how it could have failed so miserably. The client counseled the therapist not

Figure 4: Mother discounting son

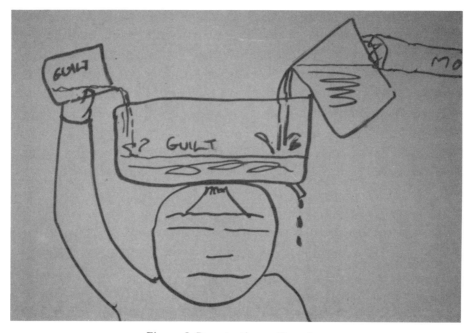

Figure 5: Perpetuating guilt cycle

to feel guilty, because "guilt is a waste of time".

This tactic was successful in redefining the "guilt" symptom and provoking a recoil by the client, who discarded a feeling state based on years of conditioning. An alteration in perception enabled him to modify his world view and quickly achieved second-order change without requiring insight. Relieved of this burden of guilt the client was able to also put aside the negative image of himself that he had incorporated from his mother's abusive language and actions.

Conclusion

In this chapter, I have sought to show how art therapy can enhance strategic therapy and how the systemic approach can be applied in therapy with individuals. The effectiveness of combining the techniques of art therapy with those of strategic family therapy should come as no surprise to art therapists. Art therapy, in theory and practice, has always been strategic. We have long recognized the power of metaphor and its communicative potential. In using art as a therapeutic modality we have traditionally given directives and created conditions that encourage clients to experiment with change. When looking at art with our clients we quite literally frame and reframe their efforts, helping them find new meanings in their work.

Therapists of all persuasions and disciplines seek to help clients discover a new lens with which to view the world and their options for change. Art therapists are unique in that they work with their client's visual representations of the world: they actually see part of the view through the lens. Their ability to make strategic adjustments to focus and aperture can exert a profound influence on both the view and the viewer.

References

Bateson, G. (1972). *Steps to an ecology of mind.* New York: Ballantine.

Bross, A., & Benjamin, M. (1982). Family therapy: A recursive model of strategic practice. In A. Bross (Ed.), *Family Therapy: A Recursive Model of Strategic Practice* (pp. 2-33). New York: Guilford.

Fisch, R., Weakland, J., & Segal, L. (1982). *The tactics of change.* San Francisco: Jossey-Bass.

Haley, J. (1963). *Strategies of psychotherapy.* New York: Grune and Stratton.

Haley, J. (1973). *Uncommon therapy. The psychiatric techniques of Milton H. Erikson, MD.* New York: Norton.

Haley, J. (1976). *Problem-solving therapy.* New York: Harper & Row.

Hoffman, L. (1981). *Foundations of family therapy.* New York Basic Books.

Landgarten, H. (1987). *Family art psychotherapy.* New York: Brunner/ Mazel.

Madanes, C. (1981). *Strategic family therapy.* San Francisco: Jossey-Bass.

Papp, P. (1980). The Greek chorus and other techniques of family therapy. *Family Process, 19,* 45-57.

Papp, P. (1983). *The process of change.* New York: Guilford.

Riley, S. (1985). Draw me a paradox?...Family art psychotherapy utilizing a systemic approach to change. *Art Therapy: Journal of the American Art Therapy Association, 2,* 116-123.

Watzlawick, P., Weakland, J., & Fisch, R. (1974). *Change: Principles of problem formation and problem resolution.* New York: Norton.

Weakland, J., Watzlawick, P., Fisch, R., Segal, L. (1982). *The tactics of change, Doing therapy briefly.* San Francisco: Jossey-Bass.

Weeks, G. & L'Abate, L. (1982). *Paradoxical psychotherapy.* New York: Brunner/Mazel.

COUPLES THERAPY/ART THERAPY: STRATEGIC INTERVENTIONS AND FAMILY OF ORIGIN WORK

"She's fat, just to embarrass me and inhibit my career." "He's thin, to spite me and he eats twice as much as I do!" "This makes our marriage a failure. How can you help us?" How many couples have come into treatment with equally impossible tasks for the therapist to solve? However, if we try not to listen to the words and just attend to the message, perhaps something can be accomplished.

Couples therapy can be exciting and challenging both for the client and the therapist. It provides a particularly creative opportunity for the therapeutic relationship. The very nature of the triadic structure of couples art therapy gives mobility and flexibility to the joining and destabilization processes available to the therapist. Treatment may be based on a variety of theoretical approaches; the concepts presented in this paper have been most helpful when combined with art therapy.

Theoretical Overview

I have freely translated notions from many authors of family treatment and I dare say they may be uneasy with my interpretations of their ideas; I anticipate incorporating other concepts as I change and learn. However, I believe that most practicing therapists educate themselves in the hopes of developing a style that synthesizes other clinicians' methodologies with their own. The individual therapist then evaluates if this "grouping" of concepts

This chapter originally appeared in *Art Therapy: Journal of the American Art Therapy Association*, 8 (2), 4-9 (1991) in a slightly different form and is reprinted with permission.

proves helpful in facilitating their clients' treatment plan. In the material below I have briefly discussed some of my convictions at this particular time.

Family functioning is an interactional system—not in the sense of the mechanical cybernetic model—but as a human system with the power to modify patterns of behaviors. Therefore, a therapist must observe the system with sensitivity to gender issues and the impingements of society. Strategic interventions which include the use of art therapy are useful and achieve a successful outcome for some families (Riley, 1988; 1990). Interventions made through an art task often help the family become aware of their redundant patterns in unsuccessful problem-solving.

In addition to strategic/systemic theories, there are multiple ways of looking at family treatment that transfer to couples therapy. Murray Bowen (1978) provides a description of the complementary nature of relationships seen in marital therapy. His explanations free the therapist from seeing one or the other partner in a judgmental manner and reinforce the stance that each member of a relationship chooses the other for the ideal "fit" to balance out their strengths and weaknesses. This balance is not obvious to the therapist or even to the clients, but with patience, the nature of this impeccable selection process becomes known.

I disagree with Bowen's proposal that individual treatment may be as effective as family or couples work; I feel strongly that the couple must be seen together. My goal is to encourage an increased individuation and differentiation for each partner. The conjoint therapy encourages and acknowledges each member's growth as well as the growth of the relationship. It does not either avoid or encourage the maintenance or dissolution of the marriage, which is always a possibility when change is experienced.

Bowen describes the process of differentiation from family of origin as one of the basic tasks that must be successfully completed to achieve adulthood and to establish a functional, intimate relationship. The growth that he refers to is an individual's internal acceptance that s/he has developed a "real self" with values and perspectives that differ from those learned in early childhood. He also discussed how, later in life, each of us is attracted to others who have achieved similar degrees of individuation from their families of origin. On this basis we seek a more or less successful relationship. Bowen (1978) observes:

> It is the basic level of differentiation that is largely determined by
> the degree of emotional separation a person achieves from his family of origin.
> Since one of the main variables that influences how much emotional separation
> (and basic differentiation) a person achieves is the amount of emotional separation

(and basic differentiation) his parents achieved, and since how much the parents achieved was influenced by how much their parents achieved, basic differentiation is determined largely by a multigenerational emotional process.... People can function at levels that are higher or lower than their basic level depending on the circumstances of the relationship system in which they are operating. (p. 98)

Since differentiation is an internal process, the external manifestations may cover up the degree to which a person has become an autonomous individual. Successful individuation does not preclude deep attachment.

Bowlby (1969), although not a family therapist, added important, fundamental understanding to the appreciation of early development. The part I emphasize, and which I feel is directly related to couples work, is an understanding (at least superficially) of touching, holding, and bonding attitudes of the family of origin. The therapist is aware that this report from the client concerning his/her childhood will be biased; however, this is still essential information. For example, youngsters who are stroked and cuddled bring a far different kinesthetic sense to the marriage bed, than those who have been treated in a distant manner, or far worse, cuddled and rejected simultaneously. Obviously, in short term treatment these profound and basic introductions into the couple's early life experiences are not going to be fully explored. However, even a modest sharing of how each partner recalls his or her childhood moments of intimacy or yearning for affection can be very revealing and helpful in couples work.

Another concept that may help the therapist induce some movement into a relationship that appears helplessly role-bound is the notion of delegation. This concept which is well described by Helm Stierlin (1981) delineates how different children in families are chosen to carry out some unfinished developmental business of a parent. These children are subtly trained to go out in the world and master the tasks that were never accomplished by a parent. The deeds they go forth to do are more or less worthwhile; indeed, how faithfully the child chooses to act on this mission varies with each and every youth. Many times I have seen clients feel ecstatic when they recognize that they no longer have to "be" for someone else (the parent), and that their own desires and goals are valid. When a wife and husband share this experience, they find strength in the mutual recognition that they no longer have to be the "chosen" one. Furthermore, this concept of a child being assigned a role to achieve gratification for a parent can be a useful subject for discussion when a couple wishes to have or has children. A session can be based on how or if the client might identify with a parent who chooses to impose a role on a child.

Within the above amalgamation of ideas let me now state that I believe that most persons are positively motivated as they attempt to solve their problems by changing their partner to "make it better". It is not the motivation that seems to go wrong, but the numerous unsuccessful attempts to achieve this goal which have failed. Therefore, it is the repetitive manner of problem solving that is the problem. This dynamic has been well documented in the work of the MRI group (see Fisch, Weakland, & Segal, 1982; Watzlawick, Weakland, & Fisch, 1974).

None of these belief systems can stand alone or can be valid without taking into consideration the social system in which we exist. Social constructionism theory expands the horizon to include not only all the factors that enter into the creation of each person's perceptions of his/her world, but also the impingement of the outside social structures that may traumatically influence a couple's world view. The theory of social constructionism (Watzlawick et al, 1974) looks at the invented worlds we all uniquely construct, the power of words to shape our thinking, and the necessity to be gender-sensitive in defining problems. Within this framework other theories may comfortably co-exist and assist a couple's therapist with the business of treatment.

Every couple, as they tell their stories and explain their world views, stimulates the therapist to respond through her experience and her knowledge, choosing what appears to be the theory, or groupings of theories, that best fit the problematic situation and the personality of the clients. The final criterion is not to mold their treatment into a theory, but to allow the couple to lead the therapist into the theoretical framework that best holds their own picture of themselves and their lives.

Role of Art Therapy in Couples Work

And what about the art? How is this component weighed in all the talk about theory and techniques? The art product is the foundation on which the theory rests. It is the window to the client's world and the resource that informs the therapist about the couple's meaning in their stories. Above all, the art tasks give the couple an action-oriented mode of problem solving. The action is based in the creative process, both in the execution of art expressions and in the invitation to be innovative in solving problems. The art process encourages the clients to move from the frame of a rigid, unsolvable problem to one that is more manageable and resolvable. The art product reveals additional meanings and invites a fresh look at long-standing beliefs.

With the encouragement of the therapist, the couple can look at their situation through the art product, create a new meaning for old patterns and invent a future that meets their desires. The therapist is able to be more effective since the information in the art expressions allows her to see the couple's world and appreciate their viewpoint. Additionally, the therapist can utilize many theories and modes of intervention, and introduce a variety of art directives that reflect the couple's story, giving new meaning to the long-standing myths of the family.

Case Example I

Cindy and Larry sat in despair in my office. They both expressed how hopeless they felt about resurrecting their dying relationship. The facts were concrete; there was no hope for change. I was to help them through this time which would probably lead to their separation. The sadness they both felt was over the fact that they still felt love for each other, but that "wasn't enough to make the difference".

The major problem was (as they presented it) the fact that Cindy was six years older than her husband. He was thirty-six and she was forty-two. Everything was tainted by the dire reality that she stayed six years older. She had "consistently" been six years older all through their seven-year marriage, the birth of their son three years ago, the blossoming of her husband's career, and her decision to retire from work and be an at-home mother. They both shared guilt over their respective ages. Larry tried to get older faster, but it never worked.

Faced with this situation, I decided not to be "helpful". I listened and empathized with their view of reality, inevitability, and clarity of the difficulties. I then asked them to return the following week with copies of their birth certificates. They were each to do their own photocopying and be responsible for bringing the copy to the session. I did not discuss with them the reason for this request and they left the session somewhat puzzled.

The following week Cindy and Larry had complied with my recommendation. Without further discussion I immediately presented them with a single sheet of 18" x 24" construction paper (they chose the color), two pairs of scissors, and glue. I asked them to cut apart their birth certificates and create a collage made of the two documents. They began their work slowly, but in due time Cindy took a decorative theme from Larry's certificate border and extended it onto hers. He took the dates of their births, cut them out, and scrambled their order. She made inventive shapes of hospital names. This continued until the two documents were unrecognizable. What resulted was a rather attractive collage embellished with a large golden seal that they had created together and placed on the bottom of the paper with the date of the session inscribed.

From this experience, Cindy and Larry seemed to simultaneously understand what they were destroying and what they were creating. They needed very few words to do this. The couple touched hands, chuckled a lot, encouraged each other's participation in the collage process, and smiled at their completed project.

As a final step I requested that they take the collage home, frame it, and place it in a prominent place, at least for a little while. They agreed and their response appeared to be one of relief, although not expressed through words, but through their heightened affect and their embrace of each other at the door as they left. They remained in treatment and never mentioned age again. Cindy and Larry were released from this dilemma and were able to move on to other difficulties in their relationship for which the "six years" issue had served as an avoidance device.

Discussion

This example addresses a basic theme in couples therapy. These two people were tormented by multiple stereotyped messages from society and their families about age in relation to roles of men and women. At the initial session, there was no time to pick apart these issues. The couple was covertly asking me to save their marriage and release them from their symbolic symptom (the age difference) that stood in the way of facing the real distress they felt. I gave them a chance to solve the problem, without interpretation, and to create a new reality for their marriage.

Symbolically through the art, the couple addressed the meta-meaning of age. They started on the path of therapy by establishing their own family interpretation of age by working on a meta-level that paralleled their trouble. Cindy and Larry presented a problem that defied a logical solution. Therefore, it was syntonic to find a solution to the problem in a non-logical way. The resolution did not need to be verbalized because by utilizing art expression, it became visual and concrete.

It is important to note that the first session in couples therapy presents the therapist with a variety of opportunities to establish a framework for the ongoing therapeutic relationship. In all cases the primary necessity is joining with each partner. However, the choice of how one joins is a constant variable. Confrontation or disbelief in the seriousness of a problem that a couple presents in the initial session is often detrimental to therapeutic commitment.

In the case example, the implied message was an ambivalent one of help/do not help, delivered equally by both wife and husband. The created a doublebind for the therapist which could only be addressed by moving to another plane (Bateson, et al, 1956). By first engaging in attentive listening and then shifting to the art task, conflicting signals from the couple were responded to in a way that allowed both Cindy and Larry to bypass their paradoxical request. Their fears of looking into other problems in their relationship were covered by challenging the therapist to solve an impossible difficulty (i.e., their age difference). The meta-message was, "By offering you this unsolvable task we will drive you away, and our relationship, even though it is far from ideal, will not be threatened by change".

The metaphoric power that lies in an art task gives the client(s) an opportunity to take charge of creating new possibilities in their problem-solving skills. What deeper level meaning this creative process speaks to in the client may never be fully understood by the therapist. She can only observe subsequent behaviors and respect the importance of the art product. The client's acknowledgment of the art mirrors the recognition that there is a profound meaning greater than the product itself. Rather than the therapist being solely responsible for triangulating with the couple and guiding the relationship in that manner (Adolphi, et al, 1989), the art becomes the third entity, one which possesses mystical skills. These skills are contained in the projective power of the art which reflects the intimate world view of the clients. For the therapist to presume to understand how the client perceives his/her world would probably prove to be faulty, particularly in the first few sessions. Therefore, the therapist observes and listens to the family story and witnesses the illustration provided through art expression.

Case Example II

The evolution of family work into conjoint marital therapy is very common. Most family treatment benefits from some adult sessions after the systems have been regulated and the children have been relieved of their delegated roles (Stierlin, 1981). It is not unusual at various times in the developmental growth of either the parents, the children, or the family for the couple to perceive that stress impacts them to an unmanageable degree. At these times of flux, couples in rigid relationships, who have not developed coping skills for change, often turn to therapy. The following case example illustrates how two apparently high-functioning adults were no longer able to maintain their facades when developmental pressures escalated.

Soon after Ellen and Craig started family treatment it became apparent that the relationship problem between these parents, not difficulties with their teenaged daughters, needed attention. The stress of adolescent rebellion had stirred up their own problems around individuation. For this reason, therapy moved to conjoint sessions.

Both Ellen and Craig were educated, financially secure since birth, committed to appropriate ethics, and rigidly programmed by their families in the "proper" roles and behaviors of each sex. They had a sixteen-year-old marriage, and although at this time they were very unhappy with each other, they had no desire for divorce. Their situation clearly indicated a need to explore their family of origin, looking at the question of differentiation theories referred to above.

We began by doing a genogram which was then amplified through art therapy in the following manner. Utilizing the usual indicators of sex, relationship through marriage, age, children, and death (McGoldrick & Gerson, 1985), the genogram also introduced color to express dominant trigenerational personality traits. For example, a circle used to indicate grandmother was colored in red, blue and a little green. It had been agreed upon by this couple that these colors would respectively show anger, depression, and nurturing. The connecting lines on the genogram that show relationships were color-coded to express behavioral traits such as affectionate, cold or violent. How they indicated these traits through a color or a combination of colors helped to clarify how the families taught their children to "be".

As Ellen and Craig explained and compared their genogram, they better understood how they were carrying on the family beliefs and how that inheritance occurred. For example, they observed that: Ellen's mother was dominant and ferociously rude; Craig's mother was passive and weak; his father was a male mirror of her mother and her father was the retiring "sweetie". What they hated in themselves were behaviors incorporated from their same sex parent; what they feared in the other was the threat of having to live with a duplication of the opposite sex role that they grew up with. Consciously, Ellen and Craig were only partially aware of these roles and dynamics.

To help make the above characteristics more visible, the next task requires them to "do a collage of your parents". Using magazine pictures each one created a composite of family traits. They were amazed when they found the many similarities in their families of origin. They also learned a great deal by being able to distance themselves from the strong personalities of their parents and felt freer to criticize a collage rather than a real person or parent. At last Ellen could say that she didn't want Craig to be a "wimp" like the picture of her father on the page. Finally, he had the courage to say that when she was like her mother, he cringed inside as he had always with his father. A major gain was achieved when the couple recognized that they both wanted the identical change to occur in the other, "don't become your parent".

Following this exploration of roles and learned behavior, the next step involved learning how to be who they wanted to be. Late individuation in adults who have neglected this process in adolescence always offers a therapeutic challenge. To fully explain the process of this treatment is too extensive for this brief chapter. However, I can note that we used art therapy to rework, from an adult perspective, real and concrete residual events of the past. Stages of development were illustrated through art tasks that reflected the most important crises and successes through their process of maturation. Seeing the past through the window of the present was very instructive.

After a six month period, their daughters showed remarkable improvement. As the parents progressed through their own individuation processes, they became more empathetic with the parallel process in their children. Separation was no longer a major threat. The couple terminated therapy with the resolve to keep on "becoming themselves". An unexpected reward was that the relationship with their own parents had become much easier. The couple no longer felt controlled and therefore could spend more pleasurable time together and interact with them from a position of action rather than reaction.

Discussion

The choice of partner is one of the most important decisions we make. It is often a puzzle to the therapist how each member of a dyad has chosen the other. However, as we look at the visual representations of the relationships and their family of origin as expressed in art, past behaviors and patterns that remain alive in the present become clear.

In the second case example, recognizing how the self often mirrors the parent, is difficult to achieve in words, but can be dramatically clear in art. It was a real triumph when Ellen was able to say "I heard myself sounding just like my mother, and I think he is acting just like his mother. I hate both those women in myself and in my husband". At this moment she was able to transcend sexual identity, recognize the source of behaviors, and move toward change. Moreover, when couples draw their families of origin in a manner that displays relationships, they are able to compare parallels in the drawings of how they, in turn, have created their own dependent relationships. With freedom to redraw, cut out, amplify, and expand a family drawing, the ability to recreate and reinvent new meanings for the process that shaped those individuals becomes a far more manageable task.

This case also presents a good example of a man and woman who, at first, seemed to have achieved full adult functioning in family and socioeconomic areas of their lives. Only under the stress that arose from confronting two teenage daughters did their undifferentiated emotional attachment to their family of origin become an issue. They experienced great frustration as their own daughters strove for differentiation from them, since their own unresolved individuation from their parents left them without the skills necessary to manage this crisis. Two generations were struggling to accomplish the same goal and, instead of differentiating, they were emotionally escalating their dependency. It was no surprise that as the couple became more aware and capable of establishing their own sense of self, the daughters made progress toward autonomy and conflicts diminished. This ripple effect is one of the ongoing pleasures family therapists experience when parents change, the children benefit.

Long term relationships that run aground after twenty or more years of commitment require a specialized approach to couples work. The most common distressor in these relationships has been given the global term "middle age crisis". However, what this term really means to each couple is entirely individual.

I believe with the majority of the couples I see, a common difficulty is that one of the partners has broken the marriage contract. Indeed, for most couples, the contract is unspoken and never really openly acknowledged, although each "promised" the other to fulfill some difficult or uncompleted desire from the other's past. The complementary relationship was built on the silent agreement that each would perform certain duties or carry emotions that would make the other feel more complete. These services were often gender-defined and usually reverberated back to family of origin belief systems.

If one member of the dyad is motivated to change the balance of their contract, then the other is deeply wounded, confused, and often angry. This major upset results when couples have not practiced solving little differences along the journey to middle age. They eventually become ill-equipped to face a major shift in the homeostasis of the marriage.

In addition, often these long-term arrangements have secret satisfactions that take time for the therapist to understand. Women and men choose partners for a variety of reasons. A motivation that is not well recognized is the satisfaction one partner gets from being able to live with an "impossible" spouse. Complementarily, the spouse continues to improve their skills at being impossible, to better satisfy the needs of the coping partner. The one up, one down dance is very lively and keeps the friction going, each knowing that s/he is alive in this contest where the sparks fly.

However, there comes a time when one or the other spouse finds a different type of stimulation which replaces the former magnetic attraction, and the marriage is in trouble.

Case Example III

A middle-aged couple, she in her fifties, he is his early sixties, requested family therapy to heal their son's behavior. The young man in his late twenties came to the first session, but he made it very clear that he was moving out of the home and he wanted his parents to deal with their relationship without him. Conjoint therapy followed.

The husband, Dr. M., was a dentist who specialized in very fine, complex reconstruction work; he was successful, had a small office staff, and a busy schedule of patients. The wife, Mrs. M., had been trained as a dental assistant and they met when she worked in a nearby dental office. After the marriage she continued to work in the husband's office. She assisted with the dentistry and bookkeeping. The couple had two children, a boy now 26 years old, and a girl 21 years old.

Dr. M. was rigidly organized, and insisted that everything be stacked, labeled, and preserved for future use; these rules applied to both the office and the home. No left over food was discarded, no junk mail was thrown away, each program on TV or movie was graded for pornography or violence. Routine was demanded and rigid time schedules followed. All of the above tasks and routines were expected of everyone else, but not Dr. M. He was chronically late and disorganized. He clearly stated that he cared for his wife, but he greatly resented her recent uncaring attitude and lack of support for his needs.

Over the last five years, Mrs. M. had shown symptoms of rebellion. This rebellious behavior was demonstrated by her deviation from the established routines. In the past, she helped her husband in the office, took his bookwork home, raised the children, stacked the papers, labelled each scrap of food in the refrigerator. She considered her role fully utilized as a woman since she had not a moment to contemplate her own existence. The couple was sexually active, and his regular advances toward her (although without romantic words or actions) impressed her as an adequate sexualized marriage.

Mrs. M. turned to her children for the fun, pleasurable outings, and the unstructured warmth she desired. However, children grow and eventually leave home. The daughter left when she was eighteen and remained very distant from the family for a few years. She refused to be trapped in her parents' relationship. The son was less determined; he served as his mother's social companion until he was twenty-four, at which time he pulled himself away. His parents felt that he had abandoned them. When the son left, Mrs.

M. found small comfort in stacking papers and doing her husband's bookwork. When Dr. M.'s rigidity kept her restricted to the home tasks, the joy and laughter in her life seemed to be entirely absent.

Motivated by sheer loneliness Mrs. M. resurrected her career and quickly found a satisfying position in a dental group practice where she used her organizational talents and developed new friends and co-workers. This change was intolerable for Dr. M. He felt betrayed and traumatized. The woman he married had fled and this new independent, rebellious wife had taken her place.

In the first conjoint session, I acknowledged that Dr. M. was the one who was betrayed. I pointed out all the wife's emancipated moves and contrasted them to the subservient woman's role to which he had been accustomed. I felt that he deserved to receive confirmation that she had broken the unspoken contract. As I noted all her betrayals, Mrs. M. glowed with pride; she was delighted to have her transgressions listed. However, how were they to stay together?

Words were not useful in this situation. This couple had built up a vocabulary of miscommunication. They loaded every statement with past events and hurt feelings to the degree that almost nothing could be said without instigating a cycle of blaming. As the therapist I was very unsure of how to proceed since their unwillingness to engage in any art expression was difficult.

In the third session a story was told by the wife that provided an opportunity to make a small change. She recounted a tale about her past birthday when Dr. M. presented her with a bag of manure as her present. She, not surprisingly, was dismayed; what she wanted was a bouquet of roses! He explained that he intended to work in her rose garden and the manure would provide many more roses than he could buy. He honestly did not understand her disappointment.

It occurred to me that he might be instructed by her reaction if it was in contrast to the real event. Therefore, I asked him to create on paper a bouquet of roses for his wife. He found a magazine picture of a rose and I helped him make the leaves and other parts of the bouquet. He then presented the gift to his wife. She was pleased and was able to tell him how much little remembrances meant to her. This was obviously a contrived art directive which only succeeded on the level of stress reduction and education. However, in the next session the wife displayed a positive and caring attitude toward her husband; Dr. M. had brought a real rose home every night since we had last met.

At this time I pointed out to him that he would benefit if he continued to be selfish. The couple looked surprised at this statement. I then inquired had the wife been affectionate and more attentive to him since he started to bring home roses? He agreed that she had been loving. So I asked had he gotten just what he wanted? He agreed again. I asked the wife could he continue to be selfish in these kinds of ways—knowing that when you are courted you are probably going to be more affectionate? She actually giggled and said she didn't mind being manipulated in this manner.

I do not propose that this one maneuver entirely changed a rigid system that had been in place for many years. However, any deviation in repetitive patterns offers hope for more change. The couple's relationship shifted slightly, but the courage and hope for change was not slight.

The conjoint sessions continued. The long term goal for Dr. M. was the readjustments required to accept the new role of his wife; for Mrs. M. the goal was to accept that her husband compulsively structured his life to contain his own insecurities. He would not relinquish these behaviors easily.

Discussion

The couple continued in therapy, making minimal use of art expressions to get past their damaged communication system. However, the impact of the art was not small just because the product was minimal.

Mrs. M. was encouraged to make some practical moves to help her husband: store his papers in large containers, hire a bookkeeper, cook only enough for a meal (no leftovers), and allow him time to talk about his chaotic childhood, a time when every aspect of his life was uncertain. There is no definitive correlation between a dysfunctional childhood and compulsive behaviors in an adult, but it did make some sense to Mrs. M. that what her husband was doing had a base in reality. She was directed to look outward from the relationship to find pleasure components he could not provide. She no longer needed to prove her competency by living up to his excessive demands; she had other areas in which to be efficient. Dr. M. slowly adjusted to having professional help take over his wife's work duties. It was hard for him to trust, but he was rewarded by a more caring wife who no longer was continuously angry.

Also, both of their children were able to visit the home without fear of losing their adult individuation. When their daughter and son felt the shift in the family system, from themselves to the parental dyad, they could relax and assume the adult/child relationship without anxiety. As a result, more laughter was heard in their home.

Each art therapy session focused on some small segment of the narrative of the session. It was sometimes just a list of grievances, other times a stack of junk mail, but the content of the drawings was symbolic of the larger issues facing the couple. Looking at these drawings out of the context of the session would be very puzzling to evaluate or appreciate. They were essential to treatment because they externalized the problem and gave the couple an opportunity to rejudge the situation from a more neutral stance.

Gradually, the silent contract in the marriage became visible through the art, and, although it was never actively discussed, it was recognized by both husband and wife. How they needed and complemented each other was no longer a secret. Perhaps the marriage remains a flawed relationship, but it does remain and it is a marriage both partners want to live within.

Conclusion

It is important for the couples therapist to be curious, modest in hubris, flexible, and, of course, enjoy conjoint work. It is also important to be aware that each person's reality is created by him/her and to understand that, at least in part, this reality may be inherited from the family of origin. Additionally, the therapist must look for the possibility of discrepancy between overt behavior and the meanings those observable actions truly represent. An ability to sprinkle the sessions with humor, be comfortable talking about sex, and realize that you are a temporary part of the system, comprise a realistic formula for the therapist interested in couples therapy.

Add to this a willingness to let the art process inform the therapist and lead the way, through images that both surprise and illuminate the couple's story. It is particularly important to look for the additional levels of meaning found in the visual expression. Material vital to both clients and therapist is more easily accessible through the image and indicates the dormant possibilities of change in the tarnished script of the relationship.

Lastly, modifying undesired patterns through a creative solution can be a festive occasion in couples therapy, especially when both the partners and therapist have the satisfaction of co-creating a new ending to a worn-out script. I paraphrase Bateson, "art" is the difference that makes the difference.

References

Adolfi, M., Angelo, C., & de Nichilo, M. (1989). *The myth of Atlas*. New York: Brunner/ Mazel.

Bateson, G., Jackson, D., Haley, J., & Weakland, J. (1956). Toward a theory of schizophrenia. *Behavioral Science*, 1, 251-264.

Bowen, M. (1978), *Family therapy in clinical practice*. New York: Jason Aronson.

Bowlby, J. (1969). *Attachment*. New York: Basic Books.

Fisch, R., Weakland, J., & Segal, L. (1982). *Tactics of change*. San Francisco: Jossey-Bass.

McGoldrick, M. & Gerson, R. (1985). *Genograms in family assessment*. New York: Norton.

Riley, S. (1990). A strategic family systems approach to art therapy with individuals. *American Journal of Art Therapy*, 28, 71-78.

Riley, S. (1988). Adolescents with family art therapy: Treating the "adolescent family" with family art therapy. *Art Therapy: Journal of the American Art Therapy Association*, 5, 48-51.

Stierlin, H. (1981). *Separating parents and adolescents*. New York: Jason Aronson.

Watzlawick, P., Weakland, J., & Fisch, R. (1974). *Change*. New York: Norton & Co.

Suggested Readings

Beach, S., & O'Leary, D. (1993). Dysphoria and marital discord: Are dysphoric individuals at risk for marital discord? *Journal of Marital and Family Therapy*, 19 (4), 355-368.

Fineberg, D., & Walter, S. (1989). Transforming helplessness: An approach to the therapy of "stuck" couples. *Family Process*, 28 (3), 291-300.

Gerson, R., Hoffman, A., Sauls, M., & Ulrice, D. (1993). Family-of-origin frames in couple therapy. *Journal of Marital and Family Therapy*, 19 (4), 341-354.

Goldner, V., Penn, P., Sheinberg, M., & Walker, G. (1990). Love and violence: Gender paradoxes in volatile attachments. *Family Process*, 29 (4), 343-364.

Lavie, Y., & Olson, D. (1993). Seven types of marriage: Empirical typology based on ENRICH. *Journal of Marital and Family Therapy*, 19 (4), 325-340.

Serra, P. (1993). Physical violence in couple relationship: A contribution toward the analysis of the context. *Family Process*, 32 (1), 21-34.

Wamboldt, F., & Reiss, D. (1989). Defining a family heritage and a new relationship identity: Two central tasks in making a marriage. *Family Process*, 28 (3), 317-336.

Willi, J., Friel, R., & Limacher, B. (1993). Couples therapy using the technique of construct differentiation. *Family Process*, 32 (3), 311-321.

Zimmerman, J., & Dickenson, V. (1993). Separating couples from restraining patterns and the relationship discourse that supports them. *Journal of Marital and Family Therapy*, 19 (4), 403-413.

SECTION TWO: WORKING WITH SPECIFIC POPULATIONS
Cathy A. Malchiodi

Most individual therapies, including individual art therapy, traditionally focus on insight, personal history, and the client-therapist relationship. In contrast, family art therapy emphasizes the interactional process of the clients, giving form to communication patterns, hierarchies and infrastructures within the client's family and world view. In this sense, the goal of family art therapy is not so much to change an individual in a family, but rather to help the client and family reinvent structure and transaction, resulting in new and more effective ways of interacting and communicating with each other.

In this section Riley demonstrates the unique value of family art therapy to help specific client populations effect change within their lives and invent new ways of interacting. The focus of these chapters is on not only what makes art therapy an effective therapy with specific populations, but also on how a specific population and/or circumstance may affect the overall family art therapy goals and design.

In the first chapter of this section, Riley presents an example of how art therapy may be used with families coping with a handicapped member. Common problems faced in raising and living with a disabled person are discussed, including the multidimensional needs of the handicapped individual, stresses faced by the parents and siblings, and effects of these stresses on the family system. More importantly, this chapter demonstrates the adaptability of family art therapy to a specific circumstance: working with several families simultaneously in a time-limited framework. The art therapy component of treatment adds the interaction necessary to successful communication between groups. It also has the additional benefit of being developmentally appropriate to a wide range of ages and abilities. If strictly verbal therapy were utilized in the circumstance Riley describes, the handicapped family member might not feel included in the activities; the art component not only enlivens the sessions, but equalizes the relationship of the group members.

One can easily see how the family art therapy approach Riley describes could be used with a variety of multifamily groups including grieving families, families with a terminally or seriously ill member, families with an alcoholic member, etc. It is obvious that families with similar backgrounds or interests could benefit from not only the interaction that a multi-group strategy provides, but also the informational exchange and mutual support that emerges as the sessions progress. With the increased emphasis in mental health on seeing more clients within shorter time frames, both practitioners and students reading this chapter may want to consider the possibilities for utilizing a multifamily group art therapy approach with families that they encounter in clinical practice.

The next chapter focuses on adolescence, and, in particular, the treatment of the "adolescent" family. Adolescence traditionally has been considered to represent the time period from 13-19 years; it is also thought to be one of the most challenging times in an individual's development as well as one of the most difficult stages to address therapeutically. Adolescence can also be a state of mind and, as Riley observes, therapists may often find that other family members may be encountering adolescent problems of their own. Family systems can be thought of as having a life of their own (Mirkin & Koman, 1985), passing through life stages similar to the stages that individuals pass through during a lifetime.

Although the adolescent child may have been identified as the reason the family has come into therapy, there are often other adolescent issues that have not been addressed within the family system. Developmental tasks of detachment, autonomy, caring for others, and maturation are only a few of the milestones of adolescence that many adult parents have not adequately handled themselves. These quickly surface through family art therapy, where group members are placed in situations of interacting with one another, and roles of authority, nurturance and responsibility are easily identified through both the process and product.

Resistance is a common complaint of therapists working with adolescent clientele. For students and beginning practitioners, how to design and use interventions to overcome resistance is often a major concern in designing effective treatment strategies. In the cases that Riley presents, she demonstrates ways to actively address adolescent resistance, whether in the adolescent client or the adolescent parent. The art process once again is used to engage the resistant clients in therapy and to equalize the communication among family members. An additional benefit of using art expression with adolescents of any age is its natural ability to tap into the creative urges common to this developmental stage, using creative propensity to encourage personal exploration (Linesch, 1988).

Figure 1: "The day it happened"; collage/painting by battered woman

In the third chapter of this section, a case of a family confronting domestic violence is examined and traced. Of family violence in general, Goldner, Penn, Sheinberg, & Walker (1990) observe that "as family therapy has widened its scope by bringing social problems like battering, child abuse, and incest into the consulting room, the violent aspects of intimate life have become more visible" (p. 343). One could also observe that art therapy has made the issue of family violence more visible through the art products created in session. The advantage of using art expression with individuals who have experienced abuse or battering is its ability to give a voice to issues that may be uncomfortable or impossible to discuss in the beginning stages of treatment (Malchiodi, 1990). In spousal violence, for example, the woman may feel embarrassed, guilty or afraid to talk about the abuse she has experienced. Through imagery, these feelings can be conveyed while also nonverbally expressing the issue of family violence. This is particularly helpful in the early stages of treatment when an abused woman may still believe that it is not permissible to talk about the abuse, but it is safe to use images to express her feelings about being battered (Figure 1).

In working with issues of violence and abuse, therapists must be cognizant of the multidimensional levels of family violence involving both gender and systemic aspects. In the seminal work, *Trauma and Recovery,* Herman (1992) observes that "the recovery process follows a common pathway... establishing safety, reconstructing trauma, and restoring the connection between survivors and their community" (p. 3). The case of Nora and her two children presented in this chapter demonstrate how family art therapy can be used as a vehicle in this recovery process that Herman describes. Through application of family art therapy techniques, Riley emphasizes the importance of safety and containment in the early stage, helping the family revisit the trauma through metaphor in the middle stage, and eventually exploring remarriage in the termination stage.

Lastly, the use of art therapy in an outpatient setting is demonstrated, with case examples involving an alcoholic family, a sexually abused child, the treatment of an adoptive family, and a suicidal adolescent. In a preface to these outpatient cases, Riley brings up a concept which may be distasteful to art therapists and mental health therapists in general: cost-effectiveness of services. In the time since this material was originally written there has been an increased focus on cost-effectiveness of services (Lipchik, 1994). Courses on brief therapies have cropped up along with advertisements hawking literature on how to prove to providers that one's mental health services are effective and solution-focused. All methods of treatment are currently being scrutinized, including art therapy, with a greater emphasis on proving the worth of specific treatment strategies with clientele.

Is art therapy really more cost-effective than other types of therapeutic intervention? There really is no hard data to prove this point; however, as Riley notes, there are several circumstances in which it has anecdotally proven itself to be cost-cutting. These include: nonvoluntary or court-ordered individuals who are not as threatened by art therapy as other modalities and, therefore, more likely to stay engaged; families with hidden abuse who may reveal more information through art-based assessment before the family is willing to talk about it, giving important data on family interactions;

adolescents, who are often identified clients in families, and who are more likely to remain and participate in art therapy because it is developmentally appropriate. Also, in general, art therapy allows for self-interpretation by the client, engaging him/her in the very first session and therefore may accelerate the treatment process. These ideas are important in both classroom and supervisory discussions as the concept of cost-effectiveness is one that will remain central to mental health service delivery in the years to come.

A Note for Instructors, Supervisors and Students

It is obviously important in working with a specific population or in a certain set of circumstances to be aware of as much as possible about them. In working with a family with a handicapped member, it may become important to know something of the handicapping condition as well as community resources for the family to consult for transportation needs, special education, and other services for the disabled person. Or, in working with domestic violence, issues of safety for the client and basic needs will become key to making initial progress; drawing a picture of what it takes to be safe will also need to be supplemented by assistance from social services, legal resources, food and clothing banks, and perhaps a shelter or safe house. Therefore, instructors and supervisors should suggest additional reading to their students or supervisees to supplement their knowledge in addition to classroom discussions of the specific populations and circumstances they see in clinical practice.

In thinking about the material presented in this section, it is important to understand what makes art therapy the therapy of choice in the situations described as well as in other possible settings and populations. It has been demonstrated in this section and the previous one that the use of art expression can enhance the therapeutic interaction, increase the understanding of the family's reality, and create movement in the therapeutic process. With families experiencing domestic violence, for example, art therapy may provide the necessary distancing from immediate trauma and a way to voice confusing ideas without words. With each of the other circumstances mentioned, there are specific values inherent to art therapy with families that support application of the art process in clinical practice.

However, on what does a therapist base selection and development of art therapy tasks with a given population or situation? The answer to this question is at the core of successful therapeutic intervention. In reading the material presented in this section, it is important to discuss and consider why art therapy was used and why a strategy for infusing it within family work was chosen. Such a classroom or supervisory session discussion can be helpful to beginning practitioners in their understanding of therapeutic intervention in general and in developing a therapeutic style and philosophy for family art therapy.

References

Goldner, V., Penn, P., Sheinberg, M., & Walker, G. (1990). Love and violence: Gender paradoxes in volatile attachments. *Family Process, 29 (4), 343-3.*

Herman, J. (1992). *Trauma and recovery.* New York: Basic Books.

Linesch, D. G. (1988). *Adolescent art therapy.* New York: Brunner/Mazel.

Lipchik, E. (1994, March/April). The rush to be brief. *Family Therapy Networker, 18* (2), 34-39.

Malchiodi, C. A. (1990). *Breaking the silence: Art therapy with children from violent homes.* New York: Brunner/Mazel.

Mirkin, M. P., & Koman, S. L. (1985). *Handbook of adolescents and family therapy.* New York: Gardner.

Suggested Readings

Cassano, R. D. (1989). Multi-family group therapy in social work practice. *Social Work with Groups, 12,* 3-14.

Cassano, R. D. (1989). The multi-family therapy group: Research on patterns of interaction. *Social Work with Groups, 12,* 15-39.

Coleman, K. H. (1988). Conjugal violence: What 33 men report. *Journal of Marital and Family Therapy, 6,* 207-213.

Gilligan, C. (1982). *In a different voice.* Cambridge, MA: Harvard University Press.

Goldner, V. (1985). Feminism and family therapy. *Family Process, 24,* 31-47.

Goldner, V., Penn, P., Sheinberg, M., & Gillian, W. (1990). Love and violence: Gender paradoxes in volatile attachments. *Family Process, 29* (4).

Goodrute, T. J., Rampage, C., Ellman, B., & Halstead, K. (1988). *Feminist family therapy.* New York: Norton.

Herman, J. (1992). *Trauma and recovery.* New York: Basic Books.

Hines, P., Richman, D., Maxim, K., & Hays, H. (1989). Multi-impact family therapy: An approach to working with multi-problem families. *Journal of Psychotherapy and the Family, 16,* 161-176.

Krpan, I., & Medved, Z. (1991). Family sculpture in multi-family group therapy. *Socijaina-Psihyatrijai, 17,* 201-211.

Malchiodi, C. A. (1990). *Breaking the silence: Art therapy with children from violent homes.* New York: Brunner/Mazel.

Malmquist, C. (1978). *Handbook of adolescence.* New York: Jason Aronson.

Masterson, J. (1985). *Treatment of the borderline adolescent.* New York: Brunner/Mazel.

Mirkin, M., & Koman, S. (1985). *Adolescents and family therapy.* New York: Gardner.

Pittman, F. (1987). *Turning point.* New York: Norton.

Wooley, S., & Lewis, G. (1987). Multi-family therapy within an intensive treatment program for bulimia. *Family Therapy Collections, 20,* 12-24.

MULTI-FAMILY GROUP ART THERAPY: TREATING FAMILIES WITH A DISABLED FAMILY MEMBER

A family with a child who has a physical handicap, a severe learning disability, or mental retardation is a family living under unusual stress that deserves a specific, focused type of therapeutic intervention. This family exists in a paradoxical situation that is not unlike the double-bind formula of Bateson, Jackson, Haley and Weakland (1956). In spite of their extraordinary burdens, they are expected by society to function at a normal level. Many families also try to meet these expectations and feel guilty when they fail to "do it all". The reality is that there are specialized, ongoing demands which must be met, such as constant medical attention, excessive need for transportation, struggles with wheelchairs and orthopedic equipment, special schools, additional financial expenditures, continuous attention in the home, and psychological stress; these burdens often result in emotional resentments and adverse reactions. Unrealistically, these families try to cope with all these distressful situations while denying the feelings which arise from trying to live normally within an abnormal situation. Families often choose one of two courses of action: they solve their problems through achieving exhausting success, or through abdicating responsibility rather than experiencing failure.

Developmental Restrictions

Trauma begins with the birth of the handicapped child. Often, this child does not meet society's stereotype of an "attractive baby". This, coupled with the overwhelming despair of having an imperfect child, often leads to

This chapter was based on an article published in the *Proceedings of the 8th Annual Conference of the American Art Therapy Association* (1977), p. 165.

155

conscious or unconscious parental and/or familial rejection of the infant. Even under the best of circumstances, the process of attachment and, later, individuation between mother and infant is distorted. Many times the baby stays in the hospital for many of his or her first weeks of life, delaying bonding. Upon arriving home medical consultations may take priority over the natural rhythm of mother's and baby's routine.

As the child grows older, the developmental steps of each member of the family are thrown off balance. The parents continue to be tied to a child who makes infant-like demands. Another crisis looms when separation is encouraged. As the disabled member struggles to achieve some accommodation to a world which uses a different standard than that which he or she is able to achieve, reality unkindly forces the person back into a dependent position. Later, even if there is an inclination to individuate, s/he cannot be free of limitations, restrictions, and biases of society. Going to school, crossing a street, shopping, or finding an accessible apartment are only a few of the challenges that must be encountered every day.

Parental Issues

The parents need to grieve and mourn the "loss" of the child they expected, and attempt to integrate this "lost" child with an acceptable image of the "imperfect" child (Solnit & Stark, 1961). This process necessitates repetitive reworking at each level of the child's and the family's development. The resentments, and possible over-protectiveness or rejection felt by the parents and the distress of the siblings are often issues which are disregarded. These buried angers and feelings that fate has unjustly singled them out for an unjust burden of sorrow may reveal themselves in displaced or maladaptive patterns. The family system becomes warped; focus may either be inordinately centered on the handicapped child or, in contrast, excessive energy is used to create defenses or denial of the problem. As Freud (1917) noted, there cannot be a "normal" family when one member needs attention and help beyond the bounds of common expectations.

Therapeutic Considerations

Considering the dynamics that exist in families living under this type of stress, the question is how to intervene therapeutically in a manner that will be helpful and include all family members? Presenting an opportunity for everyone to be expressive and still not threaten the tenuous self-esteem of the handicapped member is the central challenge. The use of art psychotherapy in a multi-family setting seemed to be a positive answer to this problem.

As I considered the design of these meetings, it seemed that the distancing and safety that expression on paper provides, combined with the benefits of multi-family exposure, would offer an optimum opportunity to invite positive change and still retain the function and balance of the system. The families would, hopefully, learn new coping mechanisms from each other, strengthen their observing egos, and gain support from others dealing with equally difficult situations while experiencing a supportive and positive introduction to therapy.

Multi-Family Group Therapy

Group process and therapeutic change is difficult under any condition, but in a multi-family situation it is often impeded by the sheer number of members. However, with art therapy the primary response lies in the individual expression through graphic form, followed by sharing of thoughts and emotions evoked by the group task. This process aids group cohesiveness, making it possible to relate simultaneously to children and adults through a task in which children are not at a developmental disadvantage. The disabled family member can also find equality through the group's acceptance of his/her creative expression.

The hospital for children which funded the program discussed in this chapter is a diagnostic and teaching center. The facility chose three families, each of whom had a disabled child who had been seen on a regular basis at the hospital in physical therapy and other therapies, such as speech or occupational. One family was also receiving psychological treatment in marital therapy.

The treatment plan was to see each family in an hour-long individual session at the first and last meetings; six one-and-a-half hour meetings would constitute the multi-family meetings. This was a brief service with the goal of more positive reorganization of individual roles and the balance of power within the family system. Hopefully, the experience would encourage a reevaluation and redistribution of values which would promote alleviation of repressed guilt, shame, anger and/or frustration caused by the accident of birth of an "imperfect" child (Bonnefil, 1977).

None of these families included members who were psychotic. All families were intact, although one set of parents was considering separation. The children ranged in age from eight to fifteen; two families had two children, one had three children. The entire multi-family group consisted of three families, with six adults and seven children (four of whom were disabled).

One family consisted of a father, mother (former nurse), a cerebral palsied, spastic ten-year-old boy, and an eight-year-old girl. The second family included a mother, father, a fifteen year-old girl and a ten-year-old sister with a chromosomal defect that causes mild retardation, mild incoordination, and a speech defect. The third family consisted of a mother, father, two boys, eleven and nine years old, and a sister, age eight. The boys had controlled celiac disease (malabsorption syndrome); their treatment restricted the diet of these children until they reached adulthood.

In two families, the parents had adequate parenting skills; in the third family, both parents displaced their anger through the older child and withdrew from active, responsible attachment to any member of the family. Two families had children who were recognizably handicapped; one family had the boys with celiac disease, a disability that was not visible to observers. This visual difference eventually became an important dynamic in the families' interaction as the multi-family group developed.

Session #1: Evaluation

The first individual session with each family was an introduction to art therapy and an exploration of anxieties and preconceptions about the forthcoming sessions. The families were asked to draw with pastels or felt pens in dyads, relating both verbally and nonverbally, as suggested by Kwiatkowska (1971), with no interpretations made. This was followed by a family group drawing with all members participating.

Observations were made by the therapist to aid her in her ability to construct future art therapy directives. When the families entered therapy, the therapist searched for some common themes and conflicts that the three families shared. Thus, some global issues were suggested to the families that could possibly be explored in future sessions.

In general, the goals of the first session were to establish an initial working relationship, to provide direct experience in art therapy, and to deal with issues of confidentiality. How the family paired, who was the leader, who was the scapegoat, and what kinds of resistance were observable were valuable pieces of information gleaned from this introductory hour.

In the initial sessions, the tasks that were proposed to the families were a help for the therapist as well as for the families. Their willingness to engage in a new activity (art therapy), their dyadic relationships and interactions when asked to draw in couples, and their ability to communicate verbally and nonverbally were all challenged in the first few tasks. The dual drawings were followed by a directive: "Draw together an island and place anything you choose on it". This island was the family's "special place" to live. They were to negotiate what would make them most content and able to exist together.

Family drawings often reveal the family system and their dominant world view. To aid in the assessment of patterns within the family system, each family member was asked to choose an individual color to use in the group drawing; observing the placement of these colors later informed the evaluation of dominant, aggressive, passive, or other personal modes of behavior within the family.

Case Examples

The family with the two boys with celiac disease, whose parents were in a conflictual relationship, drew an island in a war zone; bullets were flying and discord was rampant in the image (Figure 1). This was in great contrast to the image of the family (Figure 2), drawn by the mother which depicted an idealized harmony; the mother denied the conflict within the family and drew them in a loving relationship with each other. In reality, father and mother had withdrawn from their children; they were involved with them only around dietary difficulties and the schedule forced upon them by these needs. The parents' conflict reverberated throughout the family.

The family with the mildly retarded child was compliant and predictably somewhat overprotective of the girl. The member in this family who struggled most to find her place was the fifteen-year-old sister. She found it hard to rebel (normal behavior for an adolescent) and her attempts to individuate were ignored since attention was generally focused on her sister. The teenaged daughter was a designated parental child who was assigned the role of the strong female, while the mother was cast by the father as a delicate, less functional woman. This was a very significant aspect of their dynamics and one that was addressed in subsequent sessions.

The island this family drew was benign and without conflictual themes, with the larger drawing by the disabled child dominating the scene (Figure 3).

The third family was, perhaps, a family with what might appear to outsiders as the one with the greatest difficulties. The son's cerebral palsy made him very rigid and spastic, and he was confined to a wheelchair. He had a slight speech impairment, but in all other ways he demonstrated better than average intellectual abilities. The greatest difficulty this family demonstrated was a reluctance to let the boy test his skills and assume normal (albeit, limited) age-appropriate risks. They were unwilling to trust their son to venture forth independently. Their drawings showed a strong identification between father and son, however, not so powerful as to interfere with the parental/marital duo (Figure 4). Their drawing of their island revealed the healthiest balance between fantasy and reality of the three families. They

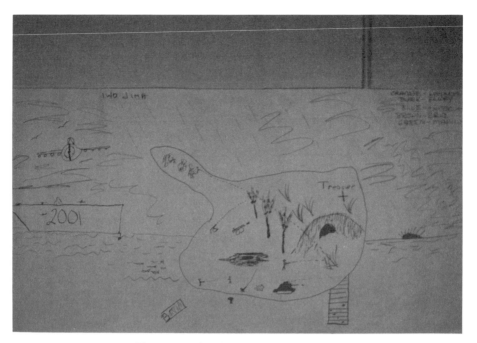

Figure 1: A family at war (family one)

Figure 2: Parents idealizing the family (family one)

Figure 3: Child dominated family drawing (family two)

Figure 4: Peaceful island (family three)

depicted less situations of conflict, equally shared the space, and devoted some attention to meeting needs rather than conducting a war.

The importance of the introductory session cannot be emphasized enough (Yalom, 1985). Without the preparation through the art tasks, the therapist would be less informed and, therefore, less effective. The family would feel less at home with the art therapy tasks and not free to question and challenge this form of intervention in a group setting. All families were encouraged to express their anxieties and to define their goals, thus placing them in charge of their own commitment. Confidentiality was reinforced and a general cooperative attitude around this venture was encouraged.

First Multi-Family Meeting: Forming an Alliance

The first multi-family session was constructed as an opportunity to provide an experience that would lead to acceptance and some understanding of each other. The families were asked to draw together as a family a picture about themselves and their activities. Unfortunately, one family was ill and did not attend this session; therefore, this same goal needed to be repeated in the second session. This session and subsequent sessions also dealt at length with the feelings around the video camera, camera crew of four, flood lights, and observers from the staff of the hospital. These seemingly impossible intrusions gradually became unimportant and almost unnoticed by the families. The decision to tape the sessions came about because of the teaching focus of the hospital.

An issue arose in the first session. The children with celiac disease (who outwardly appeared physically well) were quite anxious about associating with the boy in the wheelchair. This anxiety was exacerbated when it became apparent that the parents and siblings of this handicapped boy functioned with greater success than the seemingly "normal" children and their family. This anxiety emerged through both discussion and drawings, and was confronted in a manner that allowed expression and some resolution of these feelings.

Through exploration and comparison of the family drawings, the group addressed common interests as well as problems and stresses evoked by having to attend to the needs of a handicapped family member. At this particular session, the families were also introduced to their "new family member". S/he was a professional (social worker, speech therapist or physical therapist) selected from the staff of the hospital who wanted the art therapy experience. I felt someone would be needed as a part of each family to serve as an ancillary co-therapist in this large group. Each family decided if this therapist would be a "cousin", "uncle", etc. The person became an additional supportive figure and was useful in assisting the handicapped member, centering the family on art tasks, and making additional interpretations, if appropriate.

The group consisted of three fathers, three mothers, four boys, three girls, three co-therapists, and myself. Moving among these sixteen people were two cameramen and two assistants, and observing in the same room were eight to ten staff persons.

Second Multi-Family Meeting: Solidifying Group Process

The second session was constructed to incorporate the family who had been absent the first evening as well as to encourage greater interaction between families. The first directive involved each person drawing around his/her hand and decorating the drawing of the hand with colors, marks, and shapes. After the hands were drawn, decorated, and the person's name added, they were cut out. It was important that the drawing tasks proposed to these families were simple enough to be accomplished by the children with disabilities.

The family that had missed the first session was asked to tape their drawings of their hands on a large paper on the wall in any place they wished. They chose to put them in a cluster in the center. Then, the other families added their hands, one by one, and symbolically the group became attached. The family that had missed the first session was asked to begin the composite hand mural since the two other families would be able to attach their hands around them, thus symbolically taking them into the group. In this way, this family could actually see that they were now part of the group process. This action and the products were discussed, and how each person felt about the experience was explored.

The second part of this exercise was undertaken after the break. The families all drew their hands on a large sheet of paper on the floor. They then connected them with lines and were encouraged to move about as they desired, promoting further contact and integration between the three families (Figure 5).

Through both the dialogue about the experience and visual expression, the families began to become aware and appreciate some differences: 1) The most physically handicapped child was the most verbally assertive, capable person in this group; 2) The most stressed family in the group (having the boys with celiac disease) had children with the least obvious physical problems. All three children in this family displayed acting-out behaviors, arising from their need for attention and limit-setting from the parents; 3) The sibling of the physically handicapped child was depressed and overly-

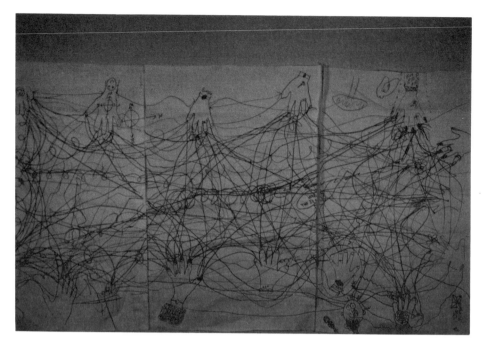

Figure 5: Everyone in group connects

anxious to please, perhaps to gain attention which was normally given to her brother. The younger girl was very dependent on her father and unable to compete in a healthy manner with her sibling. In contrast, the teenaged girl in another family was able to verbalize resentment at the lack of attention she received; she recalled a period of despair when she had even considered suicide.

Third Multi-Family Meeting:
Recognizing Adult & Child Systems

The third session was an opportunity for the children to work in one group and the parents to work in another group, and subsequently combine their products, if they wished. Disengaging the children from their families gave them a chance to demonstrate their interpersonal skills and abilities to function autonomously. This arrangement also gave the parents an opportunity to focus on adult concerns and learn from each other. They were encouraged to share other sides of themselves beyond the role of a parent of a disabled child.

For this exercise, each group was given colored construction paper, glue, pens, small pieces of balsa wood, some plastic articles, and a paper tray. They were then instructed to create anything they wished with these materials; each group worked separately on the task. The co-therapists were placed with the children's group in order to assist the physically handicapped children and to provide behavioral parameters for the children who needed them.

Without any difficulties the adults and children divided into groups and started the task in very much the same way. Each individual began with a shape and then gradually placed their three-dimensional constructed forms adjacent to another person's creation, eventually risking attaching his/her piece to a composite whole.

After the two group constructions were completed, the parents and children were invited to make a single large construction in the middle of the floor. This was accomplished mainly by the parents moving around the outside of the children's construction and connecting their pieces to the children's "city" in the center. Both parents and children admired each other's work and commented on how the final construction was more creative than its individual parts. This mutually shared experience broke down the adult-child barriers and subsequently encouraged communication between both families and generations.

Some of the remarks that were made revealed: one mother felt that she had done something totally for herself and by herself for the first time in many years; other group members commented on the excitement of free, non-judgmental creative expression; many remarked how it seemed as though everyone was the same age while doing this task.

The structure of this creative task not only equalized differences in age, but also the expectations for performance by each group member. The handicapped persons were seen as equally capable, interacting with both peers and adults. The "well" siblings were seen as autonomous individuals, and the parents became persons with unique capabilities outside of their roles as caretakers.

Fourth Multi-Family Meeting:
Experimenting with a "New" Family

The fourth meeting was designed to promote a restructuring of the three families. The goal was to encourage attachments to other adults and children outside the family, thus developing relationships with the therapeutic family as well as the natural one. This was accomplished by asking the families to form three new families. Parents and children were divided into new family configurations that were manufactured with the therapist in the therapy session. The "invented" families were instructed to work together to form a world in which they wished to live. This world was to be created on a large piece of paper with pens, pastels, and plasticine.

Again, a challenge was created through the art task. An opportunity was offered to the families to experience surrogate parents and children which would lead to a learning experience. By restructuring the families in the group, the freedom to express personal needs, to ask for connections, privacy or help, and to discuss goals, was greatly enhanced and old stereotypical mannerisms could be broken. Within the new family the need to work out old anxieties of the natural family was greatly reduced; it was easier to be straightforward in transactions and creativity was admired as all members of the pseudo family encouraged each other's contributions. Each group created a world that gave satisfaction to the individual without detracting from the larger function of the family.

The stress-free atmosphere encouraged lengthy discussion at the end of the session. The natural families related how they hoped to sustain some part of this experience in their relationships at home. They recalled their lack of tension when asking for their needs to be met in the therapeutic family. They concluded that most of the distress they experienced in their own homes stemmed from old patterns of behaviors in which actions and communications were contaminated by previous problem-laden situations. These new views of family communication and interaction were considered well-worth preserving.

The dissolution of the natural families and the recreation of a new family, with subsequent interactions and interpretations, was the therapeutic goal of previous sessions. To my knowledge this maneuver had not been tried before with multiple families in treatment. Theoretically, it put into action an accelerated understanding of how each family interacts systemically and reproduces the same problem behaviors. Through this experience, each parent and child could test what it would be like to live with a family which reacted differently. Although this was only a single session experience, the impact on the participants was powerful. It illuminated the human trait of preference for familiar burdens rather than seeking change and avoiding challenges created by new forms of stress. This realization instilled in the families a willingness to work with their own problems, rather than being jealous of other families and what appeared on the surface to be an easier life-style.

The children were anxious to return to their own parents and parents also saw their children differently. They had been exposed to parents with children with different illnesses, unfamiliar personalities and communication patterns. They also experienced a disruption of their family system that allowed them to distance themselves and develop an appreciation for their own families. The affection that parents had for their children became important, and other annoying behaviors became less noticeable.

The remaining two sessions would gradually reunite the natural families and promote an improved communication system within their structure. This separation and reintegration were parallel to the process of therapy in long-term groups (Yalom, 1985).

Fifth Multi-Family Meeting:
Rejoining the Parents & Children

During the fifth session a child and adult were asked to draw together on a piece of 18" x 24" paper. The theme of this drawing was how to achieve the changes and improvements that they sought within their own reality. The directive was given in an open-ended manner: "In your family how could things get better? What could *you* do to make it better?". Dyads of parents and children were formed and the discussion which ensued was of a heightened, intimate nature. The art products focused on difficulties in the family and explored how they each could find more functional ways of interacting. They also struggled to create a more positive environment for all family members. Later, in the group discussion, it was observed that many of the same desires for the future were commonly shared. The dominant

Figure 6: Working with what we have

167

Figure 7: Appreciating our family

Figure 8: Our family's future

themes included a search for autonomy and individuation, as well as a desire to continue this type of experience outside the therapeutic setting (Figures 6,7,8).

Sixth Multi-Family Meeting: Termination

In the sixth and final meeting, the focus was on termination and separation from the group. In addition, each member was asked for their personal evaluation of the experience.

Two large sheets of paper were placed on the wall and the families were instructed to paint a "good-bye" mural together (Figure 9). The material that emerged expressed regret that the group had ended, that the art therapy experience was over, and that they must part. The depth of the attachment to the art therapy group was surprisingly strong, considering that the experience was limited to six sessions.

Each adult family member reported gains in personal insight. In particular, the adolescent girl felt she had made an important change in self-

Figure 9: Group mural

Figure 10: Small portion of group mural,
adolescent, bird flys out of her cage

recognition. She contrasted her role as parentified child with the roles of the other children; she recognized that she could help the family and not be bound to them forever. Positive comments made by group members helped shift her view of herself and her parents supported her new role (Figure 10).

The younger children verbalized that they were sad to no longer have the opportunity and enjoyment of doing pleasurable, creative tasks with their parents and other families. Everyone agreed that this had been a unique experience.

Evaluation

Each family in the individual follow-up session felt that they would benefit from further therapy and that this idea was not something they had previously considered. They felt that art therapy was a non-threatening modality and a valuable way to interact and to make discoveries about themselves and each other.

The couple who were separating reunited for the time being, saying that they had shared pleasure for the first time in a long while. These parents of the boys with dietary problems became aware that their feelings of loneliness were due to the lack of understanding of each other and their children. In the third family, the adolescent verbalized her need for individuation, and requested differentiation from her disabled younger sister. The younger sister also showed more independent behavior.

Many issues were left unaddressed in all the families. It was recognized that more could have been accomplished over an extended period of time. This is a consideration for future groups of this nature, although the general format and dynamics of the process seemed to be successful. Importantly, the families formed a strong attachment to their co-therapist. Since these individuals were on the hospital staff and worked with the families in on-going therapy, this aspect would continue to be part of their lives. Thus, the addition of these co-therapists enhanced future treatment.

Conclusion

The multi-family experience, exploring the dynamics of a family with a disabled child, confirmed the expectation that this issue and the ensuing stress it produces can be successfully investigated with the use of art therapy in a brief format. The clarification of the family system through the art tasks, as well as observation of the personality set and assigned roles of the individual members within the system, was extremely useful. The pleasure and creativity engendered by the use of a variety of materials reinforced the families' attendance to the tasks and retained the attention of the children. Most importantly, the handicapped child rapidly became absorbed in this therapeutic approach, reducing differences and enabling the parents and the children to focus on problems and feelings in a way that gave permission for change.

It is concluded that this approach using art therapy with families under stress could be offered in many therapeutic settings to relieve some of the pressures that burden these families and inhibit them from developing successful methods of coping with serious problems. The protocol of the multi-family group can be useful with families with stress-related problems, as well as families with a disabled family member.

Reflections

Originally, this paper was written and presented in 1977. At that time there were few, if any, articles written about multi-family art therapy groups. There were many family therapists engaged in this form of treatment, but none to my knowledge with this six-session plan of observation, dissolution, and reunification of the families.

My overall goal was to help each family understand how they functioned as a system. The issue of stress created by raising a disabled child was a commonality in the group described in this paper. However, I have used this formula on other occasions in an outpatient setting with families presenting a variety of problems. The format has worked well with behavioral and psychological difficulties in families as well as the population described in this chapter.

With multi-family groups, my conviction is that the therapist must have a clear plan for the individual sessions as well as the ultimate goals of brief service. S/he must also be somewhat of an entrepreneur who is willing to move among many people and to respond to countless unexpected situations. It is an exciting, although somewhat risky, role to take. Enjoying the challenge and relying on the art expressions to help the therapy progress can result in a positive experience for all concerned.

References

Bateson, G., Jackson, D., Haley, J., & Weakland, J. (1956). Toward a theory of schizophrenia. *Behavioral Science*, 1, 251-264.

Bonnefil, M. (1977). Crisis and diagnosis: Infantile autism. *Clinical Social Work Journal*, 4 (4), 276-288.

Freud, S. (1917). Mourning and melancholia. *In Collected Papers, Vol. 4* (pp. 152-170). London: Hogarth Press.

Kwiatkowska, H. Y. (1971). Family art therapy and family art evaluation: Conscious and unconscious expressive art. In I. Jacob (Ed.), *Psychiatry and Art, Vol. 3* (pp. 138-151). Basil, Switzerland: Karger.

Solnit, A., & Stark, M. (1961). Mourning and the birth of a defective child. *Psychoanalytic Study of the Child, Vol. VI.* New York: International Universities Press.

Yalom, I. (1985). *The theory and practice of group psychotherapy.* New York: Basic Books.

Suggested Reading

Cassano, R. D. (1989). Multifamily group therapy in social work practice. *Social Work with Groups, 12*, 3-14.

Cassano, R. D. (1989). The multifamily therapy group: Research on patterns of interaction. *Social Work with Groups, 12*, 15-39.

Hines, P., Richman, D., Maxim, K., & Hays, H. (1989). Multi-impact family therapy: An approach to working with multi-problem families. *Journal of Psychotherapy and the Family*, 16, 161-176.

Krpan, I., & Medved, Z. (1991). Family sculpture in multifamily group therapy. *Socijaina-Psihyatrijai*, 17, 201-211.

Wooley, S., & Lewis, G. (1987). Multifamily therapy within an intensive treatment program for bulimia. *Family Therapy Collections*, 20, 12-24.

ADOLESCENT AND FAMILY ART THERAPY: TREATING THE "ADOLESCENT FAMILY" WITH FAMILY ART THERAPY

Conducting therapy with a family which includes an adolescent child is always a challenge. With a family of this configuration, the therapist anticipates confronting an additional component of resistance to treatment. This stance is expected since a noncompliant attitude is a normal feature of the teenage developmental process. The expectation is reinforced by the knowledge that all members of a family system are normally resistant to change, since they fear that any modification of their familiar patterns may be a threat to maintaining the family unit. However, even greater difficulties are experienced when we therapists are presented with a troubled family where both teenager and parents are functioning equally on an adolescent level.

Treatment Dilemma

Family therapy is built on the premise that there are techniques that will start a process toward symptom reduction by interrupting malfunctioning, patterned behaviors. However, in assessing an "all adolescent" family, there are more questions than answers when it comes to exact technique and applied family theory.

One treatment approach with parent/child dysfunction is to establish hierarchical boundaries, shore up the adult strengths of the parent, attend to the child subsystem and other structural aspects (Minuchin & Fishman, 1981).

This article originally appeared in a slightly different form in *Art Therapy: Journal of the American Art Therapy Association,* 5, 43-51, and in *Family Therapy: A Systemic Behavioral Approach,* Joan Atwood (Ed.), Nelson Hall Publishers.

With the family wherein the parent has not reached a level of adult psychological development, these agents of change are not particularly effective. It is useful to examine how the family art therapist can construct a treatment plan that is specifically tailored to meet the multidimensional needs of this developmentally delayed family.

Developmental Concerns

To better understand the difficulties involved in treating a family which I will call the "adolescent family", it is necessary to start by briefly re-examining the basic process of adolescent development. When puberty thrusts the child toward the next step in physical growth, a simultaneous intrapsychic realignment occurs, referred to as adolescence. In this process the youth must give up attachments to parental figures and their protective position. Adolescents turn their attention to the unexpected, uncomfortable changes they are experiencing physically and to their perceptions of themselves (Mirkin & Koman, 1985).

Detachment from the primary adults of childhood and the single-minded focus on self is recognized as the "narcissistic stance" of adolescence (Blos, 1962). Particularly in the pre-adolescent and early adolescent child (11-14 years), the pervasive feeling of emptiness and the constant introspective attention to self, limits the available empathy which may be shared with another person. It is recognized that a move from a strictly narcissistic involvement to the capacity to care for another is one of the essential tasks accomplished during adolescence (Carter & McGoldrick, 1980).

Unfortunately, many persons falter on the way to achieving the goal of empathic caring and remain at an earlier emotional stage. This is a period when it is next to impossible to expect the youth to be a "giving" person since the capacity for demonstrating caring feelings for another person has not yet been achieved (Malmquist, 1978). Now if we consider the problem of a psychologically delayed adult becoming a parent, how will that person be able to give protection and nurturance to a child when s/he is still viewing the world from a narcissistic viewpoint? The children of these adolescent-adults fare more or less well during their childhood if they maintain rigid defenses and if environmental demands are not excessive. However, as this same child moves into adolescence, where rebellion and resistance to parental authority is the name of the game, the real struggle begins. We now have a situation where both parent and child are attempting to gain sole attention for themselves, giving little or nothing in the way of empathic understanding to each other. Both child and adult are experiencing emptiness and distress which often is handled through impulsive actions that serve as a distraction from the pain. This unfortunate developmental parallel in parent and adolescent child requires a specific series of therapeutic interventions aimed at encouraging maturation in the adult while simultaneously keeping the adolescent moving along his/her own normal developmental path. This is easier said than done. Each case demands individual assessment of the developmental phase of both parent and child.

The family system referred to above is reminiscent of the environmental and systemic background of the borderline adolescent which is delineated so eloquently by Masterson (1985). The grave consequences of failure to achieve separation and autonomy by the adolescent is described by him in this manner:

> "The passage of time presents these unfortunates with inevitable life tasks and thereby faces them with truly a Hobson's choice: to avoid the challenge of growth, marriage, and parenthood with the consequent loneliness and suffering that this entails or to take on the challenge though emotionally ill-equipped. Should they opt for the latter they receive the additional dividend of becoming an appalled and helpless eyewitness to the repetition of their own unresolved problems in their children."

Classically, the borderline family was described in the literature as headed by an aggressively active mother who resists the child's desire for individuation in answer to her own needs for fusion, and a passive, distant father who encourages this symbiosis. Masterson and others have relieved the mother of full responsibility for the pathology and refuted this dynamic.

There is another very common dysfunctional family system that interferes with child development: the alcoholic or violently abusive family system, where the visible pathology is most often demonstrated by the father. In this scenario, the dependent role in the system is taken on by the mother. Many parents recall their own childhood as one where fathers were either violent or alcoholic or both—a home life where they were unprotected by mother and triangulated within the parental relationship. These adults, abused as children, who are now parents, often engaged in heavy drug or alcohol abuse during their own adolescence which compounded their developmental failures.

In many cases, it is the adolescent who is covertly encouraged by the family to attract attention and gain therapeutic treatment by engaging in various acting-out behaviors (Stierlin, 1979). Once in therapy, I have observed the parent and child expect the therapist to provide quick answers and prompt removal of symptoms. Contrary to usual treatment expectations, resistance is not encountered when the family first accepts professional help. The reluctance surfaces later when the family recognizes that they are faced with reviewing painful depressive periods of the past. Change will not occur if the adult is unwilling to rework their neglected issues of adolescence.

When considering an approach to treatment, the configuration in the "adolescent family" is fascinating because it is often a mixture of both strengths and weaknesses. As in normal adolescent development, there is the overriding component of narcissism, but one can also find adolescent idealism, creativity, intellectualization, and other positive qualities; these qualities can be encouraged in treatment and utilized to find solutions to problems. In addition, these families often fall in a grey area of diagnosis. Although they suffer from having borderline or abusive family backgrounds, they were given just enough caring from some source to give them a notion of "how it might have been better" (Winnicott, 1976).

Environmental Factors

These "adolescent families" are frequently headed by a single parent. Traditionally, these clients have separated from a mate whose behavior replicated similar stress patterns they had experienced in their family of origin. However, contrary to the notion that this pattern is fated to occur again, in many instances the mother or father is cognizant of the repetition and determined not to make the same mistake again. Although the awareness of patterns of the past may be used in positive ways, it may lead to an additional difficulty for the children. The adult, rather than risk failure, often withdraws from peer-friendships and looks to the adolescent child for companionship. This closeness increases the diffusion of boundaries between parent and child, promoting symbiosis and inhibiting differentiation.

The single-parent factor compounds the challenge of conducting effective treatment. The therapist cannot utilize the combined strengths of two parents to create a composite authority which the adolescent can either rebel against or in which s/he can seek protection. Too often a teenager in this situation assumes the role of the missing parent and is thus deprived of healthy adolescent rebellion. This assumed role adds to the confusion and power struggle. The drive to separate from the parent continues, but instead it is directed against the self (in the substitute parent role) which may turn into self-destructive, acting-out behavior.

An additional dilemma in treating these adolescents in family therapy is the reality of the community mental health setting in which they are seeking help. The restrictions on time and frequency of treatment are a serious consideration. Obviously, the most effective manner of conducting therapy for these clients is not always possible in a one-hour, once-a-week, short-term contract. Since actual contact is limited, therapists must cautiously offer therapy that can be helpful given these restrictions, and not attempt to remove defenses or weaken the needed coping mechanisms. A systemic/strategic approach is desirable because it can be designed to focus on client strengths, to reframe behavior, and to achieve symptom relief within a limited time frame (Riley, 1985).

To illustrate the systemic/strategic approach to family art therapy, I will later share some case examples demonstrating art therapy techniques which have been successful with "adolescent families" and which have resulted in a positive outcome.

Assessment

The presenting picture of the confused, frustrated parent and the defiant, rebellious adolescent is one that is painfully common in treatment. However, the original behavior that brought them into the clinic does not provide sufficient clues to understand the underlying causes of the behavior. During the initial phase of family art therapy (the joining phase), the therapist may observe an unusually prolonged and competitive struggle between adult and child; if this is the case, then the hypothesis of mutual adolescence should be considered. To explore this possibility further, the therapist may instruct the family to engage in a group art task providing an arena for enactment of the suspected behavior.

Often, the behavior seen by the therapist during a dyadic drawing demonstrates the diffusion of authority: the parent and teenager vie for attention. They may both draw or refuse to draw, grab for the same color pen, or the parent may defer to directions given by the child rather than take the leadership role. These actions along with messages conveyed through the art product may suggest that there is a parentified child functioning in this family.

After continued observation, an assessment is made of how the family patterns repeat themselves. If it is established that this is a family where both the parent and child are developmentally in adolescence, some strategic moves are necessary.

Setting Goals in Treatment.

The first goal in treatment is to create within the parent an image of competency. This will enable the parent to face the normal trials of raising an adolescent. To accomplish this goal, the therapy turns its focus to the parent and momentarily neglects the child and his/her symptoms. If necessary, the therapist invents strengths in the adult's character; paradoxically, the adolescent will often experience relief as a result of this maneuver. Shifting the system is not an easy achievement, since the family members (parent and child) are accustomed to supporting each other in an egalitarian position in the hierarchy. However, as the parent gains satisfaction and approval from others by acting more in charge, they will continue to change, and thereby gain narcissistic rewards in an appropriate manner.

Unfortunately, there often seems to be a paucity of ego strength in these individuals, and the therapist must turn to a variety of techniques to achieve treatment goals. Madanes (1981) relates how she helps a client to play-act, or *pretend*, to behave in a prescribed manner. In this case a parent is coached in how to *pretend* to be an efficient and effective adult. Following this experiment in effectiveness, the client will test if the child can perceive the difference between the farce and reality. The goal is to start a feedback loop where, as the parent "pretends" to provide structure for the family, a welcome release from stress will result. With the positive reinforcement of better family functioning, the behavior is likely to be retained and integrated as part of the "real" self. Also, "adolescent parents" feel less threatened if they are told that they only have to pretend to be grown up for the short period of their child's adolescence.

In the early stages of treatment, the therapist more openly attends to the parent while still supporting the teenager. This alliance is productive for several reasons: 1) when the therapist aligns with mother and/or father, the process leads to the parentified or symptomatic child feeling less needed and freer to be a teenager; 2) as freedom to be an adolescent is experienced by the youth, the need for acting-out behavior is reduced; 3) if the child actively participates in art therapy, but the main attention is deflected from him, age-appropriate resistance is diminished; 4) it is more difficult to assist a developmentally-delayed adult through the growth process than aid the child who is progressing normally with developmental tasks. The results: as the art therapist helps the parent gain maturation, the teenager finds it possible to achieve a more appropriate relationship with the parent.

To further the attainment of individuation, art therapy tasks are suggested which allow the client to recognize past patterns of family origin and to observe if they continue to function in the present. Seeing a parallel between past and present maladaptive behaviors provides essential information which may lead to desired changes. The therapist, when reviewing old behaviors, makes use of positive connotation, thereby creating a new reality and transforming present perceptions. By observing his/her problems represented in art products, the client may develop and utilize an ego observer. This skill of monitoring one's own behavior is one of the major tasks of adolescence, and an important step toward realizing the goal of maturation for both the parent and the child.

Case Example

Shamar, a Caucasian 13-year-old, entered treatment with her mother and younger brother, in spite of the fact that she did not feel she had any problems. She was getting satisfactory grades, she ran the family efficiently, directed her mother's relationships, and parented her younger brother competently. In contrast to Shamar's grandiose perceptions of herself, her mother, Joanne, was filled with anxieties. She tearfully admitted to being unable to set rules, oppose her daughter, or enjoy her boyfriend, because Shamar did not approve. The parents had been divorced for eight years; however, the father was still very active in the family and intruded at will. Joanne complained that "he bosses me just as my daughter does".

In spite of Shamar's protestations that she was an untroubled girl, her behavior belied her words. She prefaced every statement to her mother with the phrase, "now don't be hurt", or "don't cry, Mother, but ...". She then was able to list all her frustrations. Her problems reflected the need for structure in the home, her ambivalence in maintaining her overcontrolling role, and her desire for relief from adult duties.

As therapy progressed, the mother bootlegged many individual sessions, on one pretext or another, in order to deal with her own issues. She dwelt on her abusive and critical relationship with her father, whom she feared to this day. She said she wanted to have better relationships with men, to get out from under her ex-husband's rule, and she had other complaints that were obviously unfinished business from her own adolescence. Joanne was so fixated on her own needs that she had little time or energy left over for her own children.

The therapist found the treatment was difficult since the suggestions made by the daughter were very sensible and the contributions from the mother were much less workable. However, it would be destructive to allow this complementary relationship to continue, because no matter how well Shamar performed adult duties, she was neglecting her own normal development.

The family art therapy was very useful in achieving separation and counteracting the family members' enmeshment. The mother and daughter were artistic and were skillful in using the media provided. Each was able to see the other's product and absorb both overt and covert messages. Most importantly, the art task was often nonverbal, which reduced blaming and provided a new means of problem-solving. Joanne eventually gained respect from Shamar when she began to teach art and hold a full-time job. The girl became more cooperative when she realized that her mother had the therapist to lean on, rather than herself. During one point in therapy the mother, in her own quest for autonomy, was extremely distracted; this resulted in the daughter becoming insecure and seeking attention by getting lower grades. This action succeeded in involving the mother. In an authoritarian role, she demonstrated her concern and set rules for home study, which was a positive surprise in this relationship.

As therapy progressed, it became apparent that Shamar's mother was not going to quickly achieve the adult status that would be most desirable; therefore, the daughter's contributions to the family were honored by the therapist. Shamar remains a junior partner in the family, a role she plays openly, with structure and limitations set between the two of them. The young six-year-old brother has been given some clear rules about who is the real mother and how much authority his sister has and may use. The chances that this threesome will ever make the ideal family are extremely slim. However, the mother is now able to openly ask for individual sessions and articulate the problems she wishes or needs to address. The daughter joins the sessions every third week, where focus changes to family problems. This is the beginning of a realignment of roles to allow both mother and teenager to begin the work of individuation.

Art Therapy Expressions from Case I

A sampling of the art expressions done by the mother and daughter discussed in this case dramatizes the differences in their personalities. The first two figures were drawn in response to the question, "what are the family's problems?". In Figure 1, Joanne drew a pair of clouds obscuring the sun and producing rain. She related this image to their conflicts at home. In Figure 2, Shamar drew a picture of going shopping. The girl responded that she never got enough clothes from her mother, and, if she did cooperate, they wouldn't fight. The contrast between the empty, minimal drawing by the mother and the concrete, pragmatic statement by the daughter revealed their positions in the relationship. Figures 3, 4, and 5 are drawings done by Shamar on two different occasions while we were discussing the struggle over who would get the privacy of the one bedroom. Shamar first drew herself in pastels, a rather complimentary rendering. In a subsequent session, after some rules had been imposed, she gazed intently at her mother while drawing these two "portraits". She excused the red beard as an accident and thought the other woman was "happy". Joanne, a delicate and fragile woman with long, fine, straight hair did not resemble these renditions. However, the quality of anger and the aggressive affect portrayed were extremely confrontive and were recognized by both mother and daughter. By bringing the denied anger into the dialogue, the family and therapist had the opportunity to deal openly

Figure 1: Mother's drawing - problems, sun obscured by clouds and rain

Figure 2: Daughter's drawing - problems, Mom doesn't buy me clothes

Figure 3: Daughter's self portrait

Figure 4: Daughter's portrait of mother

Figure 5: Daughter's portrait of mother, with
beard that was a "mistake"

Figure 6: Boxing up "guilt feelings" derived from father's criticism

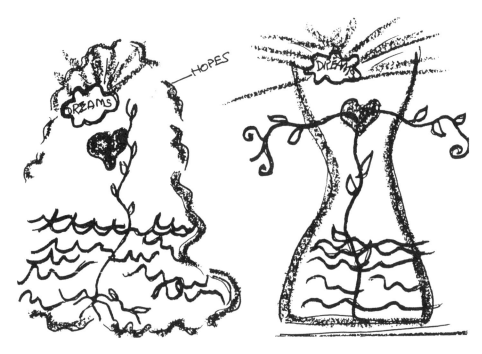

Figure 7: Mother draws "fuzzy parent" on the left and "adult parent" on the right

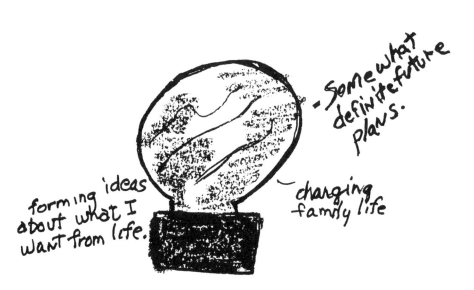

Figure 8: Final drawing - indicating a change

with conflicts. Before this session, anger contaminated their relationship, but was too threatening to risk verbalizing.

Figure 6 shows Joanne's way of dealing with her feelings about her father, feelings which she felt were identical to her emotional state with her ex-husband. She felt burdened by his characteristics of false pride, guilt, conceptions that sex was ugly, her own inability to live up to his expectations, and most of all, his violence. In an attempt to cope with these conflicts, she boxed them up and buried them. She felt that the guilt experienced in her present life was derived from past criticism. Some weeks later she drew a very different insightful rendition of the difference between a "fuzzy parent" (on the left of the page) and an "adult parent" (on the right) (Figure 7). Her explanation was as follows: "the broken pink line means no boundaries, the blue cloud is a dream world that holds back the warmth from the heart, the growth is without roots, and the blue waves show turbulence of emotions. The right drawing has a firm base, calm emotions, growth reaching out and the dreams do not stand in the way of the warmth. The most important feature is the firm, but open boundaries". The final drawing, Figure 8, indicates that the process of individuation and maturation is beginning to be realized. The words around the light bulb are: "forming new ideas, creating new relationships, some definite future plans, and a changing family life".

Art Therapy Expressions from Case II

In another session, a hypothesis for treatment was formed by the art therapist, through drawings done by a Latino father and his 12-year-old son. Over the last two years these two had lived together, had gone on Father's dates together, and had moved together from one unstable living quarters to another. The father and son had the same first as well as last name and borrowed clothing from each other. The boy's mother retained custody of his younger sister, but had turned the father out of the house because of Dad's immaturity and irresponsibility. Bob, Jr., had decided to go with his father.

The presenting complaint centered on the son's poor school performance. However, it was clear that Father did not respect the school's concern about his son, but felt he was the one persecuted and humiliated when called to school to speak to the teachers. His distress was aimed at the teachers and not at his son. He recalled how he was never successful in school and his father was never around to defend him. Figure 9 and Figure 10 were completed after the clients were asked to "show how you could help with the problem". The father drew a single horse that he jokingly said was going to escape from the corral; the son suggested that they try to be "more thoughtful, honest, kind, helpful, understanding and happy".

Figure 9: Father's solution to family difficulties - "run away"

Figure 10: Son's solution to family difficulties

Through these two drawings, we can see which person was more aware of the problem and which person was going to run away as soon as possible. Treatment focused on helping a man who never grew up to assume an adult role and appropriately support his son. The boy was encouraged to break away from this symbiosis with his father and gain an individual identity. There was progress until the father moved them away, as was his pattern. However, enough change had been made that he followed through with a referral suggestion and continued treatment elsewhere.

Art Therapy Expressions from Case III

This case was court-referred: an African-American mother and thirteen-year-old son, Jerry. He had been taken from the home six months before because of child neglect. He had recently returned to the mother's home on a trial visit; the court ordered therapy to explore reuniting mother and son.

The mother, Christi, claimed that Jerry was intractably oppositional and never did anything she demanded. The divorced father was in jail because of drug dealing and was completely out of home or family contact. The boy wished to stay at home and said he wanted to learn to control his temper. It became apparent that the mother was most interested in her job and wanted Jerry to run the house for her, to clean and cook. My perception of this case was that mother and son acted-out in similar ways with physical violence, which is often a behavior that masks adolescent depression. They both had their own forms of temper tantrums, and they both ran away from problems. They each handled stress in an adolescent manner.

To test how well they could work together, they were asked to do a dual drawing. This colorful, solid drawing (Figure 11) gave them great satisfaction, provided them with a pleasurable experience, and gave concrete proof that they could work together. The empty interior of the house was not interpreted at this time; however, the tree leaning tenderly on the house and the stop sign were all discussed at length. A positive connotation was used in reference to all images in this significant drawing, and the dyad of mother and son rallied strongly after this experience. Work was done with Mother on her parenting skills and a few individual sessions focused on her extremely immature fantasies about being rescued by a "wonderful" man.

The termination drawings are presented. Figure 12 lists Mother's appraisal "before and after therapy." Before therapy, she was "ready to give up trying, also tired of herself and losing control and hitting." She feels now that she is "happy with her attitude, has a lot of patience, can deal with most things, is no longer hitting and can show him love". These improvements were reinforced by the happiness of finding a very solid, successful man to marry, whose son happened to be her son's best friend. I mused at this coincidence that her son provided her with the man of her dreams, while providing himself with an agreeable brother.

In Figure 13, the teenager pictured the mess his room was in "before he came to therapy" and himself crying as Mother berated him. Now, "after therapy", he and his mother go horseback riding together. He claimed that these drawings indicated he felt they had moved from sorrow to pleasure. The minimal use of space and cramped imagery suggest a very careful and controlled, perhaps skeptical, expectation that this change would be permanent.

Summary

These three cases shared a broad base of commonality. Although the families were different in ethnic backgrounds, they shared similar histories in their extended families. In each case, as with countless other families seen in our outpatient clinic, the parent's childhood was extremely deprived. Role models, nurturance, and acceptance of who they were as individuals were sadly lacking. These parents passed through puberty without completing adolescent developmental tasks. In particular, the inability to identify

Figure 11: Dual drawing, mother and son - with stop sign

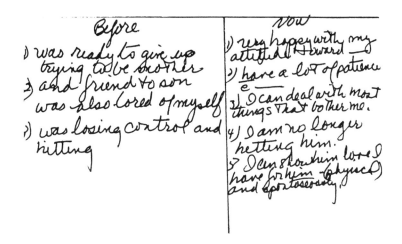

Figure 12: Mother's list - "before and after therapy"

Figure 13: Before and after therapy. Left: "crying in my room with mother yelling at me". Right: "happy, horseback riding together".

appropriate persons with whom to engage in a long term relationship was a common weakness. Because of their own identity confusions, they became parents without a notion of what parenting entailed. They did not learn these skills during their children's younger years as they were focused on their own unmet adolescent needs. When their children entered adolescence, the developmental phase forced the parents to struggle with issues of narcissism, identity and autonomy, both within themselves and in their teenaged progeny. Families attempting to survive these tumultuous times are helped by a family art therapist who is capable of setting realistic goals and adhering to a specialized treatment plan.

The combination of systemic theory and art therapy has proven helpful in treating these adolescent families. Points to consider are: 1) the parent is the main focus of treatment in the early phase of therapy; however, the art work keeps the youth involved and allows him/her to make a statement in every session; 2) the attention is directed to the parent, and it is deflected away from the adolescent, which is syntonic with developmental needs and encourages the teenager to come to the sessions; 3) as the parent is led toward achieving or pretending to achieve adult skills, the child is relieved of inappropriate assignment of roles in the family; 4) the treatment of these families takes into consideration that a compromise will probably have to be made regarding definitions of clear, hierarchical boundaries. The teenager will often continue to play a large part in the adult duties and decisions, but these activities will be overt, not covert, and therefore open to negotiation and readjustment.

The essential ingredient for the family art therapist who works with this type of family is a broad knowledge of adolescent development and the acuity to recognize the developmental delays which manifest in the adult parent. This is readily assessed through observation of the behavior between parent and child, and recognition of the problem as displayed in their art expressions in therapy.

References

Blos, P. (1962). *On adolescence: A psychoanalytic interpretation*. New York: MacMillan.

Carter, E. A., & McGoldrick, M. (1980). *The family life cycle and family therapy: An overview*. In E. A. Carter & M. McGoldrick (eds.), *The family life cycle: A framework for family therapy*. New York: Gardner.

Madanes, C. (1981). *Strategic family therapy*. San Francisco, CA: Jossey-Bass.

Malmquist, C. (1978). *Handbook of adolescence*. New York: Jason Aronson

.Masterson, J. (1985). *Treatment of the borderline adolescent*. New York: Brunner/Mazel.

Minuchin, S., & Fishman, C. H. (1981). *Family therapy techniques*. Cambridge: Harvard

University Press.

Mirkin, M., & Koman, S. (1985). *Adolescents and family therapy.* New York: Gardner.

Riley, S. (1985). *Draw me a paradox?* Art Therapy: Journal of the American Art Therapy Association, 2 (3), 116-123.

Stierlin, H. (1979). *Separating parents and adolescents: A perspective on running away, schizophrenia, and waywardness.* New York: Quadrangle.

Winnicott, D. (1976). *The child, the family, and the outside world.* Harmondsworth: Penguin.

Suggested Readings

Ackerman, N. J. (1980). *The family with adolescents.* In E. A. Carter & M. McGoldrick (eds.), *The family life cycle: A framework for family therapy.* New York: Gardner.

Erikson, E. H. (1968). *Identity, youth and crisis.* New York: Norton.

Haley, J. (1980). *Leaving home.* New York: MacGraw Hill.

Landgarten, H. (1987). *Family art psychotherapy.* New York: Brunner/Mazel.

McGoldrick, M. (1982). *Ethnicity and family therapy: An overview.* In M. McGoldrick, J. K. Pierce, & J. Giordano (eds.), *Ethnicity and family therapy.* New York: Guilford.

Minuchin, S. (1974). *Families in family therapy.* Cambridge: Harvard University.

Watzlawick, P., Weakland, J. H., & Fisch, R. (1974). *Change: Principles of problem formation and problem resolution.* New York: Norton.

ART THERAPY WITH FAMILIES WHO HAVE EXPERIENCED DOMESTIC VIOLENCE

Families who have experienced violence often seek treatment through outpatient clinic services where the focus moves from crisis intervention and case management to long-term therapy. The primary issues addressed often are those dealing with post-traumatic stress, separation and loss, single-parent family structure, and rethinking old patterns of gender-assigned roles. In addition, socioeconomic concerns enter into the field of therapeutic goals. Art therapy can address these difficulties and provide positive therapeutic experiences for both parent and children.

A Personal Construct of Art Psychotherapy

The art therapy I practice derives from my own personal and clinical observation that visual memories cannot be separated from the emotional and behavioral visual recollections which lead to the verbal explanations of events. For example, our earliest sense of self begins with the ability to retain a pictorial image of "mother". This talent for imagining, or imagery, is integrated with our thoughts whenever we describe a series of actions or interactions. When we talk about a situation we also attempt to convey the "picture" of the environment in which the behaviors occurred. The emotional quality of behaviors becomes clearer when expressed as visual metaphor: "he was as big as a bear" or "her eyes flashed red with anger" are examples

---

This chapter was originally published in slightly different form in *California Art Therapy Trends*, Evelyn Virshup (Ed.) (1993), Magnolia Street Publishers, Chicago, IL, and is reprinted with their permission.

of the ordinary use of visualization.

The art psychotherapist is a clinician who has developed the skills and sensitivity to help the client visually illustrate the stories s/he sees in her/his mind. Often additional meanings of actions emerge through the art task. Through these art expressions the art therapist is better able to comprehend the unique view of the speaker and move into his/her world. When imagery is turned into art expressions that can be talked about, the client or family and the therapist can more easily enter into a shared world reality. The synthesis of verbal communication with visual images made concrete through art expression, together with a knowledge of therapeutic theory, is the essence of art psychotherapy.

This concept of art psychotherapy also reflects a social constructionist view of "knowing" invented realities. The art therapist assists in making real the vision of events that are meaningful to the clients; in turn, we are more able to help them find an alternative to the world they originally brought to therapy. This ability to appreciate in a nonjudgmental manner the emotional, physical, and social environment of families who have lived with violence is essential to successful treatment.

The desired goal of treatment is to establish a therapeutic relationship with clients which is enhanced by the creativity of the artist/therapist who is trained to utilize the entire palette of transactions that we call art therapy. The therapist enters into the client's picture of his/her world and makes use of all the components of creativity, language, theory, and art expression. There is no division between the clinical treatment plan and the integration of that plan with the art therapy modality. The art expression is fused with appropriate theory and responds to the therapeutic needs of each case.

Introduction to Treatment

As an art psychotherapist engages in treatment of a family that has experienced abusive violence, the first issue to be considered is their natural reluctance to expose their weaknesses, their mistrust of outsiders, and their loss of dignity experienced when compelled to ask for help (i.e., therapy). This distress must be addressed early in treatment since the primary concern of the therapist is to begin to view the family's world and problems through their lens.

Introducing informal, nonstructured drawings, collage and group drawings gives the family an opportunity to express both pleasant and unpleasant memories, and to begin treatment in a nonthreatening manner. Central to the therapist's ability to understand the family's unique reality is the skill to see (through art expression) how they perceive their environment and to hear the language they use as they relate their family myths and personal explanations of events. In the process of the family's overt interpretation of their images, the art therapist attends not only to the information offered verbally, but also to the nonverbal messages imbedded in the art. The meta-message often moves the therapy in useful directions since the prohibition against words struggles with revealing issues of secrecy, shame, and repressed pain. As the family relates their stories, understanding their unique circumstances helps restore dignity and invites the trust necessary to establish a therapeutic alliance. When this first and most important step has been accomplished, the more challenging creative process of long-term therapy may begin.

Domestic Violence: An Overview of Treatment Issues

A high percentage of families who have suffered abuse in the home enter treatment at an outpatient clinic subsequent to an interim stay in a shelter for battered women and their children. During this time the degree of shock, both from the abuse and the subsequent flight from home and familiar surroundings have insulated the family from experiencing the full meaning of this move (Malchiodi, 1990). The shelter offers the protection and support needed to cushion this dramatic change of life circumstances. However, the crisis treatment is brief, and all too soon the mother may have to find housing, financial aid, schools, etc.; she and her children must adapt to a new routine of living. The challenge of living alone, making all the necessary requests for social services, as well as continuing to avoid contact with the abuser, is a very heavy burden for the woman. These anxieties and fears are transmitted to the children as they, too, face new schools and housing, in addition to the threat of confrontation by the perpetrator.

Immediate Treatment Goals

These serious circumstances call for a treatment plan with goals that are basically supportive and utilize the case management skills of the therapist. At this point the need for communication and understanding between family members is particularly critical. However, the cognitive and developmental gap between parent and child may stand in the way. Art therapy provides a therapeutic vehicle for communication and understanding that is eminently appropriate. Too often, particularly in traumatic situations, children are literally at a loss for words. They have no vocabulary for their anxieties and fears; they are confused when their world is shattered by grown-up behaviors that negate their most basic need for trust. When the child is invited to make a drawing that reflects his/her thoughts and feelings, s/he can usually find

195

their vehicle for expression through metaphor. Dragons or dinosaurs attacking small creatures or planes crashing and wiping out a village are a natural means of communicating inner states of destruction.

Each age of development will use art expression in a manner that is syntonic with age-appropriate visual language. Therefore, in a family session, the five-year-old, the adolescent, and the parent can all be "heard" through their individual art products. Each can tell a story that conveys the emotion and distress without having to be verbalized. In addition, since there is a fear of the abuser and possible reprisal, the message can be sent in a manner which is nonverbal and nonthreatening to the client.

It is also important for the art therapist to make very clear to the family that all their art work is confidential and will be kept in a safe place. If there is the slightest notion that their concrete communications could be seen by anyone outside the session, their trust and willingness to do the art will be diminished. In fact, a rather elaborate ritual of making large folders, inserting the art work, and placing it in a cupboard or drawer, can be reassuring and even give a ceremonial closure to each session. I believe every gesture from the therapist becomes significant, particularly in these families, where chaos ruled and reliability was nonexistent.

The focus of art therapy at this point should be on group tasks that illuminate the family's strengths and improve the mother's parenting skills. An additional goal of group art tasks and group sharing is to increase the abilities of the family to communicate with each other. The pleasure of creating an expressive product as a team can be very rewarding and a skill that was inhibited while living in fear and shame. Violent homes restrict the experience of pleasure and freedom of speech.

Minimal exploration for a dynamic or behavioral change is appropriate — the disruption of the life circumstances is enough to deal with at this time. Collage tasks that review past coping skills and affirmative moments experienced during a more functional period of their lives are recommended for this initial period of therapy. A focus on strengths and positive, if minuscule deviations in the abusive cycle introduces the notion that neglected talents may now be recalled and utilized to sustain change.

Secondary Treatment Goals

Therapy with a family that has experienced violence, battering and subsequent separation moves through many phases of treatment. After the family has secured housing, found schools for children, and located some financial support or a job, when the basic needs are met, the treatment can focus on additional issues that call for attention.

The recovery phase (or mid-phase) of treatment may be defined as the period that follows after the family has dealt with the initial loss, mourning and flight from the abuser. This phase of therapy is introduced when the therapist observes that the family has gained sufficient strength to consider going back into the world of relationships and inter-gender negotiations. It is time to regain socialization skills with an increased sensitivity for self-preservation. A treatment plan is implemented that will emphasize strengthening the family's skills and expanding a destructively narrow world view. In addition, the therapist and family co-create a new meaning for relationships, gender roles, and personal safety in a violent world.

Case Example/History

Nora, a young mother with two children (a daughter of nine and a son of five) sought outpatient treatment at the local community mental health center after having just terminated a ten-year marriage. It was necessary for the police to rescue her from a violent domestic battle with her husband who was hitting and choking her while kicking their daughter and son to keep them away. The argument began when Nora refused to get an abortion and the husband became enraged. The little boy attempted to defend his mother with his toy sword and the girl risked harm by telephoning the police. Subsequent to this traumatic event, the mother requested outpatient family treatment. The father refused treatment at the clinic; his contact with the children was limited to brief, monitored visits on a bimonthly basis.

Art therapy was used with this family from the beginning of treatment and greatly facilitated the grief work necessary to reconstitute this family of three as a single-parent family.

Selected Art Therapy Tasks:
Working Through a Metaphor

After four months the mid-phase of therapy was introduced. The therapist asked the family to decide on and then create their favorite fairy tale: they chose "Little Red Ridinghood". The art expression of this classic story took the form of a plasticine (an oil-based clay) and construction paper three-dimensional scene of Red Ridinghood in the forest. As the family recreated it, Grandmother stood in the doorway of her home, the wolf was in the "doghouse", and the woodsman bravely defended Grandmother (Figure 1). It was fascinating to observe the mother identifying with Red Ridinghood, the character who, as she said, "foolishly goes into the woods knowing that it was dangerous". The daughter created both Grandmother and the wolf. As the parentified child she expressed through this choice both her motherly role and the jeopardy she had been through; she also indicated her determination to contain the wolf through the metaphor of the doghouse. The son created the "mighty" woodsman who saved Grandma and killed the wolf, just as he had bravely rushed into the fray with his toy sword to defend his mother.

Figure 1, Red riding hood (center), grandmother and wolf each side,
protective woodsman in the background - plasticine and paper construction

The therapeutic value of this construction was powerful. The traumatic event was dramatically channeled into a fairy tale where the familiar story allowed these family members to re-enact their roles in a mythical setting. The mother, through Red Ridinghood, could caution herself and her children "not to go back into dangerous places when it is clearly indicated that harm will befall you" (reinforcing her newly-gained ability to see that the old sequence of harm-forgiveness-harm in her marriage was a repetitive pattern). The little woodsman (the son) was encouraged to transfer his role to a real "big man" (the therapist) who would protect him and his mother, and he could start to be his five-year-old self. He had learned to trust the help available to him through social services and therapy. The daughter could relinquish identifying with the "grandmother" who was delegated to take on the villain (the wolf/father), and who had been triangulated into a scenario of violence with her parents.

The family also enacted the drama, adjusting the fairy tale to their own needs and providing a new and safe ending to their own violent tale. The therapist was able to suggest modifications to the legend of Little Red Ridinghood, which, if made directly to the family, may have been overwhelming. By using a fairy tale, a story that has symbolic and universal significance, the therapist provided a secure metaphoric base from which the transition from mythic to personal interpretation was available to the family. Adding the illustrative quality of art forms created by the clients allowed an opportunity for further projections to be made. Hence, an ancient fairy tale becomes a modern metaphor for their situation.

Following this experience and a period of further self-exploration, a series of repetitive patterns emerged in the art expressions which indicated a need to bring the father into the therapy hour. The challenge was how to do this in a safe manner. Including the abuser in a session may be undesirable because the family is fearful of him. Also, court restrictions may not allow it. However, by utilizing art expression the abuser may safely become part of the therapy.

Facing the Abuser

Many families, who have experienced only one type of male character, such as a man who resorts to violence to win his argument, have a very limited appreciation of the broad variations in the male personality. Obviously every man does not fall into the stereotype of the man with whom they have lived and suffered (Goldner, Penn, Sheinberg, & Walker, 1990).

Limited as they are by their singular view, battered families feel more comfortable with a person who reflects abusive traits and behaviors. This return to what seems "normal" explains the redundant patterns of abuse so often observed in battered families. This observation is not meant to convey the same meaning as the outdated notion of a woman who "plays the victim" or retains a masochistic drive for suffering. It merely states that behaviors that we have grown up with do not seem strange or foreign. Since battered families need to learn to live in new ways and in new environments, it is of utmost importance that therapy for these families introduce broadened concepts of relationships and possibilities for mutual respect. It is a vital safeguard that the mother reassess what type of mate she might find attractive, and it is essential that the children find a healthy male role model before the mother establishes a future relationship.

A technique that has been very useful as an introduction to an exploration of this important issue is to ask the family to "invent a man who would suit this family". Through this task the mother and children can create a husband/father who fulfills their fantasies of a "good man". This art experience also allows the therapist to observe the family's ingrained expectations of the male/ female and the parent/ child relationships. Together family and therapist assess the mother's and child's ability to discard old and unsuccessful interpersonal patterns. Later, this same task may be repeated and the family is asked to "bring in" the abuser (on paper), to tell him their feelings and to say good-bye to issues repressed in the past.

To begin this task, the art therapist draws a large figure on a 6 foot piece of paper (such as standard white butcher paper). The outline is not definitive except for a recognizable male physical shape. The family is invited to fill in this figure with a collage (e.g., magazine images) of what they would like from a "good man" (Figure 2). The parent is put in charge of working out where to put the various images; for example, they may choose to place nurturing, protective functions around the chest near the heart, financial support pictures on the upper torso, near shoulders and arms. The family is also urged to write explanatory statements; often the art therapist may become the youngest child's scribe, writing words for the little one. Through the experience of selecting and placing the collage and defining the images through writing, the fantasy of a new mate/dad comes into the consciousness of the session.

This particular family filled in their father/husband collage with very healthy images. There were desires expressed for fun as well as love, support, sports, intellectual challenge, and relaxation. In particular, the therapist admired how the mother was helpful and generous with the space and pictures, but still maintained her own territory and adult needs. It was encouraging to see that the representations chosen were well-balanced with reality. The issue of safety was spontaneously discussed and the possibility was questioned if a "nice man", like this paper man, really existed in the world.

The mother and children also discussed what was not there, such as behaviors and traits they left out because they led to unhappiness. The "unhappy" traits that this mother and her children experienced were ones of repression, lack of respect in the marital and parental relationship, and the use of violence as a control mechanism. In particular, the dialogue around the need to be in total control versus the need for the control over one's own personal anger (violence) was a significant therapeutic subject.

It is important to examine the different interpersonal tensions that can be tolerated with comfort. Exploring exploitation and intimidation removed from the passion of the abusive family dynamics is an opportunity for learning a new way of judging behaviors and mutual respect for self and

Figure 2, Collage of the "good man"

others. The unacceptable man's (father's) traits were more easily addressed when they were viewed from a perspective of the "good" man's characteristics. This is syntonic with my approach to therapy, which is to focus on the positive, to reinforce strengths emerging from the art therapy; this stance encourages empowerment, and the will to refuse to cooperate with hurtful abuse from others in "real world" situations.

A final aspect of this task is important to mention. Constructing their own male friend out of paper was fun in and of itself. For the first time, the family could be playful and disrespectful in the presence of a man and enjoy it; they were also able to co-create a man significantly different from the man from whom they had fled.

Some Additional Observations About This Task

The longings for safety and caring from a supportive partner do not go away just because the real man had failed to meet these expectations. These wishes are acknowledged and turned into a creative art task. The ensuing family discussion turns toward a direction which opens up questions around old patterns in gender-defined roles, old patterns of reciprocal support and respect, old patterns of parenting and discipline delegated to male or female parent. These are all major areas where men and women are conflicted over issues of power and control.

Clearly, the family does not solve this complex issue through one collage, no matter how grand its size. Making the collage man "real" and "big" lends a sense of reality to this construction; however, on paper he does not threaten and is a person that the family can tailor to their needs. Another useful aspect of this task is that it makes apparent the "ghost" that is present, but not acknowledged in the sessions. An absent father often cannot be brought into therapy, but all the love, hate, drama, and authority that he once possessed are still real for the family members. Through this particular art experience, the family actively engages in a task that invites a safe confrontation of violent actions, the inequalities of power and domination in the relationship, and the fear that this pattern will occur again in the future. Also, the guilt that many women feel is often activated through this collage. When this occurs the therapist can begin to alleviate this guilt by helping the woman rebuild a more reasonable understanding of the life events that led up to this marriage (Figure 3).

Additionally, a violent relationship is not always solely violent. The partners may also experience times when love and passion dominate. To ignore these positive moments in the relationship, no matter how few or brief, is to discount the capacity of both the woman and the man to love, a denial that turns her into a masochistic puppet. There are aspects of romantic love present in these long and painful marriages, minimal in most cases, but the therapist must honor the woman and acknowledge that she has the power to love or she will ultimately feel dehumanized. The woman must be encouraged to separate out the circumstances that made her love endure such danger and learn to use this most treasured human capacity in a manner that can result in safe affection in the future (Goldner, 1990) (Figure 4).

Moving Toward Termination

At this point therapy turns to "family of origin" work. It becomes clear, in many cases, that the marital partners share similar childhood backgrounds of abuse which made violence more tolerable for them than it

Figure 3, Mother's version of the worst and best parts of her life

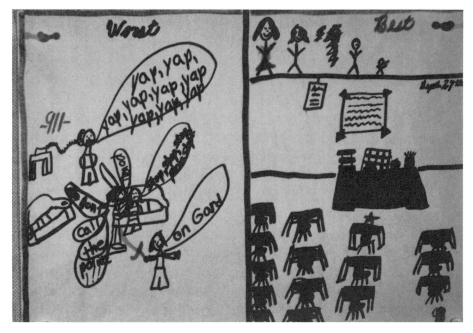

Figure 4, Daughter's version of the worst and best parts of her life

is for other individuals.

The abusive family background is often ignored or denied by clients. The source of the belief system that encourages tolerance for abusive behaviors is most easily addressed by helping the mother develop a genogram with the assistance of the children. Adding the component of art therapy to the process greatly increases the expressive possibilities by adding character traits and emotional components through color and shape of the symbols. Using collage and drawing a genogram is freely constructed on the conventional, schematic plan developed by McGoldrick (1985). I describe how to create a symbolic shape for each gender, how to connect them in marriage and how to indicate children by connecting lines. However, how the client creates or interprets these instructions is strictly personal. Some use pictures of objects or animals to reflect the characteristics of the family members, others make smiling or frowning faces, still others are so expressive that the final product resembles more a skein of yarn than a schema of the generations. This last example stresses an important point. The confusion depicted in a genogram probably reflects the confusion that exists in the family in reality.

For example, through collage, the members of the family can be described by their gender, affect, and behaviors, and the emotional temper of relationships can be demonstrated through adding color-coded connective lines. Tracing violence from generation to generation (if it exists) can give a clear picture of the abusive socialization this family experienced. The less restricted the client feels about how to create a genogram, the greater the chances that it will be personalized and the greater the amount of information that will emerge.

If there is an opportunity to create an art therapy genogram of the husband's family, similar patterns of violent relationships are often observed. Thus, the powerful force that influenced both mother and father to interact in this harmful manner is better understood. For example, the majority of people, male or female, who tolerate violent relationships have come from families of origin where stereotyped roles were exaggerated. Male gender-defined roles are cast in super-macho images and females as dependent and subservient to men. In truth, these men were generally unsure and inadequate, their self-esteem dependent on the woman's role of protecting their image. This complementary relationship is rigid and likely to become unbalanced with the slightest shift in the woman's position. The balance is maintained with either abusive behavior or threats of abuse against the woman. Moreover, this pattern has often been an established interaction, played out over several generations.

Individuating from the family of origin will be greatly helped by subsequent art tasks based on these family maps. It is a time when the mother can help her children understand the circumstances that surround this repeated behavior bequeathed from the past and can introduce a new set of values to them. As the parent teaches the child, she teaches herself! There cannot be lasting change for this client until she perceives herself through a new lens that recognizes her value as a mother, worker, companion, and citizen, and that supports her right to be an active voice in society.

Termination

The next phase of treatment begins when the family becomes involved in inventing a future, or new reality (Watzlawick, 1984). Drawings and collage of "what it will be like in one year, 10 years, etc." are vehicles for viewing change and the preparation for a new, interactive life in the community. This invented reality and projected future does not ignore hard facts of life, and the therapist returns to an earlier mode of semi-case management. Finding support groups, after-school activities, memberships in community service groups or church are all important re-entry steps. Simultaneously, helping the family to acknowledge and let go of the lingering desires to repeat old patterns and to examine the past "in the present" is the continuing task of therapy. When the family of origin is realistically evaluated and their inadequacies are seen as human, the magic and power of the family mythologies are diminished, reduced merely to a family legend. At this point, parent and child are ready to start on their own journey, plan their future, and exercise their own identity as a family (Figure 5).

Every step of this process can be recorded and amplified through art expressions; tasks can be worked on and molded to introduce a broadened world view for these restricted families. Each art creation should be one that brings therapy closer to termination. The tangible record of their work and the review of their creative expressions produced in therapy illuminates the progress as well as any remaining difficulties.

Termination is a challenge for both the therapist and the family. However, participating in the creative experience of making decisions in therapy through kinesthetic, verbal, and visual modalities keeps these families on the path of change and growth, offering a new ending to what is often a sad tale.

Conclusion

There is no one formula for conducting art psychotherapy with families who have experienced domestic violence. The examples provided here are

Figure 5, Mother sets goals for the future

suggestions for treatment that are open and flexible, leaving room for individuality. No families are alike, no family circumstances are identical, and all families have their own legends and world views. Each experience of violence hurts the family in a unique manner and cessation of that behavior is experienced by each member in their own way. Therefore, it follows that the art expressions must also be elicited and explored with a respect and appreciation for individual differences. The therapist's creativity in developing appropriate art tasks that honor individuality and parallel the family's desire for change are key in eliciting clinical issues and illuminating therapy. Art therapy is the therapy of choice because this modality allows the client to take a self-observing stance; through this distancing, the context of the art product and process may be understood, enabling the client to co-create with the therapist a more satisfactory reality for herself and her family (Goodrute, Rampage, Ellman, & Halstead, 1988).

In summary, the treatment of families who have elected to extricate themselves from volatile relationships falls into four general phases. The first is protective and crisis-oriented, often at a shelter or safe house for battered families. The second is a recovery phase that introduces the opportunity to rework old attitudes, beliefs, and gender-assigned roles both in a primary relationship and in society. The third phase occurs as the family regains its self-worth, readjusts to new living circumstances, and terminates family treatment. The last phase is individual therapy for the woman if she elects to explore the remaining areas of discomfort in her life (Pittman, 1987).

As with all problematic and potentially life-threatening situations that are brought to therapy, the issue of domestic violence must be handled with care and caution. The art therapy expressions are safeguards that help the therapist divert potentially dangerous actions and destructive behaviors, tempering the difficulty of treating these clients. For this reason, family art therapy is recommended for successful resolution in domestic violence cases.

References

Goldner, V., Penn, P., Sheinberg, M., & Walker, G. (1990). Love and violence: Gender paradoxes in volatile attachments. *Family Process*, 29, 343-364.

Goodrute, T. J., Rampage, C., Ellman, B., & Halstead, K. (1988). *Feminist family therapy*. New York: Norton.

McGoldrick, M., & Gerson, R. (1985). *Genograms in family assessment*. New York: Norton & Co.

Malchiodi, C. A. (1990). *Breaking the silence: Art therapy with children from violent homes*. New York: Brunner/Mazel.

Pittman, F. (1987). *Turning point*. New York: Norton.

Watzlawick, P. (1984). *The invented reality*. New York: Norton.

Suggested Readings

Byng-Hall, J. (1988). Scripts and legends in families and family therapy. *Family Process*, 27, 167-180.

Coleman, K. H. (1988). Conjugal violence: What 33 men report. *Journal of Marital and Family Therapy*, 6, 207-213.

Efran, J., Lukens, M., & Lukens, R. (1990). *Language, structure, and change*. New York: Norton.

Gilligan, C. (1982). *In a different voice*. Cambridge, MA: Harvard University Press.

Goldner, V. (1985). Feminism and family therapy. *Family Process*, 24, 31-47.

Hurtado, A. (1989). Relating to privilege. *Journal of Women in Culture*, 4 (11), 834-846.

Landgarten, H. (1987). *Family art psychotherapy*. New York: Brunner/Mazel.

Penn, P. (1985). Feed forward: Future questions, future maps. *Family Process*, 24, 299-310.

Segal-Evans, K. (1988). *A general heuristic model of the batterer's treatment*. Unpublished manuscript.

THE ADVANTAGES OF ART THERAPY IN AN OUTPATIENT CLINIC

Mental health and money: these do not seem to attract each other. Mental health services require money, but the relationship is hardly a magnetic one. If we art therapists are going to compete successfully in a "bearish" mental health market, then we should learn how to present our services on the basis of their cost-effectiveness. My notion is that administrators of outpatient clinics are forced by financial considerations to be as interested in our productivity as in our theoretical biases.

As therapists, we tend to feel uncomfortable when we think of our work in terms of cold, hard cash. But nowadays, we have little choice: in many parts of the country, the financial crisis in community mental health has diminished employment opportunities for all mental health professionals. Therapists find that outpatient mental health centers often prefer clinicians experienced in brief therapy with a broad range of clients. Constraints imposed by Medicaid, Medicare, and insurance companies pressure clinics to favor a cost-effective model of practice. Increasingly, clinical art therapists who aspire to work in community mental health must be able to demonstrate that their approach is effective with a large portion of the clinic population. Their practice can no longer be limited to the nonverbal and other "appropriate" clients who used to make up a large portion of the art therapist's caseload.

In spite of current financial pressures, however, clinical art therapists are playing an expanding role in community mental health. Actually, this

This article originally appeared in the *American Journal of Art Therapy*, 26, 21-29, (1987) and is reprinted with their permission.

should not surprise us, because as a therapeutic modality, clinical art therapy is often the most economical means of achieving desired treatment goals. In my experience, art therapy is readily accepted by consumers and is the treatment of choice in many situations where short-term, goal-oriented therapy is indicated. In the outpatient mental health center where I serve as a senior staff member, we have found art therapy useful in meeting the following client and clinic needs.

Nonvoluntary Families and Children

These clients, usually court-ordered or school-referred, have little interest in therapy, and because they suppose that treatment is reserved for "crazy people", they often refuse to participate. Their no-shows waste the therapist's time and involve the whole staff in nonproductive paperwork. I believe that noncompliant families and individuals are more likely to engage in treatment when offered art therapy. Their first impression is that it is "just art", and they are therefore less likely to show resistance. The therapist can join with the client through the art process and gradually steer the therapy towards the problems that prompted the initial referral.

Intake Assessments

Spontaneous drawings and other diagnostic art techniques used during intake may indicate problems that the client is reluctant to talk about. Such techniques may be especially helpful if there is a secret history of family violence or abuse, or if the client is potentially suicidal. Using art as part of the diagnostic process may lead to early identification of the problem and a prompt referral to protective services, thereby reducing the potential for further abuse and containing the suicidal impulse.

Adolescents

Adolescents are notoriously reluctant to engage in therapy, and the effective clinician must take into account their developmental needs and behaviors. Typically, teenagers want to make their own decisions; they get more pleasure from action than from introspection; and they feel more comfortable with their peers than with adults. Because art therapy is an active and largely noninterpretative technique—one consistent with adolescents' treatment needs and preferences—it works well with them.

Short-term Therapy

In clinical art therapy, the client views and discusses the art created during the session. The art task is usually perceived as nonthreatening and self-interpreted, yet it engages the client in therapeutic work from the very first session. Art therapy promotes the identification of treatment goals and accelerates the progress of treatment.

Family Therapy

In the course of family therapy, a shared task such as a family drawing or mural offers the art therapist a unique opportunity to observe interactions, form a hypothesis about the family system and create interventions to alter dysfunctional sequences of behavior (Riley, 1985). By observing patterns of family behavior as well as the content of the art, the art therapist learns about family members' relationships with each other and about the family system of which they are a part. Usually, the therapist is able to gather far more data than a strictly verbal interview would yield.

To illustrate the wide range of applications for art therapy in the outpatient clinic, I offer the following case examples. In each case, art therapy proved to be a cost-effective mode of treatment because it motivated client participation, crystallized the clinical issues, and resolved in a reasonable period of time the clients' presenting problems.

Case Examples:
Consultation with an Alcoholic Family

The Pecks were referred by a family therapist for an art therapy consultation. The family's youngest member, 10-year-old Janice, was the subject of a custody battle between her parents, and a court hearing had been scheduled to determine placement. The primary therapist had been asked for an opinion as to where the child ought to live. Thinking that family art therapy might yield information relevant to the custody issue, he asked me to perform an art therapy assessment, because he felt that through a structured art task, he could better observe the interactions and the strengths and weaknesses of Janice's family.

Janice had been living with her maternal grandparents for some time because of her mother's long-standing alcoholism. Her mother was now in a rehabilitation program, held a job, and wanted Janice to live with her. The father, also an alcoholic but not involved in any rehabilitation program, wanted custody too. The grandparents thought that Janice should remain with them, but they were willing to support Janice's return to her mother if this was the course of action recommended by the therapist.

Janice's father did not attend the session. The other family members presented themselves as follows:

Grandfather (age 63): dynamic and loud; financially successful; very concerned about his alcoholic daughter and about his granddaughter's future.

Grandmother (age 61): gentle, nurturing; recovered alcoholic for 20 years; supportive of her daughter.

Mother (age 42): living in a halfway house for alcoholics; resolved not to "slip this time" in spite of a history of repeated rehabilitation failures.

Janice (age 10): pseudomature, protective of mother and father; attached to grandparents; acutely aware of the family struggle over her future. (According to Black, 1981, children of alcoholic parents often exhibit these characteristics.)

The primary therapist remained in the room during the session, providing consistency and support, but as the consulting art therapist, I directed the therapeutic work undertaken by the family.

At the beginning of the session, the adults tensely described their inability to decide where Janice should live. Although family members tended to make statements in support of each other, they were unable to move from entrenched attitudes of blame and mistrust. Incapable of reaching consensus on Janice's future, the adults appeared ready to hand the decision over to the child herself. This was a repeated sequence, especially prevalent in interactions between Janice and her mother.

I asked the Pecks to create a family mural (Figure 1). Grandmother drew the largest form; wavelike, it reached across the paper in an apparent attempt to touch all the others. Mother drew a little house containing herself and her daughter. In the drawing, mother and daughter look as if they are the same age. Janice helped her mother with the house and added the labels *Mommy* and *me* to the portraits, but she devoted most of her attention to a sketch of her dog, who had recently run away. Grandfather made only a few small marks on the paper and added captions to the drawings of others. In contrast to his verbal assertiveness, he was the most reticent of the group in portraying his feelings graphically.

The picture was finished and the Pecks were discussing it when Mother suddenly sprang up from her seat and drew a large vodka bottle in the center, saying she felt "compelled" to complete the family mural. After a long period of silence, I remarked that Mother had strategically placed the bottle on the only area in which all four colors used by the family members intersected. (Unfortunately, this is not readily apparent in the black-and-white reproduction of the mural given here.)

Based on the mural and the family members' behavior during the session, I formed the following hypothesis. Grandmother, whose "wave" reached towards everyone else, was the caretaker, the strong member of the family system. Grandfather, surprisingly warm and supportive of the others

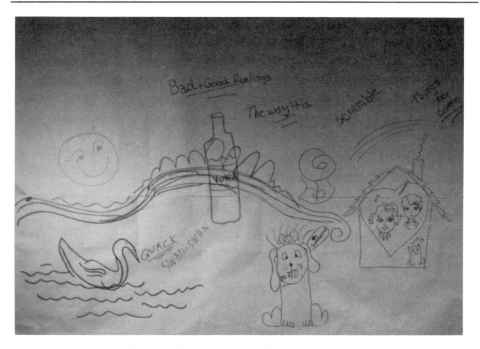

Figure 1: Family mural with alcoholic mother

Figure 2: My breasts and privates hurt

as they worked on the mural, also appeared to want to "touch" all family members with his marks and the concern was implied in the captions that he wrote. By portraying her runaway dog, Janice was conveying a message that she was not ready to assume responsibility for adult decisions; clearly, she identified with the dog's impulse to "get away" from the family problems. But it was the mother's impetuous addition of the vodka bottle that provided the most blatant clue to this family's unreadiness to make a major change. By this action, Mother signalled that alcohol still dominated the family system and that her treatment had not yet prepared her for reclaiming sole responsibility for her daughter.

From my art therapy interpretation of this mural the family therapist gleaned much that informed his subsequent work with this family. He recommended that Janice stay with her grandparents until Mother grew more secure in maintaining sobriety.

This case demonstrates how a consulting art therapist can provide an extremely valuable service to the primary therapist. The art therapist's interventions can elicit dramatic and significant information previously unavailable. Even after the consultation ends, the primary therapist can use the art work to facilitate discussion and subsequent movement in treatment

Interviewing a Sexually Abused Child

Another important use of art therapy is for interviewing child victims of abuse. Art therapy offers a means by which abused children can communicate their feelings in a safe and acceptable way. Indeed, this may be the only route to full disclosure by the child because he or she may have been threatened with dire consequences for "telling the secret" (Naitove, 1982). When children's art contains indicators of possible abuse, the therapist can explore the meaning of the image to the child and gently encourage him or her to tell what happened in the context of what the image portrays.

Figure 2 was done by a six-year-old girl instructed to "draw a picture of yourself". When asked about the picture, the child told the therapist that the "breasts and privates hurt" and that the little girl in the drawing was "running away". When the therapist wondered aloud if anyone had tried to hurt the little girl's breasts and privates, the child described sexual abuse by an adult male. Through skillful questioning, the therapist learned that the child had been repeatedly molested by an adult in her home. The child was referred to protective services and continued in therapy; eventually, the offender went to jail.

Treatment of an Adoptive Family

The practice of art therapy in the outpatient clinic is by no means limited to consultation and evaluation. In the following case, family art therapy was the primary mode of treatment and was utilized through the course of therapy.

When they came to the clinic, Anna and Tom Sommer were in the process of adopting five-year-old Jason. A well-educated professional couple, they were highly motivated to succeed as adoptive parents. They had no previous experience as parents; however, they had been thoroughly counseled by the adoption agency involved and had taken classes in child development and parenting skills. In accordance with good adoption practice, Jason's move into their home was a gradual one: six months earlier, the Sommers began visiting him at the group home where he then lived. Now he was beginning a one-year trial period in their home.

In spite of this auspicious beginning, the Sommers faced a formidable challenge in helping Jason become part of their family. During the first two years of life, he had experienced extreme deprivation and trauma. His natural mother neglected him physically and emotionally, and had involved him in adult sexual activity. When Jason was no longer of any use to her, she discarded him, abandoning him on a bench at a bus stop, where he was eventually picked up by the police. During the next two years Jason drifted through a series of temporary homes and relationships with well-meaning but bewildered foster parents who could not cope with his violent and antisocial behavior. Overwhelmed by multiple losses, Jason was extremely guarded and mistrustful, and he had lost the ability to form attachments with caretaking adults. When he turned four, his mother finally relinquished her parental rights, making Jason legally free for adoption. But she continued to play havoc with Jason's emotions by harassing him with frequent phone calls and promises she never kept.

The Sommers contacted the clinic because they wanted help in managing Jason's behavior. On intake, they reported the following symptoms: enuresis, encopresis, nightmares, and oppositional and infantile behavior. He had developed some tolerance for his new mother, but he regarded Tom with suspicion and hostility. The Sommers wanted not only improvement in Jason's symptoms, but also a way of helping him become a member of the family. The adoption would not be final for almost a year, but it was obvious that Anna and Tom had committed themselves to establishing a permanent, nurturing relationship with him.

The first few sessions were spent on assessment and in helping Jason tolerate my presence as a new (and unwanted) adult in his life. For the most part, he scribbled and drew monsters. He also threw frequent temper tantrums because he was afraid that his coming to the clinic meant he was about to lose yet another set of parents. This was not surprising, given his history: prior to the adoption, strangeness and change had almost always resulted in a new loss or trauma.

Treatment goals were to help Jason feel secure in the permanence of his relationship with adults he could trust and to help him understand that limits and rules are not always punitive. For a little boy only approaching his fifth birthday, these concepts were far too abstract: they required translation into concrete experiences. I therefore designed a series of art activities for

Figure 3: Adoptive family jails their nightmares

the whole family so that Jason, working actively along with Anna and Tom, could learn, by doing, a new way of experiencing his world.

The first of these projects addressed Jason's nightmares, which were accompanied by bed-wetting just before he woke up. I decided to use this symptom as a means of connecting with Jason's world. Accordingly, I instructed all three family members to draw and cut out their "night monsters" (Figure 3). Jason became very involved in this task and even let me help him, which reduced his fear of the new strange adult. Tom was appointed by the others the "expert in confining monsters", and he took charge of the activity. He asked Anna and Jason to let him paste all the monsters on a large piece of paper so he could "keep them under control". To confine them, he began drawing a barred cage, but then he informed the others that this task was "very difficult without help". Intrigued, Jason climbed onto his father's lap and helped draw bars to restrain the monsters.

Through this task, I made it clear that nightmares were a normal experience for all family members. At the same time, I encouraged them to use Jason's symptom to explore the process of becoming a family. Caging their monsters and giving control of them to Tom demonstrated to Jason that the family could solve problems through teamwork. As Tom assumed the role of "monster confiner", Jason moved towards him physically and broke through his initial rejection to enjoy his first experience of attachment to a father figure. Because Jason had never established basic trust in his relationships with nurturing adults, this brief physical contact was a significant step towards internalizing a lesson more appropriately learned during infancy. Fostering Jason's ability to trust adults became a guiding factor in all subsequent art therapy interventions with this adoptive family.

At the end of the session just described, Jason spontaneously asked to draw a "good monster" who would fly over him at night and keep him safe. Leaving the "bad monsters" in "jail" on the therapy room wall, he took the "good" one home and suspended it by a string from the ceiling above his bed. From that point on, Jason began art therapy sessions with a ritual of scolding the "bad" monsters he had left on the wall. For the most part, those monsters stayed confined in the therapy room; following this pivotal session, Jason reported very few frightening dreams and almost no bed-wetting.

The next task was more difficult for Jason. With the help of his new parents, he began a life-story scrapbook. Assembling a pictorial history of his life through drawings, a few photos, and cutout picture, they recreated Jason's experiences and "remembered" his painful early years. The scrapbook also contained material relating to Jason's current life and to the hopes and fears all three family members had for the future. They energetically worked on the scrapbook both at home and during therapy sessions. The activity came to symbolize the healing power of their relationship: when the memories of the past became too painful, they could turn from them to their dreams for the future as a family.

The assignment gave the Sommers precisely what they were lacking: a shared experience of Jason's early life and a chance for Anna and Tom to enter emotionally into Jason's journey through critical periods of attachment and loss. This is, of course, only a poor substitute for the real-life experience of parents and children, but it does offer the adoptive family an experiential and concrete means of establishing a pseudohistorical background together. It also hastens the adoptive family's progress through the developmental stages of coalescing as a family unit.

Somewhat later in therapy, I offered them construction paper, and they decided to build a home for the Three Bears. This became a metaphor for the permanence of the structure and boundaries of their family. They began work on the house, announcing that they intended to live there "forever". Father Bear (Tom) led them in gluing the house together with such expertise that the resulting structure was really very sturdy. When they finished, Mother Bear (Anna) placed herself at the open front door, welcoming and watching all who went in or out (Figure 4a), while Father guarded the back of the house (Figure 4b). Jason, as Baby Bear, stood on the roof with a pot of flowers and a pet bird, broadcasting the message that he was attached to the family but not yet grounded inside their home.

One problem that frequently arises in new adoptive families is that well-meaning parents become so intent on helping the child that they scrutinize and interpret his every move. It is useful to help the parents dilute this focus and provide each other with renewal and support. Therefore I encouraged Anna and Tom to spend more time on adult pleasures and on their relationship with each other. With the Sommers, art therapy resulted in an additional, unplanned dividend: it stimulated the whimsical side of their personalities. As successful professionals in business and accounting, they rarely had the opportunity to enjoy what art therapy gave them: a chance to play. This in turn fostered spontaneity in their relationship with Jason.

The last goal of therapy was to help the family deal with Jason's fear of the court hearing that would make the adoption final. I suggested that they create a large mural (Figure 5), and they literally drew their way through the court proceedings. They began by setting up the courtroom and drawing the various people involved: the judge, lawyers, social workers, and witnesses. Anna and Tom gave a step-by-step description of the process and explained what each person's role was. They drew in other adoptive families and finally themselves in front of the judge. Assuming the role of the judge, I asked Jason if he would like to live with these parents "forever". Looking confused, he at first wondered if the judge would send him away. Then he rushed to the mural and to the figures of himself and his parents he attached the exclamation "YES!".

Why was art therapy more successful in this case than a verbal approach would have been? Simply because it allowed family members to communicate with each other in a way that was congruent with Jason's level of cognitive development. His activities in each session were concrete,

Figure 4a: The house of the "three bears"

Figure 4b: Family construction of paper

experiential, and age-appropriate, and he was an active participant in working for the changes that occurred in the family system.

Adding a new family member through adoption almost always causes a great deal of stress on the family system. A child who has experienced the losses that Jason knew early in life needs help in developing trust in his new parents, and must somehow negotiate missed developmental sequences in attachment and individuation. Beginning therapy immediately after the adoption was cost-effective from the clients' point of view because early intervention could quickly focus on the essential issues even as Jason and his parents were getting to know each other, forestalling the development of rigid and dysfunctional patterns in the parent-child relationship.

Was art therapy a cost-effective means of treating this family from the clinic's viewpoint, too? It responded directly to the family's needs, engaged them as partners in the therapeutic process, and in a relatively brief period of time helped them realize their treatment goals. In short, it provided them with what, as mental health consumers, they expected and paid for.

Therapy with a Suicidal Adolescent

Outpatient therapy was requested by an eighteen-year-old Central American girl, Marie, diagnosed as having schizotypal personality disorder with severe depression. Although she slashed and burned her arms and hinted broadly of suicidal intent, she refused to be hospitalized and rejected the notion of controlling her symptoms with medication. She was functioning well enough to hold a job in a fast-food restaurant and to keep outpatient appointments. I agreed to meet with her twice a week.

At first, I found it very difficult to establish a therapeutic alliance with Marie because she was extremely mistrustful and hardly talked at all during sessions, even though she was fluent in English. Although she did not become more talkative during therapy, she did grow adept at expressing her feelings through art. Had I not tried an art therapy approach with Marie, there would have been few opportunities to assess her progress in treatment.

Marie began by scribbling in an agitated way with a black felt-tip pen; she would then immediately cover up and destroy the marks she made. I offered her materials for collage, but she only sat and cried as she used her pen to black out portions of magazine pictures (Figure 6). The first sign of progress appeared in her next production (Figure 7), completed after eight weeks of treatment. Here, she began to use collage as a means of communicating some of her inner turmoil. Her images of devil worship, hate, rejection of self and others express "unbearable pain". In Figure 8, we see the first indications of trust and the formation of a therapeutic alliance

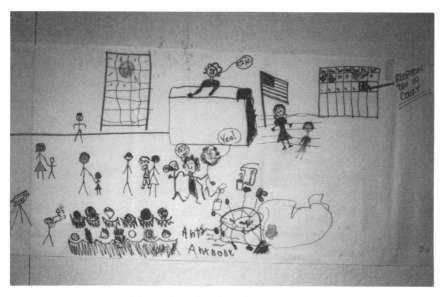

Figure 5: Role-play of the adoption

Figure 6: First art work of suicidal girl

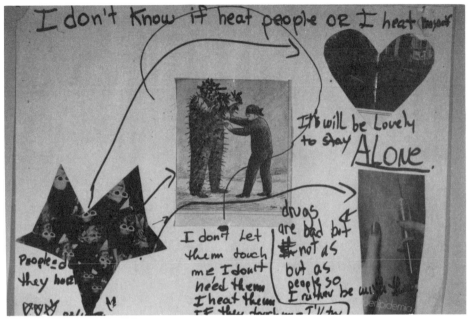

Figure 7: "I don't know if I hate people or I hate myself"

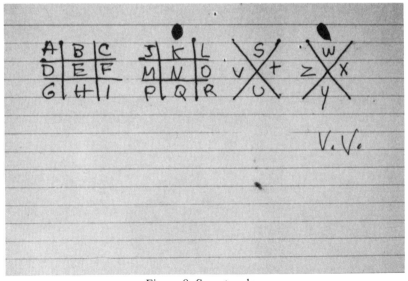

Figure 8: Secret code

after six months of treatment. The picture displays a code Marie used in all her diaries and notes to protect her privacy. She explained that in her writing, she substituted the gridlines bordering a particular letter for the letter itself, so that A would be represented by the figure   and J by   . Through the placement of tiny dots, she could differentiate A from J. By translating this code for me, Marie indicated that she was willing to let another person into her secret world.

After she completed the code drawing, Marie's self-mutilations ceased completely. In her journal, she had written that she "needed to feel something" and once the armor encasing her feelings began to crack, she became much more expressive in her artwork. As her trust in me grew, she communicated her despair more directly; she also began to bring me drawings she had done at home between sessions. In the delicate pen drawings of Figure 9, Marie used a maze to express her confusion, and by hiding the words *love, guns, death, drugs*, and *needles* along with tiny camouflaged drawings of guns and needles, she challenged me to interpret her work and help her begin to address her problems.

About two-thirds of the way through treatment, Marie brought me a Valentine on which she drew a telling portrait of herself (Figure 10). An

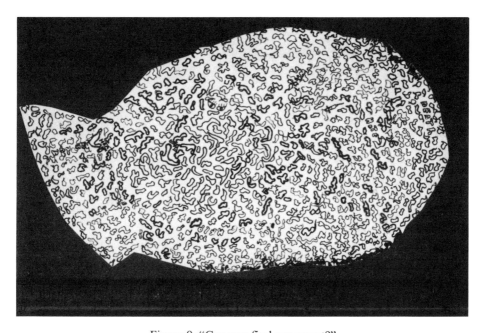

Figure 9: "Can you find my secret?"

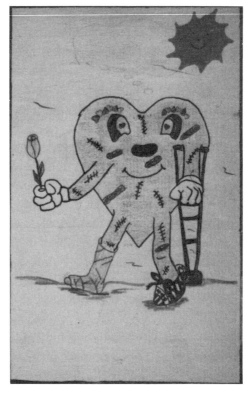

Figure 10: "Scarred but healing"

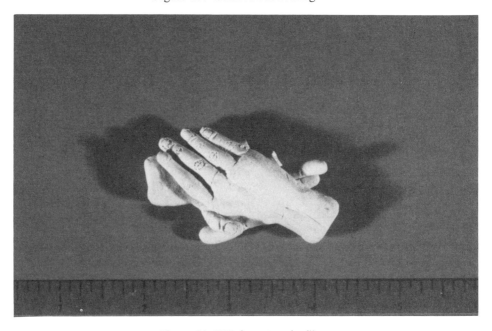

Figure 11: "We have touched"

injured heart wears a small, tentative smile and offers a rose. The scars of self-mutilation are evident, but they are healing.

We were forced to end treatment prematurely because her student visa expired and she returned to her native country. She presented me with her final piece (Figure 11) as a termination gift. These delicately articulated hands are very small (2.5 inches long) and were executed in Play Doh, a difficult medium in which to achieve such detail. The image of one hand gently holding the other symbolized her sense of the therapeutic relationship. Clearly, she had made progress from the blacked-out pictures of her early sessions.

Because of their beauty and symbolic meaning, I have kept Marie's hands in a place of honor on my desk ever since she gave them to me. Recently, she came back from Central America and asked to resume treatment after an 18-month hiatus. She was deeply moved to find her sculpture so carefully preserved, but she also wondered if I had brought it out just for her appointment. I assured her that the hands had remained on my desk since the day she left. This knowledge was evidently important to her, and I found that it helped re-establish the therapeutic alliance in spite of the long interruption.

As in the previous cases, the use of art therapy with Marie facilitated therapeutic progress that would not have occurred with verbal techniques alone. Its value from the client's point of view is plain. To the extent that it functioned as a barometer of her depressed mood and suicidal leanings, it also benefited the clinic, which had a legal and ethical obligation to protect clients from their dangerous impulses if necessary. Because Marie's conversation was barren during the initial phase of therapy, the information she shared through her artwork simply could not be obtained through other means. Until she expressed her feelings in words, Marie's art was the only way she had of communicating with her therapist. Without some therapeutic contact, an outpatient clinic could not ethically continue offering treatment to a potentially suicidal client like Marie.

Conclusion

As more art therapists become established in outpatient facilities, clinic administrators are beginning to realize that art therapy is no longer solely an adjunctive mode of treatment. It is coming into its own as a primary method of treating a broad spectrum of human problems. For many years, art therapists have demonstrated the usefulness of their approach in rehabilitation and inpatient settings. Community mental health no longer represents a new frontier for art therapists, but rather an arena in which we can address the whole range of individual and family dysfunction for which our approach has proved effective.

This knowledge will take root only if we continue to build on our professional skills as both specialists and generalists in the clinic setting. We need to document and present our treatment successes to our colleagues and to continue our search for new ways of synthesizing theory and technique.

At first blush, it may feel somewhat distasteful to sell art therapy on the basis of its cost-effectiveness. But if by cost-effectiveness we mean that art therapy meets both the needs of the consumer and the needs of the mental health service provider, aren't we really saying only that it is a valid, effective, and appropriate treatment method for many of the problems that prompt clients to seek help at mental health centers? That in itself is not an outrageous claim. It would, however, be outrageous for us to use any other criteria for measuring the utility of a therapy in clinical practice.

References

Black, C. (1981). *It will never happen to me: Children of alcoholics.* Denver: MAC Publications.

Naitove, C. (1982). Arts therapy with sexually abused children. In S. Sgroi (ed.), *Handbook of Clinical Intervention in Child Sexual Abuse* (pp. 269-308). Lexington, MA: Lexington Books.

Riley, S. (1985). Draw me a paradox?... *Art Therapy: Journal of the American Art Therapy Association,* 2, 116-123.

Addendum

Although this essay was written some years ago, it is responsive to todays' mental health concerns. This chapter speaks to the changing attitudes in federal and state governments and could be used as a document supporting the inclusion of art therapy services in future national health care systems.

SECTION THREE:
FAMILY ART THERAPY AND POSTMODERN SOCIETY
Cathy A. Malchiodi

This final section of the book focuses on some of the contemporary societal issues that have a direct effect on the practice of family art therapy in the postmodern world. "Postmodern" is a term coined to describe a society that now encompasses many diverse beliefs and differing realities. Conceptually, postmodernism first emerged as a trend in art, architecture and literature in the '70s and '80s. In contrast to modernism, the postmodernist movement disdained simplicity, clarity, analytical abstraction and order, and tended toward elaboration, eclecticism and ornamentation. If modernism favored minimalism, it could be said that postmodernism favored just the opposite and was a synthesis of many positions, including modern thinking.

Wheeler (1991) sums up the postmodernist movement in this way:

> Salient within an extremely broad range of postmodern characteristics have been an eagerness to expose or deconstruct the "real life" myths and "coded" languages of the popular media; a realization that fine art, even at its most abstract or "autonomous" cannot but exemplify the overall human realities prevalent within its time and place; the identification and analysis of the usually hidden contexts of art—museums, markets, government or corporate funding, and critics; and a recognition that in order to reflect current, ambient life, art must resist a priori dogmas about what is allowable and insist upon whatever approach—historical, psychological, narrational, political, diaristic, decorative, metaphysical, or even formal—seems best suited to the artist and his purpose. (p. 246)

Postmodernism is most boldly demonstrated in architecture where modern technological advances are combined with past styles of design and structure, resulting in something of an architectural collage. Prominent examples of this style are the AT&T Corporate Headquarters in New York by Phillip Johnson, reminiscent of Classical architecture, and the Humana Building by Michael Graves in Louisville, Kentucky, with a distinctly Egyptian flavor in combination with steel-cage technology. These structures not only demonstrate unusual and creative combinations of ideas and styles, but also the underlying concept of eclecticism central to postmodern thinking.

In general, postmodernism has become associated with a shift in consciousness in society along with the awareness that a multiplicity of realities exist. O'Hara and Anderson (1991) have observed that:

> Without noticing it, we have moved into a new world, one created by the cumulative effect of pluralism, democracy, religious freedom, consumerism, mobility, and increasing access to news and entertainment. This is the world described as "postmodern" to denote its difference from the modern world most of us were born into. A new social consciousness is emerging in this new world and touching the lives of all kinds of people who are not in the least bit interested in having a new kind of social consciousness. We are all being forced to see that there are many kinds of beliefs, multiple realities, and exhilarating but daunting profusion of worldviews to suit every taste. We can choose among these, but we cannot choose not to make choices. (p. 20)

This movement has led to a re-examination and sorting of beliefs in many fields, including the practice of psychotherapy. The traditional learning of a comprehensive model of therapeutic practice that provides all the answers has become passe leaving therapists to struggle with evolving new ways of working with their clients by synthesizing many ways of knowing. Therapy must incorporate clients' experiences that include multiculturalism, increased exposure to violence and crime, new roles and reinvented family systems, and economic changes that threaten security and livelihoods. In light of these circumstances, past theoretical models often seem inadequate to the task of addressing client needs.

In relation to the field of family therapy, postmodernism has initiated some of the most powerful developments in the profession, altering the recent course of family therapy in general. Issues such as gender and feminism, multiculturalism, and constructivism are being actively incorporated into thinking and infused within clinical interventions. Other issues, such as changes in family life, societal violence, and trends in mental health service delivery have affected the course of the development of family therapy. In the three remaining chapters of this book Riley addresses these three issues from the perspective of a family art therapist, educator and supervisor.

Postmodern Changes in Family Life

In the opening chapter of this section, Riley describes her experience working with grandparents who serve in a parental role to their own grandchildren. Changes in family structure, from the traditional nuclear family to families with single parents or to families where the grandparent(s) may take a strong role have undoubtedly become more commonplace in recent years; these are changes that family therapists must now address on an ongoing basis.

Grandparents are a resource that therapists can call upon to intervene within the family system. They are often ones that the therapist should identify, particularly if the grandchild's welfare and safety is at stake. In my own work in domestic violence I have frequently called upon a grandparent as a resource to the family decision-making process when spouse-battering and/or child abuse has upset the family system. If grandma or grandpa is a significant force in the life of a child, the child will often indicate this visually when asked to draw a family member of his/her choice (Figure 1) or may naturally volunteer information about a grandparent in an art expression (Figure 2). This may let the therapist know about a valuable source of support

Figure 1: "I fill (sic) so happy today because I am going to my graman's (sic) house to get 50$"; drawing by seven-year-old girl

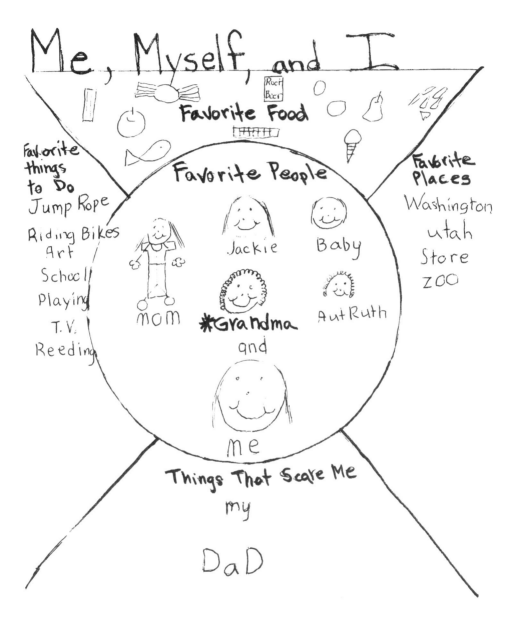

Figure 2: "Me, myself and I" depicting grandmother as favorite family member; drawing by seven-year-old girl

Figure 3: "My Dad with a hammer and a knife"; drawing by seven-year-old boy

for the child, and, in some cases, a possible alternative home for a child who has been neglected or battered, or to relieve a mother who temporarily cannot take care of her children.

During this decade therapists will certainly see a continuance of single parent households and remarried families in second and third marriages. They will also see among their clientele the parentified grandparents Riley noted as well as gay and lesbian couples raising families. The traditional idea of family has been the nuclear family with two natural parents and their children; this is no longer the normative structure in our society. During the '80s remarried families quickly became the dominant family type (National Center for Health Statistics, 1987). Given the magnitude of this situation, it is likely that any family therapist will see these families on a regular basis. The terms stepfamily, blended family, reconstituted family and remarried family have proliferated in clinical literature over the last decade. Issues such as what to call the new parent, sibling conflict, confusion over family roles, custody, and financial concerns are only a few of the topics that come to the forefront in working with changing family structures in the '90s (Walsh, 1992).

Families and Societal Violence in the Postmodern Culture

It has become a well-known fact that many of our nation's children grow up in circumstances where violence is a daily occurrence. In talking with children from violent homes over the last several years, I have heard statements that relate not only to the direct experience of domestic violence, but also general fears that relate to their home life, neighborhoods and cities. Fear is prevalent among these children, and with it they also accept the daily occurrence of violence in their lives. It is not unusual to hear these children speak of a brother who "is in jail for stabbing someone" or a father who "killed a man" (Figure 3). Additionally, it is common to hear a child say that "I'm afraid to go to sleep at night because I have scary dreams". In the last statement, the idea of post traumatic stress becomes apparent: the recurrent images that plague a child or adult who has directly survived a traumatic event.

The Los Angeles riots of 1992 as described through the eyes of Riley and her colleagues underscore the experience of post traumatic stress in the clients seen in therapy after the upheaval, chaos and fires of that time period. The visual statements made by these children and adults during an art therapy session convincingly demonstrate the importance of art expression as a vehicle for communication of multilevel experiences of confusion, fear, anger, and depression. Art therapists have long understood this innate capacity of art to give form to that which traumatizes our clients (Johnson, 1987; Malchiodi, 1990). Art making is an antidote to violence (May, 1985), given the transformative role that art plays in situations of extreme crisis or trauma. Art therapists capitalize on this power of art to transform, but with a deeper understanding of the consequences of PTSD, anxiety disorders, panic, and depression that can result from either isolated or chronic experiences with violence. It is an especially valuable way to empower children affected by family violence, violent neighborhoods and violence in society (Malchiodi, 1990).

Although the focus in the chapter on the Los Angeles riots is on broadscale violence in society, there unfortunately are other equally devastating types of violence occurring to people, particularly children. Severe neglect, emotional maltreatment and molestation are several examples of violence to children. Random violence, whether personally experienced or witnessed on television, also has a lasting effect on individuals; as clinicians we hear their fears and anxieties concerning these insecurities, especially if our clients live in communities prone to outbreaks of violence. Fortunately, as Riley has pointed out, we have in our arsenal of therapeutic weapons the art process which can give a voice to these traumatic experiences when words alone cannot adequately describe the chaotic and frightening reality of everyday life.

Postmodern Changes in Mental Health

Societal changes in recent years have had a direct impact on the practice of mental health in general. Violence, drugs, crime, and disease are certainly issues that have become a concern to practitioners who work in clinics, hospitals, shelters, and private practice. Additionally, changes have occurred on a broader scale in how mental health services are delivered. There have been modifications in state and federal regulations as well as an increase in private health corporations controlling client care. These circumstances have invariably affected how a therapist practices, including how long one can see a client and under what conditions. Therefore, it is extremely important that both advanced clinicians, as well as beginning therapists, understand these changes and how they affect mental health service delivery.

One area in particular which demands therapists' attention is their personal safety on the job. In light of the prevalence of violence in society in general and in the lives of clients seen in therapy, it is important that both clinical instructors and supervisors who are responsible for student interns address this topic in class and supervision. Topics for discussion as noted by Riley might include any and all of the following: how to handle oneself in a life-threatening situation; recognizing the potential for violent behavior in clients; understanding the signs of drug usage and overdose; and understanding current street drugs and their effects.

There is also the additional threat of disease which complicates any type of interpersonal interaction today; all therapists and students need to be acutely aware of this threat. Attention has been given to acquired immune deficiency syndrome (AIDS), and it is one obvious area that must be addressed in training programs in terms of personal safety as well as an understanding of the effects of the disease. However, there are other diseases that are even more threatening in terms of exposure, including tuberculosis and hepatitis. A working knowledge of these illnesses and safety measures to prevent exposure, especially if one works in a clinic or shelter, are of primary concern.

Art therapists reading this section may have quickly noted that there are no art-related topics mentioned. The point here is that it is quicker to visibly note that someone is intoxicated or violent rather than to look for it in the client's image. As Riley notes, "paints and markers are not a defense against guns". The issue of personal safety is a real one and one that can no longer be ignored with our students and supervisees. It is probably less interesting to talk about enhancement of self-protection than to discuss the often fascinating use of symbolic language by a client, but it is a discussion that can be indeed lifesaving in the long run.

State and federal laws governing the practice of mental health are other topics of ongoing importance. Many topics of discussion will be guided by the specific state laws in the state in which the training program is located, but some items are more or less universal. For example, many states have similar reporting laws on child abuse/neglect and domestic violence. Expert testimony has some commonalities, but when it comes to who can be an expert witness, give actual testimony and how to do so, it is probably wise for instructors and supervisors to familiarize themselves with local protocols and specific legal aspects before discussing this area with student interns.

In the postmodern world, national health care reform is still being debated as of this writing; a vast array of plans have been proposed, many as eclectic as postmodernism itself. Undoubtedly, when a decision is made regarding overall health care practices, all mental health therapists will be affected. Although the direction health care will take is not yet known, managed care scenarios may be more common. Currently, managed health care is standard for a large number of people, with "nearly half of the 178 million Americans with health insurance enrolled in some kind of managed care company specializing in mental health" (p. 22, Wylie, 1994). Additionally, licensure and certification are important issues to discuss on a regular basis with students and supervisees; advanced practitioners, whether practicing in a hospital or in a private setting, must also stay current with changes in licensure and certification regulations.

Lastly, there are also changes in how art therapy in clinical settings is provided. One obvious change over the last decade is the move to short term care and models of brief therapy. However, in contrast, much of the literature in the field of art therapy has traditionally focused on psychodynamic theories that involve long term work with clients. Although there are no easy short cuts to successful therapy, the reality of short term care remains, and therapists need to at least dialogue with each other on ways to address this problematic situation. A discussion of possible ways to adjust art therapy to solution-focused models or how limiting the number of sessions will impact the client-therapist relationship are two of many possible topics to consider either in the classroom, supervision, or in peer professional groups.

A Final Note for Instructors, Supervisors and Students

For students, instructors and supervisors who are using this section as part of a course or supervisory session, the major focus has been on developing flexibility and adaptability in one's understanding of the application of art therapy to work with families in this decade. This means not only being aware of trends in clinical practice, but also staying current with contemporary issues in society in general. Societal trends, mental health service delivery, and fluctuations in family structure are all part of this changing knowledge base. Staying current may not only involve reading the contemporary clinical literature, but also having a working knowledge of present trends in sociology, gender and cultural perspectives.

Just as artists stay in touch with and work with today's issues and ideas in their paintings and sculptures, art therapists need to stay abreast of current trends in society in order to best help their clients. In discussing this chapter, instructors and supervisors will recognize that a singular idea emerges: Are we training art therapists to deal with the real world? The "real world" keeps changing and it is most important as clinicians, educators and supervisors that we stay in touch with these changes.

References

Gergen, K. (1991). *The saturated self.* New York: Basic Books.

Johnson, D. R. (1987). The role of the creative arts therapies in the diagnosis and treatment of psychological trauma. *The Arts in Psychotherapy, 14,* 713.

Malchiodi, C. A. (1990). *Breaking the silence: Art therapy with children from violent homes.* New York: Brunner/Mazel.

May, R. (1985). *My quest for beauty.* Dallas, TX: Saybrook.

O'Hara, M., & Anderson, W. T. (1991, September/October). Welcome to the postmodern world. *Family Therapy Networker,* 19-25.

Walsh, M. (1992). Twenty major issues in remarriage families. *Journal of Counseling and Development, 70,* 709-715.

Wheeler, D. (1991). *Art since mid-century: 1945 to the present.* New York: Prentice-Hall.

Wylie, M. S. (1994, March/April). Endangered species. *Family Therapy Networker,* 18 (2), 20-33.

Suggested Readings

Garnets, L., & Kimmel, D. (1991). Lesbian and gay male dimensions in the psychological study of human diversity. In J. Goodchilds (ed.)*Psychological Perspectives on Human Diversity in America* (pp. 137-189). Washington, DC: American Psychological Association.

Gergen, K. (1991). *The saturated self.* New York: Basic Books.

Herman, J. (1992). *Trauma and recovery.* New York: Basic Books.

Jones, J. (1991). Psychological models of race: What have they been and what should they be? In J. Goodchilds (ed.) *Psychological Perspectives on Human Diversity in America* (pp. 3-46). Washington, DC: American Psychological Association.

Myers, J. E. B. (1992). *Legal issues in child abuse and neglect.* Newbury Park, CA: Sage.

O'Hara, M., & Anderson, W. T. (1991, September/October). Welcome to the postmodern world. *Family Therapy Networker,* 19-25.

Tarvis, C. (1991). The mismeasure of woman: Paradoxes and perspectives in the study of gender. In J. Goodchilds (ed.) *Psychological Perspectives on Human Diversity in America* (pp. 87-136). Washington, DC: American Psychological Association.

Terr, L. (1990). *Too scared to cry: Psychic trauma in childhood.* New York: Basic Books.

PARENTIFIED GRANDPARENTS IN FAMILY ART THERAPY

Lately, I have been thinking a great deal about the role of grandparents. Many of my clients come from families in which grandmothers are the primary—sometimes only—adult caretakers of young children. I myself am a grandmother, and after caring for my husky one-year-old grandson for only a few hours, the twinges in my back make me feel additional empathy and admiration for those grandparents who act as full-time parents.

Sadly, the histories of these grandmother-headed families are all too similar. The birth parents are often addicted to drugs, and even if they haven't abandoned their children entirely, they are incapable of functioning in a parental role because they are in jail, living with other drug users, or on the streets. They may seek to maintain some ties with the children, but they have clearly chosen drugs over family. In many cases, the grandmothers were once parentified children of severely dysfunctional parents. They now find themselves cast in a new, but familiar, role as designated caretakers, and will often take in the children of their troubled offspring, giving a new twist to an old pattern.

To some extent, this family pattern reflects the combined impact of the baby boom and the drug culture of the '60s and '70s. Many baby boomers became yuppies, but a large number never stopped taking drugs and are now incapable of caring for their children. The children either become wards of the state or are adopted by family members—most frequently, grandmothers.

In time, the children of such a family may become difficult for a grandmother to handle, and school officials or friends may refer her to our

This article originally appeared in a different form in the *American Journal of Art Therapy, 28,98 (1990)* and is reprinted with the permission of Vermont College of Norwitch University.

clinic for family therapy. Treatment is complicated by the fact that both the children and the grandmother feel grief for the absent birth parent. The children may believe that they were not valuable enough for their mother to choose them over drugs, thus suffering a blow to their self-esteem. The grandmother may feel that she herself failed as a parent—her child, after all, is an addict—and that she must atone by succeeding the second time around. Another complicating factor is the large age gap between the generations: some grandmothers may not have enough physical stamina to keep up with the demands of parenting young children. These problems may lead to anger, miscommunication, and difficulties in setting limits for increasingly oppositional children. A grandmother may become angered and frustrated by her reduced ability to cope, and the children may come to feel that the anger is directed at them. The children may escalate their misbehavior in order to attract attention. They may feel embarrassed because they were abandoned by their birth parents and because they have an adoptive mother far older than their peers' parents.

Another common troubling issue is secrecy. If the birth parent is in jail, what have the children been told? Does grandmother share all communications from the birth mother with the children and let the children talk with her when she calls? Do stresses and strains of puberty evoke the grandmother's memories of her own child's sexual misadventures? Many family secrets may lay buried under three generations of myths in a family system where generational boundaries are undefined.

As a family art therapist, I am frequently called upon to perform a case management role when these families first come into treatment. Building an effective support network is an immediate goal. For example, Big Brother/ Big Sister programs can introduce the children to adults close in age to their birth parents. Extended child care can take some of the burden off the grandmother and involve her with community professionals and other parents. Parent support groups can help expand her knowledge of child development and effective limit-setting.

After casework needs are dealt with, I see grandparents and children together and use art work to bring the missing parent or parents "into treatment". Collage and drawings are able to evoke memories of old times, feelings never before expressed, and the anger and frustration both generations feel over being abandoned. Not until the absent parent has been recalled and made "real" through art can a grandmother fully assume the role of parent to the children. As the grandmother recalls her relationship with her daughter or son, the grandchildren acquire some insight into her loss even as they cope with their own. Communication often becomes easier when there is tangible art work to discuss. Miscommunications can be clarified as family members explain to each other what their art work means.

Two Heroes

There are all sorts of variations of human behavior that we therapists are privileged to observe as we share in the lives of our clients. There are methods of dealing with life's challenges which are more memorable than others; the two cases I will discuss were unforgetable. These two clients displayed sheer, unmitigated bravery—how rarely we are privileged to spend time with a warrior who keeps on fighting even when wounded and outnumbered.

Case I

The intake form indicated that my new family consisted of Chuckie, who was four years old, and grandmother, Esther, sixty-three, with whom he lived. Chuckie's preschool had drawn the line! Either Chuckie came to counseling or he was out. They reported that he hit and bit the other children, was noisy and over playful, and still enuretic at age four and a half.

Grandmother worked as a case manager in a residential facility for pregnant girls. She picked Chuckie up at the preschool every day and they went back to her tiny apartment. They had lived together since he was born; Esther was his legal guardian. Her daughter, Chuckie's mother, had moved to the East Coast when he was about a year old.

At our first session I opened my office door to greet the new clients and encountered a short, square package of dynamite that charged into my room and began a detailed inspection. Following at a much slower pace came a woman who appeared to be very elderly. She also was quite square, walking with slow, careful steps on legs and ankles that were markedly edemitus. She looked far older than the sixty-three years I had read on her chart.

Our relationship started on an uneven keel. Although our ages were not so far apart, and I had been a clinician for many years, I was a child in life's experiences compared to this client. However, she generously took me down the path of her life, and I admiringly listened to her tale.

Chuckie had started acting-out about three months previous to this meeting when he learned that he was probably going to join his mother, her new husband, and his two children in New Jersey. His beloved grandmother, who was his real mother in his eyes, was not included in this move. Every moment of his life (outside of day care) he had spent with Esther. They ate together every day and he decided what they ate. They watched TV together every evening and he decided what they watched. They took little outings on

Sunday and he decided where they would go. They went to bed together every evening and he decided on the time. I remember well when Esther reflected on how they each put on their diapers and snuggled down together for the night.

Perhaps this family script sounds unhealthy from a therapist's perspective, but I soon learned that her physical health was so poor and his physical energy was so great, and finances were so limited, that a great deal of this intimate way of living was inevitable. Esther recognized their enmeshment, Chuckie's behavioral changes, and her own limitations. She courageously told me that she knew she would not be able to care for Chuckie much longer. Her heart was failing and fluids were accumulating in her body. Her greatest fear was releasing the boy to the new husband and his children; she trusted her daughter, but would the others take in this "little outsider"? Since Esther had legal custody of the child, no one could take him away. However, she was concerned that he would be increasingly unable to separate if he remained with her during her declining years.

The task of therapy was to prepare Chuckie for (1) his first visit with his mother and new husband in Los Angeles; (2) if this meeting went well in everyone's estimation, to prepare Chuckie to leave grandmother to go to live with his mother and her new family.

The early sessions could only be described as stormy. Tasks involved: drawing the new home (which included the fear of the new Dad); drawing two homes, one here and one there (fear of the move); drawing school and what to do with fists (not hit). The drawings focused on as many of his little world circumstances that he could relate to, in hopes he could begin to comprehend all the changes that were in store for him (Figures 1 and 2).

During the course of therapy, Esther related some vignettes of her life. She was educated and worked in San Francisco as a young woman. When the hippie era began, she enthusiastically engaged in every drug on the market. Addicted to heroin and drinking heavily she soon gave up working and lived a casual life. Men came and went, some paid, some did not. She was in and out of jail until one day she found out that she was accidentally pregnant; she immediately became sober and produced a healthy daughter, Lilly. They lived together in the same symbiosis as I described with her grandson; Esther worked hard at manual labor and was their only support. They did resume drug use after the girl was older, but true to the family script, when the daughter became pregnant, both women became sober and remained sober after Chuckie's normal birth.

Shortly after Chuckie's birth Lilly met a man who, after a short time period, became her husband. Mother and daughter decided that her marriage

Figure 1: Dual drawing of new home, Chuckie's home

Figure 2: Dual drawing of new home, Grandma's home

would have a better chance if Lilly moved to New Jersey. Esther assumed full responsibility for Chuckie, although her health had been undermined by drug abuse, alcohol, neglect, jail, poverty, and self-sacrifice. Despite her health, she took loving care of the child; she also found a new job, never drank or abused drugs again, and spent most of her income on his needs.

The most striking aspect of this case was the tremendous selfless love that Esther had for her grandson. She said she never knew that she could care so much. Therefore, her major goal was to see him settled in his new home before she died. She put aside the pain of giving him up, the lonely years ahead, and her declining health—she only wanted the best for him.

She took her poor sick body to New Jersey to visit the new home and meet the other children. She was not graciously received there, although her daughter's husband was willing to take Chuckie in. Esther became fearful that he was too much of a disciplinarian for her grandson. While on this trip she observed that he was strict and structured with his own children; in contrast, Chuckie had never had even his slightest wish contested. Esther feared that Chuckie would not be able to thrive in this type of environment.

Over the course of six months we worked on all the issues of separation. The ongoing art task became to "create a book of memories" that Chuckie could take with him when he left. During each session we added drawings, collage, snapshots, and memorabilia from home and wrote a short "memory story" about an important event or situation. For a four-year-old it was important to stay with one task; to give the book permanence and importance required repetition.

The book was an agonizing task for Esther. Each page took something from their past and concretized it as a step toward separation. She knew that her love would be part of the child, but since he was so young, that memory might be overridden in the coming years. In contrast, the four years would have to sustain her into the future.

After Chuckie moved away Esther became ill and did not come to the clinic for some time. When she did return for a few visits to terminate, I could actually feel the grief in the room—it was palpable. She had lost a great deal of weight and aged ten years. I found myself worrying over her diet and her medical needs as well as mourning her loss. As Esther grieved, she found some small consolation in working on her own memory book of Chuckie. I was grateful I could give her all Chuckie's art work done in therapy as an addendum to her book (Figure 3).

In a few months Esther gave up therapy and tried to find some new direction by helping the girls she worked with find a better life. She identified with their pregnant, unmarried situation and was very understanding of the pressures that encouraged teenagers to use drugs and have sex. She wrote to Chuckie regularly, but seldom had return correspondence from his new family.

(Figure 3: Therapist mothering grandmother)

Case II

The second grandmother I will discuss is a woman who refused to cooperate in family therapy. She did come to the clinic from time to time when it was necessary to review plans and programming for her grandchildren. The clinic and I had some lively disagreements about how she was labeled; resistant, uncooperative and other negative terms were used. However, I had a different view which is supported by her responsibilities.

Alita was a young grandmother and at fifty-four years old she was keeping a part time job, caring for her schizophrenic daughter and the daughter's three children. Two of her grandchildren had difficulties, genetic and/or emotional due to the mother's disturbance and use of drugs during her pregnancies. The schizophrenic daughter was living with Alita while going to day treatment. Alita's oldest grandson, Leopold, attended middle school and was gang-oriented. Her next youngest grandson was severely damaged by cerebral palsy and required a great deal of attention because he could not talk or respond nor did he have any control of his body functions; he also required a special semiliquid diet and had to be fed. Amin, the youngest granddaughter, age eight years, had been diagnosed ADHD, due to her mother's crack habit during pregnancy; this child was very anxious about revealing family secrets and violent in temper.

Both Leopold and his sister were clinic clients. Leopold was in the early adolescent group, and Amin in the after school socialization program. The boy was my client and my first impression of him was memorable. He said, "My name has two meanings. Leopold means 'lion' and Leopold was a king—I'm both!" His lion ran with the neighborhood gang; his king came to therapy. The lion was brave enough to facer the rigor and rituals of the gang culture. The king, on the other hand, was capable and superior, coming to therapy only to please his grandmother and make me feel useful! He also came to the clinic to walk his sister there safely for her therapy sessions.

The focus at the clinic was on family treatment. Alita's daughter, Carmen, attended the day treatment program, but she was not capable of making decisions on any level. Therefore, we turned to the grandmother, Alita, for family sessions with the children. She refused to attend regularly and complied only when necessary. She did come to the first session and when the clinic treatment threatened to terminate treatment if she did not attend one family group session in the socialization program.

I met Alita several times and was impressed by her intelligence and energy. She had a youthful appearance, was well-groomed and had stylishly cut hair dyed a brilliant red. She clearly stated that she had enough to do and did not have the time to come to the clinic. She said she expected Leopold and Amin to share in the care of the disabled brother; she protected them from their own mother by having her sister, the childrens' aunt, come over on evenings when she went out to socialize. She had both men and women friends and enjoyed her part time job. When I considered her life-style, her high self-esteem, her feelings of being loved and expressing love that Leopold and Amin attested to in therapy, I decided that she did not need to hear our advice; in contrast, we needed to learn why she was so remarkable. Just to review her responsibilities and the manner in which she managed a schizophrenic daughter, the severely disabled grandson, and two emotionally distressed children, all with good spirits, is a lesson for us all to respect.

Therefore, this family therapy "failed" and I supported its failure. It also became one of my major learning experiences as a therapist—we must not impose our own cultural ideas of therapy when it is inappropriate.

Conclusion

In both these narratives the women were strong beyond normal standards, in my opinion. They defied the stereotypes of poverty, welfare-dependence, and irresponsibility. I consider them and their many prototypical sisters the real warriors in our society, fighting a war against social conditions without surrendering an inch of their territory.

If we try to limit our thinking to Ericksonian developmental cycles and the white, middle-class norms, we are not practicing therapy in the world of today. I think that if we were to take a look at all the developmental information and worn-out labels, cut them into confetti, and let them fall, we would have a more representative picture of today's society. Children grow up too early, becoming children who have children, and grandmothers raise not only their own offspring, but also the children of their children. Under these circumstances the life cycle does not complete a gratifying continuum; rather it spirals back on itself in ways that challenge therapists to take a new look at the generational patterns.

The number of families headed by grandparents is increasing astronomically; they now represent about thirty percent of my caseload of family art therapy clients. It is inevitable that families will experience great distress when generational roles are disturbed and one generation is missing. The combination of support from outside sources and the emotional relief offered through family art therapy can make a difference in the lives of these grandmothers and grandparents, breaking long-standing family patterns. I have great respect and regard for the grandmothers who assume the responsibility of raising their abandoned grandchildren; their burden is enormous. As one said to me in our last session, "I can't stop getting older and who will take them (the grandchildren) if I go? They have nobody but me".

ART CAPTURES THE IMPACT OF THE LOS ANGELES CRISIS

On April 29, 1992, long-standing unresolved frustrations, angers, and inter-racial tensions erupted into violence, arson, and rioting in the city of Los Angeles and across the nation. Triggered by the court decision concerning the police handling of Rodney King, protest and unlawful, destructive actions were set into motion. Involvement in the crisis was brought home to every citizen in a more personal way than ever before. Most of us were overwhelmed and traumatized by the unbelievable actions of the police seen in the countless television reviews of the Rodney King beating video. When the riots began, the media gave 24-hour exposure on every channel and brought the fires, looting, and the angry despair of the crowds into every home. Criminal and outraged reactions, positive and negative actions by citizens, and deeds of cowardice and bravery were all placed before our eyes for four days and nights of curfew and restricted activity. However one evaluates this extraordinary event, what is undeniable is that everyone felt as though they were on the frontline of this revolution.

We therapists were particularly disturbed by the feelings of emotional stress, helplessness and confusion experienced by our clients. For example, children were encouraged to loot with their parents, and those who did not saw others gain desired goods in this manner. The public also observed individuals who lost control and beat others without clear provocation, citizens who allowed their emotions to transcend reason. In contrast, others rescued

This chapter was originally published in a slightly different form in *Art Therapy: Journal of the American Art Therapy Association, 9* (3), 139-144 (1992) by Shirley Riley, Mindy Newborn, Yoko Takasumi and Jane Walter, and is reprinted with permission.

men and women from their cars or from fires without a thought for their own personal safety. During normal times, it is possible that one would not be able to differentiate between these "heroes" and "villains" if one saw them on the street. All ages shared in this extraordinary revolution of values and behaviors. In particular, the conflicting messages and the fear of danger and violence were beyond the life experience of the young and evoked terror and despair in the elderly.

Words alone cannot express the impact of the images evoked by this crisis: the fires, the mobs, the beatings, the angry faces of the crowds. For a fortunate few, the opportunity to explore these images and to find some words that helped to make some of the stress more manageable was provided by art therapists and art teachers in the schools and in the clinics. In addition, the city responded to volunteers who came into the community and offered workshops and time for expressive arts. The need for these services still continues and the interest in the therapeutic power of art has not been forgotten, although there is a denial and repression in the larger system which continues to ignore a long-term resolution of the core problems in this situation.

A selection of drawings done by children and adults after the L. A. riots is offered along with brief commentaries by each therapist.

Post Traumatic Stress in an Adult Client

Figure 1 is a drawing by my client, a 50-year-old woman who suffered many days of serious depression and dissociative reaction, when riots evoked in her the feelings of attack, fear, and lack of security; these paralleled similar feelings experienced in her youth. For her, red is rage and green is abandonment; hence, the fire and burning houses were experienced on an external and internal level in her red and green renderings of the riots.

Many persons with post traumatic stress disorders relived their traumas when faced either with the reality of the riots or the images seen on television. The visual impact of rage and violence evoked memories of similar situations in the lives of persons damaged or abused in the past. The riots became a powerful metaphor for their own painful experiences. The closer the destruction of the city to the real life experience of the individual, the more s/he suffered a reaction. In particular, abreactions and regression were stimulated in veterans of Vietnam and more recent conflicts.

I believe that many of us who had experienced slight or moderate trauma in our lives were also shaken by the incidents. I use myself as an example; my family was part of the Bel Air fire which took 600 homes, 300 in our immediate vicinity. During the riots, we relived that terrible experience

Figure 1

Figure 2

as we grieved over the damage done to people and property in our city; past and present resonated for many citizens, including myself.

Adolescent Boys in a Therapeutic School

Figure 2 was drawn by a 14-year-old Black/Hispanic boy, a client of Mindy Newborn, an art therapy trainee. He has spent most of his life in juvenile hall and foster homes. Both his parents have been in and out of jail for as long as he can remember. He repeatedly expressed his anger at being a poor Black male in a White society in which he feels victimized.

The day after the L. A. riots the boy was extremely angry because, as he said, "I wanted to go looting, but my aunt wouldn't let me". He was also angry about the police and their violent reaction toward African Americans in Los Angeles. He was asked to do a drawing about how he was feeling about the riots. Without hesitation, he drew a road leading to a burning city; on one side of the road there are signs warning, "At this point turn back", and "Welcome to L. A.". In the distance is South Central Los Angeles burning, with people running away. The other half is Beverly Hills; there are no fires and many armed police are guarding the area. He put himself in the center of the page on top of a sign warning, "Risky". The boy explained that, "the rich people in Beverly Hills get protected by the police just because they're white and rich, even though their buildings weren't on fire. The poor minorities in South Central get no help from the police while their buildings burn down." There was a disgusted resignation and sadness in his voice as he spoke about the riots. When I asked him about the Black fist rising out of the burned structures, he responded by saying, "We're fighting back. Just wait."

Figure 3, another boy's collage of a child floating through the sky, corresponded to his feelings of helplessness during the riots. When I asked him how that child might feel, he replied, "scared and alone". All of his drawings about the riots indicated feelings of isolation and sadness.

Figure 4 illustrates the work of an 18-year-old white male who has experienced physical and sexual abuse from the time he was three. He was placed in foster homes at the age of four and has been in and out of juvenile hall. He was extremely verbal and responded to the riots with feelings of outrage and anger directed toward the police. He was very proud of being able to get away with looting merchandise from some stores in Los Angeles during the riots. He said, "I looted because it was a chance to get a hold of things that I never get a chance to get a hold of. It had nothing to do with Rodney King. It was about, 'let's get what we can get and get out'. "

His drawing (Figure 4) shows Hollywood before and after the riots. His depiction of "During" shows his experience of looting at a Radio Shack,

Figure 3: "Scared and alone"

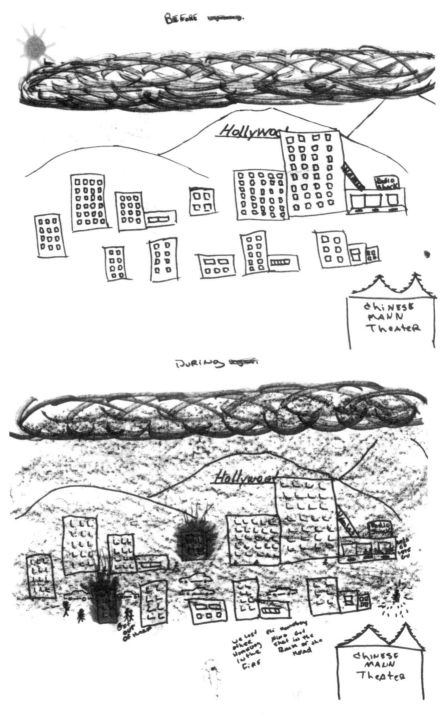

Figure 4: Hollywood before and after the riots

fires raging, and blunt descriptions of death and destruction. He said, "I feel hurt by it (the riots), but I also feel good because people were striking back".

An Outreach Program for Adolescents & Children

Figures 5 through 10 were drawn by adolescent girls during a crisis intervention session at Gardena High School, a part of the L.A. Unified Schools for pregnant minors. The therapist was Yoko Takasumi, LCSW, A.T.R. The teacher reported that these girls did not have much to say when she attempted to talk to them that morning; however, given the opportunity to express their feelings and impressions through images, they were able to express themselves dramatically. The art also stimulated verbal expression and discussion in the group. The students were asked to draw their impression of the crisis, including what they saw and how they felt. When they were finished, they were asked to title their drawings.

Figure 5, "Simi Valley vs. L. A.", drawn by an 18-year-old girl, expresses her disbelief and anger over the "not guilty" verdict for the Rodney King case. She also commented that because everyone was looting, it almost seemed OK to steal. The group related to her feelings of confusion and her mistrust of the justice and police systems. Some of the students also offered the explanation that they believed that the jurors were bribed.

Figure 6, created by a 17-year-old girl, is a composite of images which most impressed her about the crisis. "There were fires and lootings everywhere. The news crew was busy televising. All the markets in South Central L. A. were destroyed." This image also refers to the White truck driver who was brutally beaten by Black gang members, an image that became representative of the racially oriented violence. On the upper left corner is an image of Rodney King who spoke on television, pleading for peace. His words, "Can't we just get along" serve as the title.

Figure 7 titled "Corner of Florence & Western" drawn by another 17-year-old girl, focuses on the truck driver who was beaten. The brutality and lack of response from law enforcement frightened her.

Figure 8, drawn by a 16-year-old student, makes a distinctive statement about what it was like for people dependent upon welfare checks and food stamps. The government checks were not delivered on time because of the disruption of the postal service. When a few check cashing businesses reopened after the riot, everyone rushed to cash their desperately needed checks; the result was a large crowd with long lines. This picture reminded some group members of the feelings of panic they experienced while standing in long lines in markets miles away from their homes.

Figure 9, titled "Black Community is Burnt, Reconstruction Begins:

Figure 5: "Simi valley vs L.A."

Figure 6: "There were fires and lootings everywhere"

Figure 7: "The guy that got beat-up at the corner of Florence & Western"

Figure 8: Trying to cash a cheque

Figure 9: "Black community is burnt, reconstruction begins: we all learn

Figure 10: The mall burned up

This is the
bad man getting near
the house.

That's me
crying Out
there
burning the
house.

Figure 11: This is the bad man getting near the house

We All Learn", was drawn by a 16-year-old girl. The police vehicle arrives too late, trash and money are scattered about a ruined building while more fires are burning in the background. Her drawing skill does not match her cognitive awareness of the beginning reconstruction efforts. The group talked about how some store owners offered the looters whatever they wanted in exchange for protecting the building.

Figures 10 and 11 are samples from a second grade, orthopedically handicapped class at an elementary school in Gardena. Most of the children in the class suffer from neurological damage and are functioning below grade level. The teacher was very relieved when art intervention was offered to deal specifically with the riot, because she was unsure of how to help the children talk about their feelings. The children were asked to draw what they saw or how they felt about the unrest.

A 7-year-old boy saw the fire at the mall (depicted in Figure 10) when he went to Burger King with his uncle. He kept repeating, "This is fire burning, y'all". He did not stop until he had filled the entire mall with colors of fire as if he needed to discharge anxious energy. He finished off with blue, which he said was water.

Figure 11 was done by another 7-year-old from the handicapped class. He pictured the blackened figure as the bad man who sets the house on fire, and himself as crying. He kept laying on colors heavily for a long time, unlike his usual simple drawings with happy stories; the layers of colors may have reflected his own layers of anxiety.

This population of vulnerable children tended to personalize the trauma more readily than others, by internalizing the external events of the riots. For example, both boys imagined themselves as being in the fire. Art was helpful in this circumstance, expressing their fears and separating their feelings from reality. It was observed that children who were encouraged to externalize their inner distress over the crisis regained equilibrium more rapidly than those who did not participate in the therapeutic art activities.

Community Mental Health; Day Treatment Programs

Both Figures 12 and 13 were drawn in a community mental health center during the time of the uprising. The art therapist was Jane Walter, MA, A.T.R. This culturally-diversified clinic population experienced its share of the devastating effects of the turmoil, looting, smoke-filled skies, and tensions. One client, on her way to the clinic, was terrorized by a mob when they entered her bus with baseball bats, breaking windows and wounding a passenger. The damage and violence spread far beyond the inner cities; the tension and fear were experienced by all of Southern California.

Figure 12 was drawn during the third day of the uprising by an art therapy group of adult clients in an outpatient community support setting for the chronically mentally ill. Typically, this population experiences great difficulties joining with one another through art. Residual symptoms of their illnesses and side effects of medications are often evidenced by the clients through withdrawal, rigid defenses, and disconnected thought processes which impede the ability to link feelings to internal and/or external stimuli.

This group drawing reflects the degree of anxiety felt concerning the riots; this otherwise detached and withdrawn group attempted to bind together in a supportive circle of hands in order to provide comfort and create a safe place. Words were later added to the images and stimulated a discussion about the riots. One group member finished the group discussion by saying, "It is too bad that everyone can't come to the same conclusion about what our communities need to do".

Figure 13 was drawn on the sixth day after the riots during a children's group treatment program. This culturally diverse group was comprised of boys, ages 10 through 12 years, who were experiencing behavioral difficulties related predominantly to attention deficit disorder and oppositional defiance.

The group of boys was requested to "draw how the city should be rebuilt after the riots". The children took the directive one step further by

Figure 12: Adult group supporting each other after the riots.

Figure 13: "Draw how the city should be rebuilt"

offering solutions as to how the city could prevent future incidents of this nature from occurring. All group members unanimously agreed that City Hall was the most important building in the drawing. They reported, "It should be there to help people with problems and for keeping peace". Another group member retorted, "City Hall should also allow people to come any time during business hours to discuss the problems they are having in their community". Lastly, a boy commented, "Yeah, but City Hall also needs to listen and do something about the problems before riots happen again".

Postscript

My motivation for gathering these examples of art expressions made after the crisis was derived from my continued amazement and respect for the impact of artwork created by clients who normally have great difficulty in communicating their inner experiences. Through clinical contact and supervision, I observed how my colleagues successfully utilized imagery during times of crisis. It seemed important to me to share these drawings with art therapists and other professionals outside our sadly torn community of Los Angeles. It brings to mind the many other crises that have impacted the people with whom we work; these crises were more clearly understood when expressed by them through their art. If we art therapists ever need confirmation of how important our services are in the therapeutic world, moments like these reconfirm the unique contributions we make to our field.

Since this historic event, in 1992, Los Angeles County experienced the Northridge and Santa Monica earthquakes. It was interesting to observe that the stress-management county teams included art making as a needed component in all their interventions. The art was utilized to externalize the trauma, however, few art therapists had the opportunity to stay with the victims and provide sufficient time to process the drawings.

Nevertheless, we saw the acceptance of art as therapy throughout the immediate relief efforts offered to the public. Perhaps in the future it will not take a disaster to bring the attention of the community to the therapeutic value of clinical art therapy.

THE CREATIVE MIND

For many years art therapists -HLM have claimed that using art expressions in the therapy session helps the client reach their goals in a timely manner. However, the question of why this "making of marks" brings self-knowledge to the client has only recently been justified by some discoveries in the field of psycho/neurology, which will be lightly touched upon in the following discussion. As an art therapist I have become fascinated by the principles of brain-mind-body and I am convinced they provide the rationale for the use of imagery through the introduction of the language of art in therapy.

The following explorations are intended to enlarge the landscape of the practice of art therapy and to introduce some concepts from which our profession can profit.

The Nonverbal Beginnings

If we start by recognizing that in our first three years the world is experienced mainly through our visual and other somatic senses, before we are verbal, a clue is discovered as to why our mind finds image-making and image-recalling a natural state. Not until the corpus callosum comes on-line around the third year of our lives do the left and right brain have the ability to have a conversation. The acquisition of verbal ability begins to give names to the emotional life that we had known so intimately in our most formative infancy. Our somatic, kinesthetic, auditory, visual world now have words, but the basic knowledge of relationships and a sense of security have already been firmly laid into the memory banks and will remain as body knowledge all the rest of our lives. (Bowlby, 1969) It follows that visualization is not a stranger to our knowing the world, only that society has superimposed the value of words over imagery and we tend to disregard the information that is not "rational and explainable".

The capacity to first know relationships and environment without words and later on be able to name and evaluate our inner images, is to become an interactive human being. We are the only primates that acknowledge, or are able to verbalize, that the inner world is as important as the outer world. At least I have not heard to the contrary from our primate relatives.

I was further intrigued when I learned that the images that the brain holds in memory are no less real in our mind than the actual images the visual senses receive through our eyes from the outer world. Thus, in therapy we are not only examining with our clients their perceptions, but also their inner images that are inaccessible to us unless we offer tools that enable them to actualize those images.

The Brain, Images and Art Therapy

The potent ability of imagery to convey meaning and impact the discourse with greater import, has been a primary belief for art therapists. However, the mechanism of how we actually observe objects visually has not been of major concern. It becomes unreasonable to imagine that what you see and I see is identical after we learn how visual images are stored and retrieved in the brain. How we make choices and how emotions influence our decision-making is another puzzle. There are many more mysteries about our mind left to uncover, but I have been most intrigued by the use of imagery and the process of visualization.

I would like to digress and share a few quotes from some of the authors whose observations have made a major difference in the way I perceive my clinical practice and have added to my conviction that art is a viable language in therapy. Damasio (1994) has given examples of how some persons whose right hemisphere of the brain is injured, still seem to function without damage when challenged with purely intellectual tasks. However, their decision-making ability was repeatedly very poor. He (Damasio) explained that we need both the right brain's emotional intelligence and the left brain's intellectual (verbal) intelligence to work together in order to make successful judgments. Without the emotional input that sends signals of warning or confirmation, signals which remind us of how it "felt" when a similar situation arose, we do not have intrinsic memories from the past to help us make correct choices. Emotional feelings integrated with past decisions, either satisfactory or not, are signals that inform us to proceed or take care. Right brain-injured persons did not have this capacity. Therefore, these men or women would repeatedly make the same poor choices, as they lacked emotional intelligence from the right brain and limbic system interacting with left brain abilities. They were cut off from their emotional intelligence (Damasio, p. 245).

This translates, in the profession of clinical art therapy, into the ability to appreciate the creative process in a new manner (Malchiodi, 2002). When we ask our clients to project an image (right brain activity) and contemplate the meaning of the image (left brain activity) we are offering an opportunity for an integrated experience that can lead to new creative choices. As the client considers change, they can also attend to and make visible their emotions that are part of past experience and present responses. In the course of this process, all aspects of the decision-making process can be examined. (A caveat: there is not an absolute clear division between the processes of the two hemispheres. However, in general, there are areas of activity that are more active in different sectors of the brain that correspond to the above simplified explanation. In this paper the designations right and left are used as metaphors for the more complete explanation, which I quote below.)

> Siegel explains: In the right hemisphere are fast acting, holistic processes. This side specializes in representations such as sensations, images, and the nonverbal meaning of words. An example is the contribution of the right hemisphere for the understanding of metaphor, paradox, and humor.

> On the left side of the brain are the slowly-acting, linear, sequentially active, temporal processes. The left brain "packets" information as basic information. Our language-based communication is dominated by this linear mode of expression. This is quite distinct from the analogic representations seen in a artist's painting." (p. 179)

This information can be shared with the client in a form that makes sense in the context of how they are addressing their difficulties or questioning the mode of art therapy. When our clients ask about the benefit of artmaking, if they are able to understand a layman's description of the mind, they, too, will be excited about its potential. The issue of pathology becomes moot. As a therapist, I am also more excited about the therapeutic potential of this concept, and this stimulates and heightens my attention. In collaboration the client and I weigh their choices in the light of bringing forth the emotional signals as well as the rational information that are stored in the neurological imprints created in the present and informed by the past.

Images and Vision

Another amazing mind-brain activity is that of vision. We art therapists take for granted that looking at the client's art is a major part of sharing information in the therapeutic process (with the exception of special situations such as blind clients). We might assume that we, client and therapist, are both seeing the same art therapy image and have a mutually shared visual perception. Not true. Ramachandran (1998), the neurologist, informs us that we should let go of the notion that we have images in the brain and begin to think of symbolic descriptions.

I quote, "....viewing any object evokes a pattern of activity (in the brain). As we look at any object a different pattern of nerve activity is elicited, 'informing' higher brain centers about what you are looking at. The patterns of activity represent the visual objects but do not have any resemblance to a photographic image" (p. 66).

To confound us even more, we learn that there are sorting and discarding centers in the visual cortex where useless information is put aside and simplified— similar to how a cartoonist can imply a whole body with a few lines, relying on the mind to insert the rest. The edited message is then sent to over thirty centers that appear to be highly specialized for extracting different attributes from the visual scene, such as color, depth, motion, and the like (p. 72). Why is this information something an art therapist should think about?

If one believes as I do, that we are collaborative partners with our clients, then we must not make assumptions until we share our views. Now we have to be aware that since no brain is alike, we actually may not be seeing (visually) the identical client-created image until we have a dialogue about the product, and even then we can never see "exactly". Every image has a unique meaning to the artmaker, and now we are forced to accept that their vision is also unique. As Bateson (1972) said long ago "It is a difference that makes a difference" (p. 453). Therapists must now explore how the client "sees" the world before we can begin to hear their narrative.

Some therapists may not want to practice in a landscape that is so alien that the therapist must accept that seeing, knowing, and language are all unknown until they are described. Perhaps it is more challenging, but it is also more stimulating. If we are doing therapy by listening to our own words and seeing only through our own lenses, we might as well sit alone with our own projections and not confuse our clients.

Body Memory

Briefly, I would add the concept of "body memory", based on the notion that the body informs the mind and the mind informs the body— there is no division. For example, when a cold is coming on, we anticipate the heavy feelings of discomfort, lassitude and desire to retreat into a warm, safe place. Accompanying these symptoms is also often a state of mild depression that is part of the immune system slowing us down, and in most cases we react to these symptoms. On the contrary, in clinical practice we find some men and women who refuse to submit to this warning or simply cannot stop their routines to be ill. That form of denial is not unusual and most persons survive a cold. However, when the body advises the brain that all is not physically well on a more serious level, and the mind rejects the signals, we have troubles ahead (Sternberg, 2001).

If this is a chronic state of affairs, the client may benefit from an art therapy which provides a means to actualize messages sent by the body. For example, some of their physical feelings and the accompanying emotions could be indicated on a neutral (unisex) body drawing. On the simple body image the client could localize and acknowledge the pain or site of the disease and make decisions as to how to proceed with seeking help. The surrounding emotions concerning illness can also be projected onto the drawing. Emotional and physical states are not disunited. The drawing gives the client the chance to speculate where the resistance lies in acknowledging illness and the accompanying emotions that are stimulated. Recognition of this complex interaction between body and mind and the natural reluctance most persons have to facing illness will not produce a physical cure, but it may reduce stress factors that do influence the immune system.

Unattended stress and denial can undermine the ability of the immune system to successfully combat disease, while even more dangerous is denying the need to seek treatment. When a client can visualize the disease and feel they have some control over treatment, they may be able to take a more realistic approach to healing (not curing) their problem (Sapolsky, 1998).

Another form of body memory may be observed when an abused child may, in adulthood, still resist physical caresses. Since the earlier experience of physicality was harmful, the body reacts to touch as though it would be painful. The body has to learn to trust as much as does the personality. Art media cannot cure this grave situation, but it can introduce the subject of touch and pressure by examining a variety of media and exploring the associations the touch evokes. That could open the door to exploring the next level of reactions to kinesthetic stimulation and the earlier experiences of abuse. Past traumatic events often surface (often in drawings) and should be resolved, but not without providing a form of control that releases the experience of the trauma in controllable increments. A therapeutic procedure that allows a learned skill of self-regulation must be put in place. By allowing the trauma imagery to emerge gradually, and the intrinsic body memories to be safely experienced and then integrated into the here and now, the emotional/kinesthetic neuronal tracts in the brain can learn new patterns (Siegel, 1999, p. 221).

Art therapy is an action therapy, which, through the use of tactile and visual senses, provides the possibility to add body memories to the therapeutic dialogue. If the body memory evokes repressed memories of early trauma, then the imagery can be projected in a visible fashion and a controlled entree into painful recollections is possible (Van der Kolk, et al., 1996).

Language

Words have a life of their own as well. Each of us learns meanings assigned to words within our singular culture; the culture of the family and the culture of the surrounding society. As therapists we cannot assume that when we use words that our client attributes the same meaning to the words as we do. I often use the challenge of "imagine the word 'father'" to prove this point. No two persons will bring forth the same image, even if they are of the same family. Each family member will assign emotion and meaning to a "father" image in an individual manner.

The Mind-Brain-Body Synthesis with Art Expressions

So now we are in an unfamiliar world of therapy: the neurons in our brain are sorting and firing, our emotions are conversing with our intellect; our words are retaining individual meaning; our body is retrieving memories. It seems both our clients and ourselves may be in a foreign land unless we find a mutual language to facilitate communication. The task of exploring uncharted territory with everyone we see is exciting but also a challenge.

What do we do when we are lost in a foreign country? We buy a map, and ask questions. This notion seems amazingly simple, but we have the ability to do this in therapy as well as in an unfamiliar country. If, as therapists, we take a "non-knowing" stance (Anderson & Goolashian, 1985), are curious, and open to reading the client's map, we can enter into the imagery of our clients and wait to discover if our visions are similar. We can rely on the art images produced by the client to illuminate their vocabulary and we can continue the dialogue until we understand their significance. A rudimentary education in mind-body research can provide the rationale to regulate our reactions to our clients' artwork, and help us to be patient as we learn to speak the language of our clients. (Riley, 2001, pp. 236-252)

Case Examples

The examples that follow are taken from my practice and show how psychoneurology is not an esoteric theory, but one that can be used in both the process of assessment and in the practice of therapy. The language of art evokes reflections on the manner in which we know the world through our mind and our body. When the concepts of neuro/psychology guide the treatment the road map is not hard to follow, and my clients and I travel together.

MARY

My first use of this approach was with a bright and accomplished doctoral candidate in one of the major universities in our area. Her husband, who was eager to file for divorce immediately, had recently summarily abandoned her. Not surprisingly she was devastated and somewhat in shock since she still loved him in spite of his abusive nature. We spent some time with this issue of loss, anger, and trauma, and in due time Mary began to pay more attention to herself and her own reactions. Her approach to creating her reality was to analyze every thought and reaction, intellectualize her every emotion, and generally make herself more miserable. Mary had programmed an answer for every situation, answers that did not seem to make a difference when seeking solutions. Thus she raised her stress level by trying to reduce it with a purely factual evaluation.

As I was thinking about her exaggerated determination to understand intellectually exactly every process of her life, an image came to my mind. I wanted to share it with her. By now we were well connected, had a strong working relationship and Mary was used to my flights of fantasy in the sessions. Based on my confidence that she would not be thrown off by my strange way of communicating, I looked at her in a puzzled manner. "What?" she said. I told her that I was having an optical hallucination when I looked at her. "How?" she asked. "When I look at you I see a very strange shape to your head. The left side seems so distended and the right side is caved in and perhaps even atrophied! I wonder if your brain is causing this abnormality." Mary looked at me with that "come off it look". Then we both laughed and then became serious. We talked about the emotional intelligence of the right side of the brain, and the need for both hemispheres to work together to make successful decisions. There is no clear division of labor in the brain, but she had been ignoring the input from her right brain "emotional intelligence".

I had her look at Damasio's book, *Decartes Error* (1994), in which his explanation made clinical and neurological sense of my imagery. She made a drawing of the lopsided head and then created on the drawing a corrective surgical procedure. With scissors and glue she removed a piece of the left bulge and attached it to the right side, which then made a more normal balance and a metaphor for using both sides of her intelligence.

For Mary the notion of emotional input aiding her intellectual reasoning made a significant impact. In addition, she appreciated how the art helped her make a conscious effort to move from left brain to right, and then toward integration of both capabilities. Moreover, she understood that "left and right" was a form of metaphor for her neglect of her feeling by her rationalization and intellectualization. She started to slow down and listen to the messages that advised her to remember the feelings aroused when she made certain decisions, and the consequences when she disregarded the warnings from her emotional wisdom. It was interesting that this introduction of a new reality into her decision-making gave her the capacity to evaluate her past marital relationship more clearly. She allowed herself to feel all the past hurts and disappointments in that relationship, and she no longer was convinced that she loved her ex-husband in light of her new understanding. She had spent years analyzing why he operated the way he did, and forgot to check on why she was the way she was.

In our next phase Mary was focused on finding her own solutions and gave up trying to find answers for her exiting husband's behaviors. She described how tense she felt most of the time, at work or play. She said that "it was as if a spring was about to unwind and when it did (she) would fly apart". This imagery was an invitation to a representational drawing, one that she did with passion. Her "spring" was very different than my expectations. Instead of it unwinding with an upward thrust, it unwound downward. It pierced her genital area and shattered her boundaries, and then zoomed upward. This led to long conversations about her desire to have a sexualized relationship because that might unwind the spring and keep her focused on her doctoral research. She had had little success with this solution as she pursued men relentlessly and with little discrimination. The men she chose were not kind men and this resulted in even more stressful incidents.

The therapeutic dialogue was not making much progress until we turned to a discussion of how repeated stress, without a period of relief, builds up hormones in the brain such as glucocorticoids, until there are hormonal reactions that prolong the distress and diminish functioning rather than solve it (Sapolsky, (1908). Seeking more stress to alleviate stress didn't make much sense when translated into possible reduction of brain functioning. This information she related to her relational problems with men.

We looked at her behavioral patterns and ways she had decreased stress in the past; she remembered that she could sometimes "unwind the spring" with a contemplative hour at the seashore. The repetitive motion of the waves breaking on the sand calmed her. At that moment she opened her art therapy drawing pad and showed me her "wave" drawing. She said that after our previous discussion of psychological and physiological effects on the brain, she found relief in this representation, and subsequently found that recalling the imagery was sufficient to gain control over her "spring". She had found her way to self-regulate. Mary felt that when we had our discussion of the hormonal reaction to repeated stress she had gained a tool that appealed to her "left brain's" desire for knowledge. That information combined with a "right brain" appreciation of representations in her artwork enabled her to invent a new approach and secure a more serene tempo.

This is not to say that Mary was a totally different woman after this experience, nor did she or I want that to happen. What it did mean was that she used the language of art in her daily life; the images that arose she did not neglect and this, in turn, enriched her decision-making capacities. It was really delightful for me to explore with her my introduction to mind-body interactions, and see that it made positive sense to both of us.

DON

In this incident a young man was unable to verbalize his loving feelings toward his wife. She was quite frantic because, in her world, the sex act was a declaration of love from a man and was the cornerstone to her self worth. In her marriage she demanded the security, both verbal and physical, she lacked as a child. Don was terribly confused with his conflicted feelings of wanting to express his affection sexually, and his paralysis in doing so. The discord continued and the marriage was in jeopardy. A point of change was instigated when I asked him to explain how he had expressed his feelings growing-up. He said he was not allowed to show strong feelings and was sent to his room if he attempted to do so. He immediately said "I don't want to blame everything on my childhood. I have gone through all of that". What he hadn't gone through was the way the brain lays down patterns of behavior and responses to which we react even if we have "insight". (Siegel, 1998) We discussed this responsive pattern and the research that claims that patterns can be undone. We had a semi-scientific conversation of how neurons that fire together over a long period of time tend to persist in this pattern.

Don decided to draw his neurons and then redirect them. Somehow that drawing gave him the sense that he was in charge of his reactions. Later on he drew doors; open, closed, slamming, opening, a door theme that opened the dialogue to attachment theory. The drawings were rather fanciful, where the neurons were charging down to a hand opening the door. He refused to be "sent to his room" (emotionally) any longer. He could appreciate in a new way that even though he had been raised in a caring home the demonstration of affection was unavailable to him. Love was always at long distance. He was offering this same form of distant emotional attachment toward his wife.

His ability to be expressive came about slowly, but with some other way of understanding his dilemma he felt less self-blame. He could imagine changing brain patterns rather than feeling hopelessly deficient and condemned to remain that way the rest of his life. The language of art reinforced his mastery over a longtime habit of being reclusive rather than face rejection. This movement came about by being engaged in active expression, which tied to active change in behaviors. His wife realized that she, too, had to deal with her present-day expectations that were based on past interactions.

GERIATRIC GROUP

The last audience one would expect to respond to diagrams of neurons and neuron transmitters would be a group of elderly Alzheimer's clients. This proved to be untrue. In our early-onset group, where the members are in first or second stages of memory loss, we did some exciting work. A young doctor-student was visiting the facility to satisfy his community service at medical school, so we pressed him in as a co-therapist. I was eager to try out the notion, that these clients, who came from educated backgrounds— such as an MD, an accomplished actor, and a former CEO —would be interested and stimulated if they were offered a visual representation of the process of retrieving memories, and the damage that dementia inflicts on the process.

On a large piece of paper the medical student drew the neurons firing and explained what happens when a process, such as dementia, injures that sequence. The two other co-leaders helped the clients if they were having troubles hearing or needed some part of the discussion repeated. However, the group was absolutely fascinated with his explanation (which was scaled down to more simplistic terminology, but not avoiding real information). One man said, "at last I am getting some information here that I have been waiting for!" The members were then asked to respond by drawing how they thought their brains might look. This degree of response was a surprise to the staff, and led to a higher form of communication during the rest of the activities.

At the group's request we continued the medical discussion the next week. I asked our new medical co-leader to show how the brain informs the body and the body informs the brain. He made a great schematic, and gave a clear, simple educational talk as he drew the process. I felt that it was an important procedure to make visible the subject of body memory because there was such an emphasis on intellectual memory. The clients believed that when that skill diminished there was little left to help function. In this group most members had some motor retardation, some had less facility to direct their hand coordination, and others had well-functioning physical control, and all struggled with memory. They felt they were incompetent and had "lost it all" when they forgot a name or an event, they had never heard of body memory.

What we emphasized in this group was that if we lose one function we haven't lost it all. The body can have memories, as well as the recall sections in the brain. This idea was stimulating for the group, and they saw themselves through a larger lens than before. The discussion that followed was so lively that the director watching from behind the one-way mirror was amazed. The group appreciated that they had a variety of functions that could augment memory— if they lacked extrinsic memory, they still had procedural memory. In fact, in that regard, it was noticeable how polite and formal most of our clients were, most of the time.

We brought the drawings back for the next few groups and tacked them on the wall. We were curious to test if the information was retained. Much to our satisfaction, most of the eight group members had recall and positive emotional responses to the illustrations. However, it was necessary to have the illustrations to trigger the memories of the past session. This is another example where bringing a fresh reality into the therapeutic process can give unexpected payoff.

I have not yet had a negative experience in sharing these mind-body notions with clients, but also I have been very aware that, as with every intervention, it must be done with caution and in the context of the therapeutic environment.

IRENE

A brief description of the illustration displayed below: it is a brain drawing of a young woman who is struggling to become an "American" woman, while her family is determined to keep her in their Middle Eastern culture. They immigrated to the USA when she was a child. The drawing illustrates her dilemma, which we confronted in the early phase of treatment. In the drawing she chose those traits of her culture that she would like to keep, and she rejected those features that she disliked. She was desperate to discard the suspicious, judgmental behaviors that she felt her parents had taught her. She fluctuated between hysterical reactions and closed-down isolation. I was interested to note how her drawing concentrated her feelings all in one area of the right hemisphere. She did not show much intellectual consideration of the consequences of her behaviors in her daily living.

She said she needed to cut this inherited belief system from her brain, and would do anything to be happy. Therefore, we did a "lobotomy" drawing in which there was a blue image made at the base of the brain. I want to assure the reader that my pastels are not strong enough to be a surgical tool, yet, however strange this intervention may seem, it was fully directed by her and made a difference to her control of her circumstances. She used this metaphor to strengthen her move to independence by "cutting off" the old patterns and moving into a more cognitive, critical evaluation of her options.

Summary

Making an art form takes movement, tactility, vision, memory, and imagery, and, in the doing of this, all of the brain functions that I have mentioned are brought into play. The emotional intelligence is stimulated as the image retrieves memories and associations, while the process engages the cognitive capacities and self-regulators, as well. The drama is played out with all the senses adding texture to the dialogue. The therapeutic conversation can be wordless, or it can be through verbal metaphors that later become concrete expressions. With an attitude of freedom and willingness to be informed by our clients, we have a special form of therapy that can be useful to all ages of participants and can fit a broad range of difficulties. Learning about brain function may not change the way an art therapist appears to be conducting her sessions, but it requires a shift in epistemology that is reflected in the therapy (Kaplan, 2000, pp. 55-76). For me, it has provided scientific reassurance that reinforces my confidence in the value of adding the language of art to the therapeutic discourse. In addition, I am comfortable sharing some of this layman's knowledge of mind-brain-body with my clients. They in turn appreciate that their attention to their images and a synthesis of emotional and cognitive awareness is valuable and will likely lead to alternative solutions to old problems.

I have concluded that my theoretical stance can be summarized as a

"Postmodern, inter-relational co-constructive belief system, coupled with psycho-neurology and expressive arts therapies". It sounds complicated, but is practical and pragmatic and opens possibilities for new ideas in art therapy.

References

Anderson & Goolishian, (1985). Human systems as linguistic systems: Preliminary and evolving ideas about the implications for clinical theory. *Family Process* 21, 43-56.

Bateson, G. (1972). *Steps to an Ecology of Mind.* New York: Ballantine.

Bowlby, J. (1969). *Attachment.* New York, Basic Books.

Damasio, A. R. (1994). *Descartes' Error. Emotion, Reason and the Human Brain.* New York: Avon Books.

Goleman, D. (1995) *Emotional Intelligence.* New York: Bantam Books.

Kaplan, F. (2000). *Art, Science, and Art Therapy.* London: Jessica Kingsley.

Malchiodi, C. (ed) (2002) *Handbook of Art Therapy.* New York: Guilford.

Ramachandran, V.S. & Blakeslee, S. (1998). *Phantoms in the Brain.* New York: Quill William Morrow.

Riley, S. (2001) *Group Process Made Visible.* Philadelphia, PA.: Brunner/Routledge.

Sapolsky, R.M. (1998). *Why Zebras Don't Get Ulcers. An Updated Guide to Stress, Stress-related Diseases, and Coping.* New York: W.H. Freeman and Company.

Sternberg, E.M. (2001). *The Balance Within.* New York: W.H. Freeman and Company.

Van der Kolk, B., McFarlane, & Weisaeth, L. (1998). *Traumatic Stress.* New York: Guilford.

FAMILY THERAPY: ATTACHMENT, TRAUMA AND PSYCHONEUROLOGY

The last decade has confirmed the value of looking at the influence of the family on its members as a primary influence for life-long behaviors. This more recent confirmation of the influence of the family comes from research done in the field of neuropsychology. By the use of scanning techniques scientists have confirmed that the brain maturates in the presence of relationships, particularly the early relationships that are experienced (usually) within the family. The development of the brain and the formation of strengths and resiliencies have been demonstrated through the exploration of the early attachment patterns between child and caretaker. These patterns last a lifetime, although they can be modified through powerful relationships later in life. Given the recent proof of the impact of the first three years of an infant's life, we again look to the parent-child relationship for basic understanding of the individuals that comprise the family (Shore, 1994).

Because of the emphasis on family interactions as the formation of the basic skills needed to have a productive life, family therapy has added meaning and importance. Neuroscientists and trauma specialists can show brain scans that demonstrate how the brain is constricted under abusive situations, and family therapists can see scientific evidence in the brain of the behaviors that are the outcome of this abuse. It is important that the information in both fields of family art therapy and neuroscience be shared and since they compliment each other. I believe that family art therapist can greatly benefit from a beginners course in psychoneurology. Understanding the importance of attachment and the effects of trauma can sensitize the family therapists to aspects of the family system that may have gone unnoticed without this knowledge.

Attachment Theory and Neuroscience

Attachment theory and neuroscience explain, to a degree, why children in the same family have varying abilities to function successfully in relationships. We have a better understanding why buried memories of the environment in infancy set patterns in the present generation that then emerge in the families of following generations. In every family the primary caretaker (who, for reasons of brevity, we will call mother) reacts differently to each child she rears. Either by her (his) predilection or circumstances, child number two will have a different attachment experience than child number one, and so on through the family configuration. These patterns are handed down and subsequent relationships are unconsciously created on the template of the original relational model. The family has a general blueprint of beliefs, but the early attachment experience modifies that model for each individual, and gives the therapist the conceptual challenge of recognizing generalities and specifics in each family member (Bowlby, 1988).

When, in the family session, the members are asked to construct their autobiographical story, the parents are also invited to recall their relationship to their parents or even their grandparents. The narrative becomes thicker and richer as the historical illustrations and reflections continue in the family group. The importance of a congruent autobiographical narrative has assumed new importance. A congruent life story, or a disorganized story, assumes that the narrative arises from an individual who has had secure attachment or insecure attachment experience and will parent as they have been parented. Siegel (1999) proposes;

> . . .an attuned relationship would involve the following fundamental elements: congruent, collaborative communication, psychobiological state attunement, mutually shared interactions that involve the amplifications of positive affective states; and the ensuing development of mental models of security that enable emotional modulation and positive experiences for future interactions.(p.118)

Cozolino (2002) adds;

> Interestingly, the positive or negative nature of a parent's childhood is not the predictive feature correlating with his or her own child's attachment pattern. What does seem to matter is the coherence of the narrative created, not the exposure to trauma or loss during childhood. This strongly suggests that that the processing and integration of childhood experiences is the relevant variable in a parent's ability to be a safe haven for his or her children. (p.206)

With the creation of the Adult Attachment Interview by Main and her colleagues (1993), the family therapist has a new tool to evaluate the strengths and weaknesses that the family members bring to the therapy. Listening to the family story, and discussing the visual illustrations of the story, helps the therapist estimate how secure the attachment patterns have been in the family.

Systemic family theories referred to throughout this book do not suffer from incorporating attachment theory into a systems viewpoint. Most of the systems premises reinforce and demonstrate the validity of the recent knowledge even before there was clarity about the centrality of attachment and neuroscience.

Seeing the family together in session will give clues that are very difficult to discover in individual treatment. Since early attachment patterns are laid down in the first eighteen months to three years these experiences are stored in intrinsic memory, memories not available for recall later on. An individual in therapy may talk about their family but the information the therapist and client would like to explore about those early formative months are not retrievable. However, in the en vivo family session, the therapist can observe the interactions that are indicators of bonding and communication, and what one person cannot remember about the interactive relationships of his or her early life some older person in the family may. Art tasks that invite family members to work together as a group, or in dyads, can also help in the assessment. Cozolino (2002) writes;

> Recent research suggests that attachment patterns formed in childhood may be relatively stable into adulthood. They have been shown to impact experiences of romantic love, interpersonalattitudes, and the sense of self." (p.208). "Secure attachment represents the optimum balance between sympathetic and parasympathetic arousal, whereas their imbalance correlates with insecure attachment patterns. The balance of these two systems established early in life translates into enduring patterns of arousal, reactivity to stress, and possible vulnerability to adolescent and adult psychopathology.(Shore 1994, in Cozolino, 2002, p.209)

Seigel, (1999) addresses the issue "heredity vs. environment" throughout his book the Developing Mind, (p.23) He proposes:

> *The mind develops at the interface of neurophysiological processes and interpersonal relationships* (Italics mine). Relationship experiences have a dominant influence on the brain because the circuits responsible for social perception are the same or tightly linked to those that integrate the important functions controlling the creation of meaning, the regulation of body states, the modulation of emotions, the organization of memory, and the capacity for interpersonal communication. (p.21)

In light of these quotes from scientists that have been deeply invested in research concerning attachment and interpersonal relations, we must again return to the importance of the family where most persons first experience their world and form the neuronal patterns that are present throughout their lifetime. Family has to be interpreted in as broad a context as possible. The definition of the "family" in our society can be as expansive as can be imagined. The person or persons that are the caretakers, even institutions, become the primary influence on the infant. The theory of attachment and the theory of family systems reinforce each other, in both theories the healthy adjustment of the parent is seen to be reflected in the function of the whole family of which the child is the most vulnerable member. Within the family system the primary neurturing role may be shared by more than one person as well as the belief system reflected by the actions of the family members. In our society of varying economic stabilities, the chance of one primary caretaker taking full responsibility for the child is less certain than in some generations. However, if we look back historically and think of the prevalence of wet nurses and nannies in many of our cultures, we can see that our contemporary family is not unusual in their choice to share the responsibility of raising the child with many persons, even someone outside the family of origin. Parent education suggests that a stable relationship with the mother benefits the child; economic demographics suggest that that is often not an option.

The family therapist should understand the importance of secure attachment, insecure attachment, and disorganized attachment, and, evaluate what interventions would best aid the family to repair their relationships when there is a need. If necessary, the task may be to find ways to have the family compensate for unavoidable societal or economic difficulties that interrupt even the best intentions of the family raising children. Difficulties that are imposed by the external world require the therapist to deal with that reality as well as the resultant disorder to the internal system that impacts each family member. Fortunately, along with the research that validates the importance of early secure attachment, the neuroscientists have discovered that neuronal patterns can be modified throughout the life span. The family therapist who has restored stability to the family system has aided the possibility that there will be an atmosphere that allows attachment patterns to be established. It is unreasonable to imagine serene bonding in the midst of chaos

The importance of bringing the family, in every way possible, into the treatment session, either in person or in art therapy representations, takes on new weight when we read the serious effects the caretakers have on children. Shore (2003) states:

> The central thesis of my work is that the early social environment, mediated by the primary caregiver, directly influences the final wiring of the circuits in the infant brain that are responsible for the future social and emotional capacities of the individual. The attachment relationship thus directly shapes the maturation of the infant's right brain, which comes to perform adaptive functions in both assessment of visual and auditory socio-communicative signals and the human stress response. (p.112)

The responsibility and the treatment goal of the family therapists has become a central core in the attempt to give families an new outcome to the failed narratives of the past.

Psychotherapy

Psychotherapy can provide an experience that stimulates thinking differently about behaviors that previously were not questioned. As the family learns together new patterns of relationships the neuronal tracts that record these chemical and emotional responses are activated, while the old patterns become less automatic because of disuse. Cozolino (2002) reflects:

> Psychotherapy is an optimistic endeavor that demands the probability of change. . . recent research reflects   openness to the brain's role in all domains of human experience, including love, empathy, and spirituality. There is also new optimism concerning the brain's ability to remain flexible and to benefit from enriched environments throughout life. Psychotherapy is just such an enriched environment. (p. xiv)

In the art psychotherapy session communication between members can be constructed in ways that parallel positive interactions and are created in a manner that will encourage self esteem, modulation of mood states, and identification of automatic arousal processes. For example, if parents are helped to hold the gaze of their child briefly, and then look away for a moment, and then reengage; they engage in an interactive process that allows arousal, then repose, followed by a readiness to reengage. This enactment imitates an early attachment pattern replicated as a form of reparation of lost opportunities. This physical exercises could be followed by an art task created by the child and caretaker; a task that insures a positive outcome which, again, makes visible a reparative attachment activity (Riley, 2001, pp. 34-48).

Art Therapy

The family art therapist has the advantage of providing parent-client psycho/ education about the brain/mind functions by simplified illustrations, drawn spontaneously in the session, which can clarify complicated concepts. Equally simple explanations of how their interactions form neuronal patterns in all the members helps the family appreciate how important they are to one another. The focus on neurons and brain helps the family move away from reporting negative incidents and to form a focus that is a common endeavor. This by no means eliminates the more common techniques of providing opportunities to create alternative viewpoints and unique outcome narratives as a goal for family treatment. What is added is information that introduces new concepts to the family and explains some repetitive patterns that have become problematic. I have recently used informal drawings of the brain or the neurons firing, to as diverse a population as; a 7 year old girl dealing with her disturbed brother; adult clients struggling with relationship problems; and older persons confused and anxious about the diagnosis of Alzheimer's disease they received. They all responded with interest and used the information for themselves in ways that were productive.

Case Example 1

A 7 year-old girl requested her own therapy because her brother had "his" therapist. She lived in an intact family with two loving, intelligent, and sensitive parents who understood her unspoken need to have attention that paralleled her brother's. She is an unusually intelligent child and seemed developmental ahead and appropriate in all her reactions. Her only difficulty at home was a problem sleeping the night through in her own room without getting up to sleep on the floor of her parent's bedroom. What Susi was confused about was finding a rationale for her brother's autistic-like hyper-active behaviors which she sensed were not like other 9 year-olds. It seemed important that I find an approach that would deal with this situation in a way that a seven year-old could understand. The parent's gave permission to discuss this sensitive issue with Susi, which they had not been able to do up until now. My goal was to find ways to let Susi illustrate her emotions about her brother problems and for her to come to an age appropriate understanding of some of her brother's rather bizarre behaviors to which she was exposed daily. She was not sure if that was the way she was supposed to act, or if her perception that she was the "different" one, and that her brother was more acceptable to her family. She was not sure whether she was "different" or he was.

Figure 1 is a jar that holds her good feelings and her bad feelings. She identified each color as a particular emotion and where and when it occurred. The bad feeling was about her brother, Mark, when he couldn't settle down to play with her. She placed a lock on the side where she could open the jar and let the feelings out when she chose to.

Figure 2 is a drawing of emotions and where they are felt in the body. The lines that are wiggly are bad, when they are resolved they are straight. She could demonstrate where in her body she felt the stress and talked about feeling better when she could see them on the page. She needed no prompting to do this mind-body work that might be a challenge to others.

Figure 3 is my explanation of her brother's disability. I told Susi a story about how are brains function with electricity, and how we all need to have that "charge" to keep us thinking and moving. I then drew the two brains with lightening emanating from one brain, and soft electrical waves emanating from the other. Before I could ask a question Susi said the "lightening" brain was Mark's, the other brain was hers. We then discussed how he had a different "charge" that made him so jumpy,

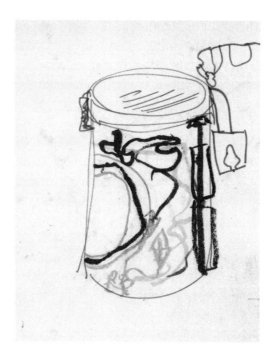

Figure 1: Jar of feelings

Figure 2: *Please go away*, Bad feelings are "loopy", good feelings are straight.

Figure 3: brothers' brain, left; 7 year old girls' brain, right

and she did not have to either try or be as jumpy as he was, or feel bad that he could not stop when she wanted him to. This was so clear to her that she could explain it to her parents and often went back to the drawing to refresh her memory. I felt it was a comprehensible explanation for a seven year old that was not pejorative of her brother, and opened the door for further discussions around the subject of self regulation, both his and hers. The parents were shown the "brain" drawing by Susi and they used the visualization in further talks with her when she had questions. Up to this point Susi had imagined (I believe) that in order to get the same level of attention as her brother from her parents, that she had to act as hyperactive as he did. This intervention allowed both parents and Susi a channel of communication that, up to this time, was extremely difficult. My intercession was stimulated by my readings of brain functions and neurology and reduced to a simple symbol that was based on reality.

Case Example II

A young woman of 30 had recently decided to divorce. She had been ambivalent about this decision for several years and spoke about her recurrent physical symptoms that overwhelmed her in the midst of her busy career. When the "attack" put her out of commission, she reported that her heart beat irregularly and fast, she had stomachaches, and felt like a "burning lightening rod" entered her body from the genital area to her throat. I matched these symptoms to the function of the vegas nerve that often produces these reactions under extreme stress, and she was very stressed. I speculated how I could share this hypothesis with her. We had approached her conflicts in many ways, but little relief had been achieved. She continued to blame herself for not solving all her difficulties immediately.

To shift the focus from her critical stance of herself to another field of action, we discussed the function of the vegas nerve and its relation to health and clearer cognition when the cortisol levels retuned to normal. (This explanation was only partially true in a scientific manner, but true enough to give the client a notion of how stress related activity can do damage to the mind-body function).

After this discussion we decided together to make the vegas nerve the client while she went on vacation from being hyper-anxious. My client drew the imagined vegas nerve within her body and illustrated the symptoms. She then drew a person with the same organs and nerves when they were in repose. She several times drew the non-functioning body under stress, each time making "corrective" marks on those areas where she had experienced distress. She felt she was taking over the automatic responses in her body and reducing the vegas nerve's control of her symptoms.

On her own she decided to visit the beach and contemplate the waves and the ocean, which had calmed her before, and then drew the sea and the motion of the waves in her art therapy journal. She felt she had created a "counter-stress" medication for her vegas nerve over-activity. She would go to this drawing when she felt herself becoming tense and it acted (she said) in the same way the actual waves at the ocean did for her. I thought it might be the semi-hypnotic action of the waves that may have been helpful. The rhythmic drawing of the waves sent the same relaxed feeling throughout her sensory organism, and perhaps was self-hypnotic. The client talked about this notion and agreed it was a self-soothing devise she had been utilizing over the years.

The client had externalized her stress-related symptoms and found her own solution, since she had moved the symptom from her inner world to the outer world where she could be active in their control and treatment. Other therapies followed, but the debilitating physical symptoms greatly diminished.

We agreed that the vegas nerve had been a responsive client.

Trauma

Traumatic events often bring families into therapy; this field has also made many gains over the last decade, particularly validating the efficacy of the use of non-verbal, visual communication for the primary channel for release of memories locked in the amygdala. Goleman (1995) writes:

> One way to get at the picture (of the trauma) frozen in the amygdala is through art, which itself is a medium of the unconscious. The emotional brain is highly attuned to symbolic meaning and the mode which Freud called "primary process", the message of metaphor, story, myth, and the arts. This avenue is often used in treating traumatized children. Sometimes the arts can open the way for children to talk about a moment of horror that they would not dare speak about otherwise. . . (p. 208) (The therapeutic avenue of art is equally valid for adults.)

Steele (2002) states:

> For children, as well as adults, traumatic   memories are encoded in images because trauma is a sensory experience rather than a solely cognitive experience... We must be able to see what children see as related to themselves and to the world around them as a result of their exposure. Drawing provides this opportunity to view the experience and see it as the child (adult) sees it. The art provides the stimulus for the victim to tell his or her story and in essence make us a witness to the fear, terror, worry, hurt, anger, revenge, accountability, and overall victimization. (p. 143)

The family is often the site of recurrent trauma. Either by neglect or abuse, meant or not, the child is the hapless victim of constant assaults on his or her safety. In a home whether caretaker is deliberately abusing the child, or is seriously out of tune with a child's needs, the multiplicity of the incidents that are traumatic lead to life-long damage. Among the many neuronal systems that diminish normal processing in the brain of the traumatized is a reaction that is specifically interesting to the art therapist.

van der Kolk (2003), points out that in a study of traumatized individuals:

> . . .there was decreased Broca's area functioning and increased activation of the right hemisphere. This would imply that is difficult for traumatized victims to verbalize precisely what they are experiencing, particularly when they become aroused. . . The person may feel, see, or hear the sensory elements of the traumatic experience, but be unable to translate the experience into communicable language.

> To help traumatized individuals process their traumatic memories, it is critical that they gain enough distance from their sensory imprints and trauma-related emotions so that they can observe and analyze these sensations and emotions without becoming hyperaroused or engaging in avoidance maneuvers. (p.187)

Helping the family by using art media to solve their shared trauma or that of an individual member, is neurologically valid as well as assessable to a layman's understanding of the process of trauma on the brain, and is more accepted since the traumatized victim has initiated the art expression. The fact that it has something to do with the amygdala is inconsequential to treatment, unless later on the therapist feels that an explanation can further the goals. (The neurological interest is held by the therapist). Art Therapy can approach the traumatic experience non-verbally and allow the person to gain the distance from the experience before the process of verbalization and the route to integration. Art can open the way for intrinsic memories to surface through the image, even, in some cases, memories that were acquired before verbalization during the first two years of life. The earliest memories are often carried as body memories and have no verbal translation. The more we are aware of why the addition of art to the therapeutic conversation makes sense neurologically and physiologically the more we can continue to explore new frontiers and broaden the rationale for the use of art therapy. The recognition of the serious impact of low-grade, but multiple traumas, have on children makes us pay closer attention to family systems or early environmental stressors. The life long damage is greater than was considered some years ago.

There are many approaches to helping a person through their traumatic experience which are not useful but have become a part of the general belief system. These approaches need to be avoided (van der Kolk, (2003), p.173). The therapist can educate the family and bring the proper approach to healing into the support system that is needed by the traumatized member. An educated family can be helpful, one without knowledge can be well meaning but destructive to the person's recovery.

The Art Therapist

The additional advantage for the family therapist to acquire some education of brain function and the recent advances in attachment theory is to broaden concepts for the therapist herself. Scientific information has not always been welcomed in the art therapy community. Malchiodi (2003) reminds the art therapist that;

> Art therapy has historically resisted an association with science and favored a more art based stance in its philosophy and practice. However, recent scientific findings about how images influence emotions, thoughts, and well-being, and how brain and body react to the experience of drawing, painting and other art activities are clarifying why art therapy may be effective with a variety of populations. As science learns more about the connection between emotions and health, stress and disease, and the brain and the immune system, art therapy is discovering new frontiers for the use of imagery and art expressions in treatment. (p.1)

Family art therapists in particular should feel comfortable with the material referred to above since the foundation of attachment and brain formation lay in family interactions which is their field of interest. Not only is it responsible to keep up with the advances in the mental health field, it is also stimulating and creative to find ways to share this knowledge with the families served. In the hands of an educated therapist imagery can help in the readjustments of relationships, and art tasks can modify archaic learning by encouraging right-left brain activity, and discussions about the client's imagery can bring change into the awareness of all members of the family. Family therapy has always been an economic approach to therapy since it helps many persons simultaneously, now the therapist can be even more efficient as he or she becomes more educated.

For the family art therapist this is a time when the neropsychology of mind-brain-body integration can bring new confidence in the efficacy of promoting art tasks, imagery, and conversations about the art product. Understanding why the use of art in the conversation makes the family sessions more useful brings an air of assurance into the art therapy field, which benefits art therapists as well as their clients.

References

Bowlby, J. (1988). A secure base; Parent-child attachment and healthy human development. New York: B asic Books.

Cozolino,L. (2002). The neuroscience of psychotherapy: Building and rebuilding the human brain. New York: W.W.Norton.

Malchiodi, C.A. (2003). The handbook of art therapy. New York: The Guilford Press.

Riley, S. (2001). Group process made visible: Group art therapy. Philadelphia, PA.:Brunner-Routledge.

Riley, S. & Malchiodi, C. A. (1994). Integrative approaches to family art therapy. Chicago, IL: Magnolia Street Publishers.

Shore, A.N. (1994). Affect regulation and the origin of the self: The neurobiology of emotional development.. Hillside, N.J: Erlbaum.

Siegel. D.J. (1999). The developing mind: Toward a neurobiology of interpersonal experience. New York: The Guilford Press.

Solomon, M.F. & Siegel, D.J. (2003). Healing trauma: Attachment, mind, body, and brain. New York: W.W. Norton.

Steele, W. (2003) Using drawings in short-term trauma resolution. (in) C.A. Malchiodi. Handbook of art therapy. New York: The Guilford Press.

Recommended Reading

Damasio,A.R. (1999). The feeling of what happens: Body and emotion in the making of consciousness. New York: Harcourt Brace.

Sapolsky, R.M. (1999) Why Zebras don't get ulcers. Stress, stress related diseases, and coping. New York: W.H. Freeman & Co.

CHANGE: THE REALITIES OF
THE MENTAL HEALTH PROVIDER'S WORLD

An article in a Los Angeles newspaper reviewed the state of affairs concerning the 1.75 million children living in poverty in the State of California as well as the 48,000 in foster care. Proper care was found to be sadly lacking and in fact diminishing. The funds that support family and child services and mental health for general programs that come from both state and federal levels is rapidly eroding. The population that was formerly housed and served by hospital settings is now directed to find help in outpatient clinics. The clinics, in turn, are urged to do short-term therapy with only severely disturbed people and to disregard pleas for preventative work. To make the circle complete, many hospitals are under-utilized because they require insurance coverage to pay for the cost of service and insurance companies are cutting back payments. As the brunt of demand for treatment falls on the community mental health centers, they are caught in the bind of providing services in response to dollars rather than patient needs.

For example, if the clinic has received a grant for families with child abuse, those are the families served. Other families with equally serious problems are put on a waiting list that moves at a Dickensonian speed through the system. The novel *Little Dorrit,* by Charles Dickens, reflects our current welfare system in a way that seems almost prophetic. Dickens emphasizes how poverty breeds isolation, which in turn leads to an impasse of paperwork and bureaucracy preventing any attempt to escape poverty. This struggle reduces the individual to a state of helplessness and prolongs the poverty it

This article originally appeared in a slightly different form in *Art Therapy: Journal of the American Art Therapy Association*, 6 (3), 99-102 (1989) and is reprinted with permission.

supposedly was designed to remedy. The incredibly slow pace of governmental agencies and social services compounds the despair of the person trapped in the system.

In addition to these hard facts, this neglect often leads to more severe problems. In Los Angeles we have the ever-widening influence of drugs and gang violence moving from the inner city and permeating the whole population of the metropolitan area. Drugs, crime, and broken homes are not special only to Southern California, however. Across our nation we have many areas where mental health workers in a dysfunctional system attempt to give aid to persons overwhelmed by all-too-powerful and adverse agencies.

The situation today is one which forces us to evaluate our standards and to question the following areas: 1) Are we training therapists in our educational settings to deal with the real world? 2) Have we modified our theoretical base and therapeutic techniques to be as effective as possible, given the populations we serve? 3) Are our national professional organizations (such as the American Art Therapy Association) recognizing and supporting the changing demands on mental health clinicians?

As a family therapist who has been employed by the same community mental health center since 1975 in their Family and Child division, and who has taught in a master's level clinical art therapy program for approximately the same length of time, I would like to share some thoughts on these three areas that affect our future.

Education

The challenge for educational programs training at the master's level is to maintain the ground work required in the core curriculum adopted by the American Art Therapy Association as well as address the content that is necessary for state licensing requirements. It may be that we have to increase the educational subject matter covered in our art therapy programs to prepare students for new demands placed on them in practicum. The intern must bring to the practicum a much broader knowledge than was needed in the past. S/he will be exposed to more severely pathological clients earlier in his/her training and will need broader support systems.

In addition, somewhere we must find the time to educate our students on how to deal with some of the issues listed below:

1) **A greater emphasis on and familiarity with legal matters**. Well in advance of practicum, students must understand all reporting laws that concern abuse. The ethical responsibilities for child and elder abuse and laws protecting clients who are threatened or are threatening violence are quite clear. However, the responsibility of the therapist in legally protecting her/

himself and the client, especially in cases where the records may be subpoenaed for child custody or in contested divorce, is an area that is rarely discussed in class.

There are different approaches to the issue of how much clinical observation or second party reporting should be entered into progress notes. If the therapist is called to court and held accountable for incidents written into the record, the whole matter of confidentiality has to be considered. Each agency has a policy and, hopefully, legal counsel to advise and deal with these contingencies.

Students must be educated how to ask for help if they are called to court, but better still, to ask for instruction on how to avoid going to court unless it is absolutely necessary. If the art therapy product is regarded as part of the case record, the students should be very clear what they can say about the art expression and how much of the client's verbal references they remember or have recorded regarding each art task. Emotional and psychological support should be given students when they anticipate having to give testimony in court or have dealings with attorneys seeking information. Their status in a court battle or the pressures that may be brought to bear on them is not part of what we usually discuss when advising students about their training in the field.

2) **Training the clinician in self-protection**. From 1988-1989, the state of California eliminated eighteen million dollars from the mental health budget and has continued on this path into 2004. These cuts resulted in the closing of many centers that cared for severely and chronically mentally ill patients. When these unfortunates became street people, needing medication, having no place to turn where their level of disturbance could be monitored, often these multiple difficulties resulted in an outburst of violent behavior. In February 1989, a counselor was stabbed to death by a patient who felt frustrated by the system. Of course, that was not the first time that a therapist was placed in mortal danger as a result of the uncontrolled behavior of a client. However, what is so painfully apparent at this time is that the safety devices that might be life saving such as a panic button system or a security guard, cannot even be developed since there are no funds to implement them.

What should training programs do? Paint and markers are not a defense against guns. We must teach our students the procedures regarding self-protection as well as techniques in restraining violent people. We must alert them to defend themselves against the dangers in society: the neighborhood, working late hours, the necessity of having colleagues close by. Informally, therapists can provide a guard system for one another. A class on self-protection like this may be more valuable than any one of us can imagine at this time! If the school cannot provide this service, the intern should be encouraged to request training from the agency or hospital.

3) **Recognition of client behaviors that suggest substance abuse**. Another area that can be addressed by education is the recognition of the common use of street drugs by clients. The treatment of persons who abuse drugs can be learned from texts, other clinicians, and in supervision. However, what is often missing is help in learning to quickly recognize the behavior of a client who is high on drugs or experiencing hallucinations due to a chemical reaction. Other clients may be unable to think clearly because of drug-induced brain damage and therefore act irresponsibly. Learning to recognize when a client has used alcohol or street drugs or both, and signs of chemical imbalance, is a course that could be titled "Saving Your Life". This title is facetious, but self-protection and awareness of potential violence in mental health settings must also be part of our curriculum.

New Techniques and Goals in Treatment

The second section of this chapter examines therapeutic techniques adapted to the changing populations seen in mental health settings; it examines a more personal, individual concern. Each therapist is challenged to move from tried and true formulae for treatment to unexplored and unfamiliar interventions. This shift is not always desired by the practitioner. However, regularly reexamining the theoretical, technical, and creative approach to performing therapy is a task even more important than it has been in the past. If society, the economy, and the increase in violence have radically changed the world in which our clients live, how can we assume that the "old way" we have worked with people will continue to be effective? It is up to each therapist to consider how, or if, modifications in technique and theory could enhance his or her effectiveness with patients.

For myself, the struggle has always been my reluctance to fit everyone I see into a crisis or short-term therapy framework. However, I have very little choice in this matter, except in private practice, because the clinic has a state mandate to limit treatment and to set short-term goals. This is not always successful, and it is unrewarding and disappointing to offer a service that appears inadequate in meeting the needs of the client. However, my responsibility is to find the most effective approach to brief therapy that fits my belief system and, more importantly, is responsive to my clients' goals.

A few techniques that I frequently use are identified below. Each art task and construct is designed to enrich a limited once-a-week treatment schedule and to keep the clients' attention focused on alternative solutions to their problems.

288

First, I use many more art therapy homework tasks. Often I suggest an art therapy journal which will focus on helping the individual(s) observe their own and their families' patterns of behavior. That task may be coupled with a prescribed family ritual, formulated to interrupt redundant behaviors. Thus, the individual has his/her own focused task and the whole family joins together in different ritualistic tasks. This has proved to be fairly effective, particularly because the art work has a therapeutic component all of its own. This, in conjunction with the active participation required in a family ritual, is useful.

For an individual I may prescribe a ceremony that requires the person to construct a small box (usually one created in the therapy session) dedicated to the storage of a specific emotion, e.g., anger. Each morning the client is instructed to draw the anticipated situations during that day that will evoke angry reactions. These quick drawings are then placed in the box for safe keeping. The client is asked not to stop being angry, but to store it in the box for one tremendous blowout at the clinic. This massive discharge (which rarely happens) could be channeled into an art piece that expresses anger visually, with the therapist providing safety and containment.

For families, any ritual that I would suggest would be specifically tailored to their problematic behaviors. Therefore, it is difficult to generalize regarding how it should be designed. In one instance, I encouraged both parents to get up at 5:30 a.m. and enthusiastically insist that their daughter have her temper tantrum early in the morning. In that way they would have it behind them and could proceed with the day's activities. This procedure successfully failed as the parents substituted other limits rather than the "dawn patrol", to quote the father.

These hometasks are generally designed to highlight the undesired behaviors and place them in a new time frame as well as emotional context. Under these changed circumstances, the behaviors are usually discarded. For example, the aversive circumstances (5:30 a.m.) and prescribing the symptom (the tantrum) are the underpinnings of reframing the symptom-saturated interactions.

To simply prescribe a period of time to talk to each other does not impact the family sufficiently to invite compliance. To ask them to order their favorite pizza, turn off the TV, sit around a table, and *not* talk to one another is more likely to result in their "breaking the rule" and talking. The question is *what* will they talk about. If it is only blaming, this is not a profitable move. To inhibit a blaming session, the therapist could prescribe blaming one day and praising the next, observing that it is a gesture of giving attention to another rather than the self. This could be encouraged as a enactment within the session, to "practice" blaming. A shift in interpretation of a behavior allows new material to enter into the family interactions. The next move is to turn blame into a positive action and then bring it back to self-evaluation which is now no longer a negative attack.

I developed a second technique in response to my own confusion in keeping track of the chaotic life histories of many of my clients. A large percentage of the older adolescent youths whom I see in treatment have lived more lives in their limited years than most of us ever will. They have "done it all" by age sixteen. Also they have begun to say "no" to a variety of toxic substances. The one "no" they cannot control is the "no" that their parents must say for themselves to their own addictions. Many adolescents and children have, to all intents and purposes, lost their parents to the streets, to drugs, or to jail. Often these youths survive in spite of the neglect, some more successfully than others.

I felt that a technique was needed to enhance understanding and appreciation of the catastrophic events and traumas my patients had survived. By drawing on a long scroll of paper, a chronology of their life is recorded. By reliving the events of their life through art and gaining some psychic distance, they can achieve some overview of their strengths as they struggle with adversities. Teenagers also can see how they were too young to have the power to change many of their life events. This experience of reliving their own history generally offers an opportunity to relinquish guilt and to mourn and later cease to resent the parents who failed them. The scroll becomes a visible record of a battle that has been successful and a journal of triumph over impossible challenges. Thus, an important goal may be reached by these young people as they gain a sense of self-worth and personal pride in their endurance.

Perhaps the greatest change I have experienced over the last few years has been the manner in which I view a family constellation. I rarely see an intact family, in the traditional sense, of a married couple with children living together with long-term commitment. For example, the emergence of a grandparent as parent (and often an unwilling parent for several reasons) is a common family configuration. This often leads to a situation where a youth actively seeks a home environment less stressful than the grandparent's home; this may be manifested by running away. I have supported that activity if I feel that I can set up a system where the client lets the grandparent family know where s/he has run in exchange for reducing the demand that they return home. This encouragement is given sparingly and only on a case-by-case basis.

A case example: An adolescent whose mother and father were entirely out of the picture lived with her grandparents who were chronic, but not violent, alcoholics. There was no alternative living situation other than foster placement, which would have been more destructive. The girl found a friend who would take her in, and, with the grandparents' consent, I supported this "run away". During this search for a home many of her friends rejected her, but she persisted until she found a pseudo-foster home for herself. The grandparents approved of the family and were relieved to give up the responsibility of her care.

Often in a case like this the weekly therapy session becomes the only time when grandparents and grandchild can meet on neutral ground and examine issues within the protected environment of the clinic. Helping the grandparent to help the child "run away" keeps a relationship alive and provides both generations with a feeling that they have maintained some power while preserving their attachment. "Running away safely" is the treatment goal.

There are many other situations where I can only provide limited services because the larger system has more control in the patients' lives than I have. For example, I see a foster mother and eight foster children in a family group session. Each of these boys and girls has a history of abuse and neglect that would qualify him/her for individual therapeutic attention. However, considering that they will live together as long as the court allows and that the clinic would be hard pressed to find eight individual hours for these needy children, we do family group art therapy. It is extremely useful that each member can draw about his or her own troubles and also about mutual attempts to reduce stress in the foster home. I do not feel that this is poor treatment, but I do feel a sense of helplessness when a child is removed from the foster family by the court and there is no opportunity to clarify any progress or to deal with separation. So again, therapists are confronted with compromise and questions concerning choices of treatment.

Throughout all the examples cited above, and in many other cases too numerous to mention, the one constant has been the use of clinical art therapy. More than ever the clients need permanence and a safe place to be expressive. The real and metaphoric values of externalized expression of problems through art that can be brought to a future session or taken home as a transitional object, have proven worthwhile. Another component of an art task lies in the duplicity of the work. Many families are court-ordered into treatment and are therefore resentful and resistant to treatment. When they are asked to engage in expressive activity, it is my observation that they are often more compliant. The pleasure component in working together with media, keeping eye contact to a minimum as they focus on the drawing, provides a more positive experience for the reluctant client.

I believe that each of us has an arsenal of creative ideas which will result in the therapeutic modifications we desire. If the real world of clients is acknowledged and incorporated within the framework of treatment, there may be a greater success rate for the families as well as increased satisfaction for the clinician.

State and National Professional Organizations

The individual therapist seeks support and confirmation from peers and the group that represents him/her professionally. If there is a lack of awareness on the state and/or national level of life on the frontline of mental health service, there will also be a breakdown in understanding the needs of the professional practitioner. Rather than maintaining a stance that is separate from other mental health disciplines, it would be useful to be educated as to the manner in which all the disciplines are changing. State and national professional conferences can no longer dwell solely on clinical presentations, but should give participants practical information: how to write grants, where to find legal advice, how insurance coverage has been challenged, how to lobby, etc.

The AATA should be particularly courageous in these areas, taking the position of leading the members into professional changes that may be unpopular or uncomfortable for many, but necessary. Of course, these changes cannot be legislated without due process, but the members must be clearly informed if there is a threat to their future by neglecting to take a certain action. The leaders who have been elected by the membership must also be willing to research the current climate of the mental health community at large and inform members about the steps necessary to protect their economic as well as their human lives.

It is important that the art therapy journal and professional publications publish material that reflect new trends in mental health. Learning about changes in therapeutic theories and techniques is not only intellectually challenging, but at times an economic necessity. An art therapist who is unaware of current directions in the field of mental health is at a disadvantage when interacting with other professional colleagues. Publishing the contemporary speculations on treatment allows the practitioners in our field to examine theories and to make decisions about their validity. The irresponsible position is not to take the chance of exposing readers to what may, in the long run, be "trendy". The market place is interested in hiring individuals who are cognizant of current trends and talk intelligently about them with other professionals. By being aware of various forms of treatment, therapists may then justify the individual choices they have made to be effective therapists.

Cultural diversity is another growing factor in our society. The national organization must be willing to demand fair representation of all ethnic groups on its various administrative committees. If the membership has not elected persons who can voice the concerns of minority groups, then consultants can be brought in to enlarge the world view of the executive committees. There are many other solutions which may be more inventive, workable, and answer this need. These solutions will not arise spontaneously, but must be nurtured by leaders on a national and local level.

In the long run the national and state art therapy groups must change their thinking from linear to systemic. We can start with students in our training programs, who eventually graduate and join the ranks of the mental health service system; these graduates will interface with the larger social system and will be supported and informed by their own state and/or national professional organization. All of these worlds are interlocking and cannot be viewed as functioning independently. This concept is not original nor unique, but to adopt and practice this viewpoint seems to be difficult for many students as well as professionals.

Summary

The day the mental health worker was stabbed to death in Los Angeles a ripple effect started, impacting the entire state of California mental health services as well as highlighting both economic and moral awareness of our profession. My hope is that through education, professional techniques, and social awareness, and guided by the direction and support of state and national professional organizations, we can start a serious movement toward change. The only real armor against fear is knowledge; knowledge of how to stay alive and useful in a system that at this time in history seems to be threatened. The struggle is worth the price and invites growth and change, providing another challenge for each art therapist's creativity.

Bibliography

Ackerman, N. J. (1966). *Treating the troubled family.* New York: Basic Books.

Ackerman, N. J. (1980). The family with adolescents. In E. A. Carter & M. McGoldrick (eds.), *The family life cycle: A framework for family therapy.* New York: Gardner.

Ackerman, N. J. (1984). *A theory of Family systems.* New York: Gardner.

Allman, L. (1982). The aesthetic reference: Overcoming the pragmatic error. *Family Process, 21,* 43-56.

American Art Therapy Association. (1990). *Code of ethics.* Mundelein, IL: Author.

Anderson, H., & Goolishian, H. (1988). Human systems as linguistic systems: Preliminary and evolving ideas about the implications for clinical theory. *Family Process, 27,* 371-394 and 43-56.

Anderson, H., & Goolishian, H. (1990). Beyond cybernetics: Comments on Atkinson and Heath's 'Further thoughts on second-order family therapy', *Family Process, 29,* 157-163.

Anderson, W. T. (1990). *Reality isn't what it used to be.* New York: Harper & Row.

Andolfi, M., Angelo, C., & de Nichilo, M. (1989). *The myth of Atlas.* New York: Brunner/Mazel.

Andrus, L. (1990). Art therapy education: A tool for developing verbal skills. *Art Therapy: Journal of the American Art Therapy Association, 7.*

Bateson, G. (1972). *Steps to an ecology of mind.* New York: Ballantine.

Bateson, G. (1979). *Mind and nature.* New York: E. P. Dalton.

Bateson, G., Jackson, D., Haley, J., & Weakland, J. (1956). Toward a theory of schizophrenia. *Behavioral Science, 1,* 251-264.

Beach, S., & O'Leary, D. (1993). Dysphoria and marital discord: Are dysphoric individuals at risk for marital discord? *Journal of Marital and Family Therapy, 19* (4), 355-368.

Berger, P., & Luckman, T. (1966). *The social construction of reality.* New York: Anchor Books.

Bing, E. (1970). The conjoint family drawing. *Family Process, 9,* 173-194.

Black, C. (1981). *It will never happen to me: Children of alcoholics.* Denver: MAC Publications.

Blos, P. (1962). *On adolescence: A psychoanalytic interpretation.* New York: MacMillan.

Bonnefil, M. (1977). Crisis and diagnosis: Infantile autism. *Clinical Social Work Journal, 4* (4), 276-288.

Bowen, M. (1978). *Family therapy in clinical practice.* New York: Jason Aronson.

Bowlby, J. (1969). *Attachment.* New York: Basic Books.

Bross, A., & Benjamin, M. (1982). Family therapy: A recursive model of strategic practice. In A. Bross (Ed.), *Family Therapy: A Recursive Model of Strategic Practice* (pp.2-33). New York: Guilford.

Byng-Hall, J. (1988). Scripts and legends in families and family therapy. *Family Process, 27,* 167-180.

Carter, E. A., & McGoldrick, M. (1980). The family lifecycle and family therapy: An overview, in E. A. Carter & M. McGoldrick (eds.), *The family lifecycle: A framework for family therapy.* New York: Gardner.

Cassano, R. D. (1989). Multi-family group therapy in social work practice. *Social Work with Groups, 12,* 3-14.

Cassano, R. D. (1989). The multifamily therapy group: Research on patterns of interaction. *Social Work with Groups, 12,* 15-39.

Cecchin, G. (1966). Hypothesizing, circularity, and neutrality revisited: An invitation to curiosity. *Family Process, 26,* 405-413.

Coleman, K. H. (1988). Conjugal violence: What 33 men report. *Journal of Marital and Family Therapy, 6,* 207-213.

Connell, G., Milton, G., & Whitaker, C. (1993). Reshaping family symbols: A symbolic-experiential perspective. *Journal of Marital and Family Therapy, 19* (3), 245-254.

Corey, G., Corey, M., & Callanan, P. (1988). *Issues and ethics in the helping professions.* Pacific Grove: Brooks/Cole.

Damasio, A. R. (1994). *Descartes' Error. Emotion, Reason and the Human Brain.* New York: Avon Books.

Duhl, F., Kantor, D., & Duhl, B. (1973). Learning, space, and action in family therapy: A primer of sculpture. In D. A. Bloch (Ed.), *Techniques of family psychotherapy: A primer.* New York: Grune & Stratton.

Duncan, B., Parks, B., & Rush, G. (1990). Eclectic strategic practice: A process constructive perspective. *Journal of Marital and Family Therapy, 16,* 165-179.

Efran, J., Lukens, M., & Lukens, R. (1990). *Language structure and change.* New York: Norton.

Epston, D., & White, M. (1991). *Experience contradiction, narrative and imagination.* Australia: Dulwich Center Publications.

Erikson, E. H. (1968). *Identity, youth and crisis.* New York: Norton.

Fesh, V. (1993). Poststructuralism in family therapy: Interrogating the narrative/conversational mode. *Journal of Marital and Family Therapy, 19* (3), 223-234.

Fineberg, D., & Walter, S. (1989). Transforming helplessness: An approach to the therapy of "stuck" couples. *Family Process, 28* (3), 291-300.

Finkelhor, D. (1983). *The dark side of families.* Beverly Hills, CA: Sage.

Fisch, R., Weakland, J., & Segal, L. (1982). *The tactics of change.* San Francisco: Jossey-Bass.

Freud, S. (1917). Mourning and melancolia. In *Collected Papers, Vol. 4* (pp. 152-170). London: Hogarth Press.

Garnets, L., & Kimmel, D. (1991). Lesbian and gay male dimensions in the psychological study of human diversity. In J. Goodchilds (ed.) *Psychological Perspectives on Human Diversity in America* (pp. 137-189). Washington, DC: American Psychological Association.

Gergen, K. (1991). *The saturated self.* New York: Basic Books.

Gerson, R., Hoffman, S., Sauls, M., & Ulrice, D. (1993). Family-of-origin frames in couple therapy. *Journal of Marital and Family Therapy, 19* (4), 341-354.

Gilligan, C. (1982). *In a different voice.* Cambridge, MA: Harvard University Press.

Golann, S. (1988). On second-order family therapy. *Family Process, 27,* 51-57.

Goldenberg, I., & Goldenberg, H. (1991). *Family therapy: An overview.* Belmont, CA: Wadsworth.

Goldner, V. (1985). Feminism and family therapy. *Family Process, 24,* 31-47.

Goldner, V., Penn, P., Sheinberg, M., & Walker, G. (1990). Love and violence: Gender paradoxes in volatile attachments. *Family Process, 29* (4), 343-364.

Goleman, D. (1995) *Emotional Intelligence.* New York: Bantam Books.

Goodrich, T. J., Rampage, C., Ellman, B., & Halstead, K. (1988). *Feminist family therapy.* New York: Norton.

Goolishian, H., & Anderson, H. (1992). Strategy and intervention versus non-intervention: A matter of theory. *Journal of Marital and Family Therapy, 18 (1),* 11.

Haley, J. (1963). *Strategies of psychotherapy.* New York: Grune & Stratton.

Haley, J. (1973). *Uncommon therapy.* New York: Norton.

Haley, J. (1976). *Problem-solving therapy.* New York: Harper & Row.

Haley, J. (1980). *Leaving home.* New York: McGraw Hill.

Hare-Mustin, R. (1987). The problem of gender in family therapy. *Family Process, 26,* 15-27.

Herman, J. (1992). *Trauma and recovery.* New York: Basic Books.

Hines, P., Richman, D., Maxim, K., & Hays, H. (1989). Multi-impact family therapy: An approach to working with multiproblem families. *Journal of Psychotherapy and the Family, 16,* 161-176.

Hoffman, L (1981). *Foundations of family therapy.* New York: Basic Books.

Hoffman, L. (1990). Constructing realities: An art of lenses. *Family Process, 29,* 1-12.

Hoffman, L. (1993). *Exchanging Voices, a collaborative approach to Family Therapy.* London: H. Karnac Ltd.

Hurtado, A. (1981). Relating to privilege: Seduction and rejection in the subordination of white women and women of color. *Journal of Women in Culture, 14* (11), 834-846.

Imber-Black, E., & Roberts, J. (1992). *Rituals for our times: Celebrating, healing, and changing our lives and our relationships.* New York: Harper.

Johnson, D. R. (1987). The role of the creative arts therapies in the diagnosis and treatment of psychological trauma. *The Arts in Psychotherapy, 14,* 7-13.

Johnson, D. R. (1991). Introduction to the special issue on the creative arts therapies and the family. *The Arts in Psychotherapy, 18* (3), 187-190.

Jones, J. (1991). Psychological models of race: What have they been and what should they be? In J. Goodchilds (ed.) *Psychological Perspectives on Human Diversity in America* (pp. 3-46). Washington, DC: American Psychological Association.

Junge, M. (1985). A book about Daddy dying, A preventative art therapy technique. *Art Therapy; Journal of the American Art Therapy Association,* (pp. 4-10).

Kaplan, F. (2000). *Art, Science, and Art Therapy.* London: Jessica Kingsley.

Kerr, M. E. (1981). Family systems theory and therapy. In A. S. Gurman & D. P. Kniskern (Eds.), *Handbook of family therapy.* New York: Brunner/Mazel.

Krpan, I., & Medved, Z. (1991). Family sculpture in multifamily group therapy. *Socijaina-Psihyatrijai, 17,* 201-211.

Kwiatkowska, H. Y. (1962). Family art therapy: Experiments with a new technique. *Bulletin of Art Therapy, 1* (3), 3-15.

Kwiatkowska, H. Y. (1967a). The use of families' art productions for psychiatric evaluation. *Bulletin of Art Therapy, 6,* 52-69.

Kwiatkowska, H. Y. (1967b). Family art therapy. *Family Process, 6* (1), 37-55.

Kwiatkowska, H. Y. (1971). Family art therapy and family art evaluation: Conscious and unconscious expressive art. In I. Jacob (Ed.), *Psychiatry and Art, Vol. 3* (pp. 138-151). Basel, Switzerland: Karger.

Kwiatkowska, H. Y. (1975). Family art therapy: Experiments with a new technique, In E. Ulman (Ed.), *Art Therapy in Theory and Practice.* New York: Schocken.

Kwiatkowska, H. Y. (1978). *Family therapy and evaluation through art.* Springfield, IL: Charles C Thomas.

Kwiatkowska, H. Y., & Mosher, L. (1971). Family art evaluation: Use in families with schizophrenic twins. *Journal of Nervous and Mental Disease, 153* (3).

Kwiatkowska, H. Y., Day, J., & Wyneem L. (1962). *The schizophrenic patient, his parents and siblings: Observations through family art therapy.* U. S. Department of Health, Education & Welfare, Public Health Service. Washington, DC.

Lachman-Chapin, M., Stuntz, E., & Jones, N. (1975). Art therapy in the psychotherapy of a mother and her son. *American Journal of Art Therapy, 14* (4), 105-116.

Landgarten, H. (1975). Group art therapy for mothers and daughters. *American Journal of Art Therapy, 14* (2).

Landgarten, H. (1987). *Family art psychotherapy.* New York: Brunner/ Mazel.

Landgarten, H. (1991). Perspective: Family creative arts therapies: Past and present. *The Arts in Psychotherapy, 18* (3), 191-194.

Lavie, Y., & Olson, D. (1993). Seven types of marriage: Empirical typology based on ENRICH. *Journal of Marital and Family Therapy, 19* (4), 325-340.

Levick, M., & Herring, J. (1973). Family dynamics—as seen through art therapy. *Art Psychotherapy, I (1),* 45-54.

Linesch, D. G. (1988). *Adolescent art therapy.* New York: Brunner/Mazel.

Lipchik, E. (1994, March/April). The rush to be brief. *Family Therapy Networker, 18* (2), 34-39.

Madanes, C. (1981). *Strategic family therapy.* San Francisco, CA: Jossey-Bass.

Malchiodi, C. (1990). *Breaking the silence: Art therapy with children from violent homes.* New York: Brunner/Mazel.

Malchiodi, C. (ed) (2002) *Handbook of Art Therapy.* New York: Guilford.

Malmquist, C. (1978). *Handbook of adolescence.* New York: Jason Aronson.

Masterson, J. (1985). *Treatment of the borderline adolescent.* New York: Brunner/Mazel.

May, R. (1985). *My quest for beauty.* Dallas, TX: Saybrook.

McGoldrick, M. & Gerson, R. (1985). *Genograms in family assessment.* New York: Norton.

McGoldrick, M. (1982). Ethnicity and family therapy: An overview. In M. McGoldrick, J. K. Pierce, & J. Giordano (eds.), *Ethnicity and family therapy.* New York: Guilford.

McNamee, S. & Gergen, K. (1992). *Therapy as social construction.* London: Sage Publications Ltd.

Minuchin, S. (1974). *Families and family therapy.* Cambridge, MA: Harvard University Press.

Minuchin, S. (1984). *Family kaleidoscope.* Cambridge, MA: Harvard University Press.

Minuchin, S., & Fishman, C. H. (1981). *Family therapy techniques.* Cambridge: Harvard University Press.

Minuchin, S., Montalvo, B., Guerney, B., Rosman, B., & Schumer, F. (1967). *Families of the slums: An exploration of their structure and treatment.* New York: Basic Books.

Minuchin, S., Rosman, B., & Baker, L. (1978). *Psychosomatic families: Anorexia nervosa in context.* Cambridge, MA: Harvard University Press.

Mirkin, M. P., & Koman, S. L. (1985). *Handbook of adolescents and family therapy.* New York: Gardner.

Mueller, E. (1968). Family group art therapy: Treatment of choice for a specific case. In I. Jakab (Ed.), *Psychiatry and art: Proceedings of the IV International Colloquium of Psychopathology of Expression* (pp. 132-143.) Basel, Switzerland: Karger.

Myers, J. E. B. (1992). *Legal issues in child abuse and neglect.* Newbury Park, CA: Sage.

Naitove, C. (1982). Arts therapy with sexually abused children. In S. Sgroi (ed.), *Handbook of Clinical Intervention in Child Sexual Abuse* (pp. 269-308). Lexington, MA: Lexington Books.

Neimeyer, R. (1993). An appraisal of constructivist psychotherapies. *Journal of Consulting and Clinical Psychology, 61* (2), 221-234.

Nelson, M. (1984). *Family therapy: Concepts and methods.* New York: Gardner's Press.

O'Hara, M., & Anderson, W. T. (1991, September/October). Welcome to the postmodern world. *Family Therapy Networker,* 19-25.

Palazzoli, M. S., Cecchin, G., Prata, G., & Boscolo, H. (1978). *Paradox and counter paradox.* New York: Jason Aronson.

Papp, P. (1976). Family choreography. In P. Guerin, Jr. (Ed.), *Family therapy: Theory and practice.* New York: Gardner.

Papp, P. (1980). The Greek chorus and other techniques of family therapy. *Family Process, 19,* 45-57.

Papp, P. (1983). *Getting unstuck.* Seventh Annual Family Therapy Networker Symposium. Unpublished paper.

Papp, P. (1983). *The process of change.* New York: Guilford.

Penn, P. (1982). Circular questioning. *Family Process, 21,* 267-280.

Penn, P. (1985). Feed forward: Future questions, future maps. *Family Process, 24,* 299-310.

Pittman, F. (1987). *Turning point.* New York: Norton.

Pynoos, R., & Eth, S. (1986). Special intervention programs for child witness to violence. In M. Lystad (Ed.), *Violence in the Home.* New York: Brunner/Mazel.

Ramachandran, V.S. & Blakeslee, S. (1998). *Phantoms in the Brain.* New York: Quill William Morrow.

Real, T. (1990). The therapeutic use of self in constructionist systemic therapy. *Family Process, 29,* 255-272.

Riley, S. (2001) *Group Process Made Visible.* Philadelphia, PA.: Brunner/Routledge.

Rubin, J. (1978). *Child art therapy.* New York: Van Nostrand Reinhold.

Rubin, J. (1987). *Approaches to art therapy.* New York: Brunner/ Mazel.

Rubin, J., & Magnussen, M. (1974). A family art evaluation. *Family Process, 13* (2), 185-220.

Sapolsky, R.M. (1998). *Why Zebras Don't Get Ulcers. An Updated Guide to Stress, Stress-related Diseases, and Coping.* New York: W.H. Freeman and Company.

Satir, V. (1982). The therapist and family therapy: Process model. In A. Horne & M. Olsen (Eds.), *Family counseling and therapy.* Itasca, IL: Peacock.

Segal-Evans, K. (1988). *A general heuristic model of the batterer's treatment.* Unpublished manuscript.

Serra, P. (1993). Physical violence in couple relationship: A contribution toward the analysis of the context. *Family Process, 32 (1),* 21-34.

Simon, F.B., Stierlin, H. & Wynne, L.C. (1985). *The Language of Family Therapy: a systemic vocabulary and source book.* New York: Family Process Press.

Sluzki, C. (1992). Transformations: A blueprint for narrative changes in therapy. *Family Process, 31,* 217-230.

Sobol, B. (1982). Art therapy and strategic family therapy. *American Journal of Art Therapy, 21* (2), 43-52.

Solnit, A., & Stark, M. (1961). Mourning and the birth of a defective child. *Psychoanalytic Study of the Child, Vol. VI.* New York: International Universities Press.

Stanton, M. (1984). Fusion, compression, diversion, and the workings of paradox: A theory of therapeutic/systemic change. *Family Process, 23 (2).*

Sternberg, E.M. (2001). *The Balance Within.* New York: W.H. Freeman and Company.

Stierlin, H. (1979). *Separating parents and adolescents: A perspective on running away, schizophrenia, and waywardness.* New York: Quadrangle.

Tarvis, C. (1991). The mismeasure of woman: Paradoxes and perspectives in the study of gender. In J. Goodchilds (ed.) *Psychological Perspectives on Human Diversity in America* (pp. 87-136). Washington, DC: American Psychological Association.

Terr, L. (1990). *Too scared to cry: Psychic trauma in childhood.* New York: Basic Books.

Thomm, K. (1985). Circular interviewing: A multifaceted clinical tool. In D. Campbell & R. Droper (Eds.), *Application of Systemic Therapy: The Milan Approach.* London: Grune & Stratton.

Tinnin, L. (1990). Biological processes in nonverbal communication and their role in the making and interpretations of art. *American Journal of Art Therapy, 29, 9-13.*

Van der Kolk, B., McFarlane, & Weisaeth, L. (1998). *Traumatic Stress.* New York, Guilford.

Varela, F. J. (1989). Reflections on the circulation of concepts between a biology of cognition and systemic family therapy. *Family Process, 28,* 15-24.

Wadeson, H. (1973). Art techniques used in conjoint marital therapy. *American Journal of Art Therapy, 12* (3),147-164.

Wadeson, H. (1976). The fluid family in multifamily art therapy. *American Journal of Art Therapy, 13* (4), 115-118.

Wadeson, H. (1980). *Art psychotherapy.* New York: Wiley.

Walsh, M. (1992). Twenty major issues in remarriage families. *Journal of Counseling and Development, 70,* 709-715.

Wamboldt, F., & Reiss, D. (1989). Defining a family heritage and a new relationship identity: Two central tasks in making a marriage. *Family Process, 28* (3), 317-336.

Watzlawick, P. (1984). *The invented reality.* New York: Norton.

Watzlawick, P.,Weakland, J., & Fisch, R. (1974). *Change: Principles of problem formation and problem resolution.* New York: Norton.

Watzlawick, P., Beavin, J. & Jackson, H. (1967). *Pragmatics of human communication.* New York: Norton.

Weakland, J., Watzlawick, P., Fisch, R., Segal, L. (1982). *The tactics of change, Doing therapy briefly.* San Francisco: Jossey-Bass.

Weeks, G. & L'Abate, L. (1982). *Paradoxical psychotherapy.* New York: Brunner/Mazel.

Wheeler, D. (1991). *Art since mid-century: 1945 to the present.* New York: Prentice-Hall.

Willi, J., Friel, R., & Limacher, B. (1993). Couples therapy using the technique of construct differentiation. *Family Process, 32* (3),311-321.

Winnicott, D. (1976). *The child, the family, and the outside world.* Harmondsworth: Penguin.

Wooley, S., & Lewis, G. (1987). Multi-family therapy within an intensive treatment program for bulimia. *Family Therapy Collections, 20,* 12-24.

Wylie, M. S. (1994, March/April). Endangered species. *Family Therapy Networker, 18* (2), 20-33.

Yalom, I. (1985). *The theory and practice of group psychotherapy.* New York: Basic Books.

Zierer, E., Sternberg, D., Finn, R., & Farmer, M. (1975a). Family creative analysis: Its role in treatment. Part 1. *Bulletin of Art Therapy, 5* (2), 47-63.

Zierer, E., Sternberg, D., Finn, R., & Farmer, M. (1975b). Family creative analysis: Its role in treatment. Part 2. *Bulletin of Art Therapy, 5* (3), 87-104.

Zimmerman, J., & Dickenson, V. (1993). Separating couples from restraining patterns and the relationship discourse that supports them. *Journal of Marital and Family Therapy, 19* (4),403-413.

magnolia street publishers

Art As Therapy With Children   **EDITH KRAMER**

Kramer's discussions of sublimation, art and defense, aggression, and the role of the art therapist have not been surpassed by other authors. This profoundly wise volume offers inspiration and genuine assistance to the fledgling clinician as well as to anyone else working with children who wishes to understand how and why art can have such a profound effect. (color illustrations, 238 pages) ISBN 0-9613309-4-5   **pa. $21.95**

Art Therapy in Theory & Practice   **Ed. ELINOR ULMAN & P. DACHINGER**

Since its first publication, this volume has been used continually as both a textbook and a resource. Many of the chapters have become indispensable classics which continue to define the field of art therapy. Elinor Ulman shows great skill, perception and eloquence as both a writer and editor. (color illustrations, 414 pages) ISBN 0-9613309-8-8   **pa. $29.95**

The Artist in Each of Us   **FLORENCE CANE**

This book represents 25 years of the practical experience of a pioneer whose new methods bridge art education and art therapy. Cane considers both the psychological and technical factors of learning and personality growth. She gives us a careful step-by-step account of her teaching methods with a number of fascinating case studies. (color illustrations, 370 pages) publ: Art Therapy Publications, ISBN 0-9611462-0-6   **pa. $24.95**

California Art Therapy Trends   **Ed. EVELYN VIRSHUP**

So many times we, as Americans, have noticed that California is a place where experimentation, innovation and creativity are not only allowed but actually accepted and even expected. This edited work is by 35 of those Californians who are setting trends in their field of the arts and creative therapies. A sampling of the issues: Group Art Therapy, Adolescence, Masks, Psychodrama, Sand Tray Work, Dissociative Disorders, Survivors of Sexual Violence, Abused Women and Children, Families in Recovery, Women Writing and Healing. (431 pages) ISBN 0-9613309-3-7 **pa. $29.95**

Childhood and Art Therapy: Notes on Theory and Application   **EDITH KRAMER**

Edith Kramer has been educating art therapists since 1959 and is considered a master in her field. This new edition has been updated and revised and is an excellent companion to Art as Therapy with Children. (color illustrations, 300 pages) ISBN 1-890374-00-8 **pa. $21.95**

Drawing Time: Art Therapy in Prisons and Other Correctional Settings
Eds. DAVID GUSSAK & EVELYN VIRSHUP

This book includes some of the most startling, unique and beautiful artwork to come out of our correctional institutions to date. The issues dealt with are working in maximum security prisons, hospitals, court-ordered schooling, incarcerated abused women, aging prisoners and much more. (color illustrations, 259 pages) ISBN 0-9613309-9-6   **pa. $31.95**

Dynamically Oriented Art Therapy: Its Principles & Practice
MARGARET NAUMBURG

As a pioneer in this field of psychotherapy, Margaret Naumburg's approach to art therapy is psychoanalytically oriented; she recognized the fundamental importance of the unconscious as expressed in the patient's dreams, daydreams and fantasies. In this work, three case histories of emotionally disturbed women are used to illustrate the various ways in which the process of dynamically oriented art therapy can function in the treatment of depression, ulcers and alcoholism. (color illustrations, 168 pages) ISBN 0-9613309-1-0   **hd. $36.95**

Fun To Grow On: Engaging Play Activities for Kids with Teachers, Parents and Grandparents
VIRGINIA MORIN

This marvelous book suggests 167 fun activities for adults to share with children ages 3 to 10. Used extensively in the *Theraplay* programs, these games delight little ones and are a lot of fun for grown-ups too! They foster closeness and cooperation and facilitate interaction. (126 pages) ISBN 1-890374-01-6   **pa $12.95**

The Gestalt Art Experience: Patterns That Connect   JANIE RHYNE

Based on gestalt psychology and therapy, the focus of this book is on direct and immediate experiential insights gained through creating art that expresses and clarifies personal problems and potential. Emphasis is on exploring present life style and discovering possibilities for self-actualization. (revised edition, color illustrations, 225 pages) ISBN 0-9613309-6-1   **pa. $26.95**

Mind Over Matter: The Uses of Materials in Art, Education and Therapy
DON SEIDEN

The material and exercises in this new volume will aid in establishing a base for an art therapist or art educator who seeks a meaningful connection to the use of materials in their work. Don Seiden is a well known and highly respected artist, therapist and professor at the School of the Art Institute of Chicago. (publication Summer 2001) ISBN 1-890374-02-04   **pa. $18.95**

Shattered Images: Phenomenological Language of Sexual Trauma
DEE SPRING

Dee Spring has specialized in the treatment of post-traumatic stress and dissociative disorders for more than twenty years. Her pioneering efforts in this field have gained international recognition because of her unique treatment style which includes art therapy, imagery and hypnosis. She presents a treatment model that simultaneously helps the therapist stay on track amid the myriad crises encountered with sexual trauma victims and creatively explains the complex, multi-level treatment process. (305 pages) ISBN 0-9613309-2-9   **pa. $29.95**